MARY PICKFORD REDISCOVERED

RARE PICTURES OF A HOLLYWOOD LEGEND

KEVIN BROWNLOW

INTRODUCTION AND PHOTOGRAPH SELECTION BY
ROBERT CUSHMAN

HARRY N. ABRAMS, INC., PUBLISHERS, IN ASSOCIATION WITH

THE ACADEMY OF MOTION PICTURE ARTS AND SCIENCES

CONTENTS

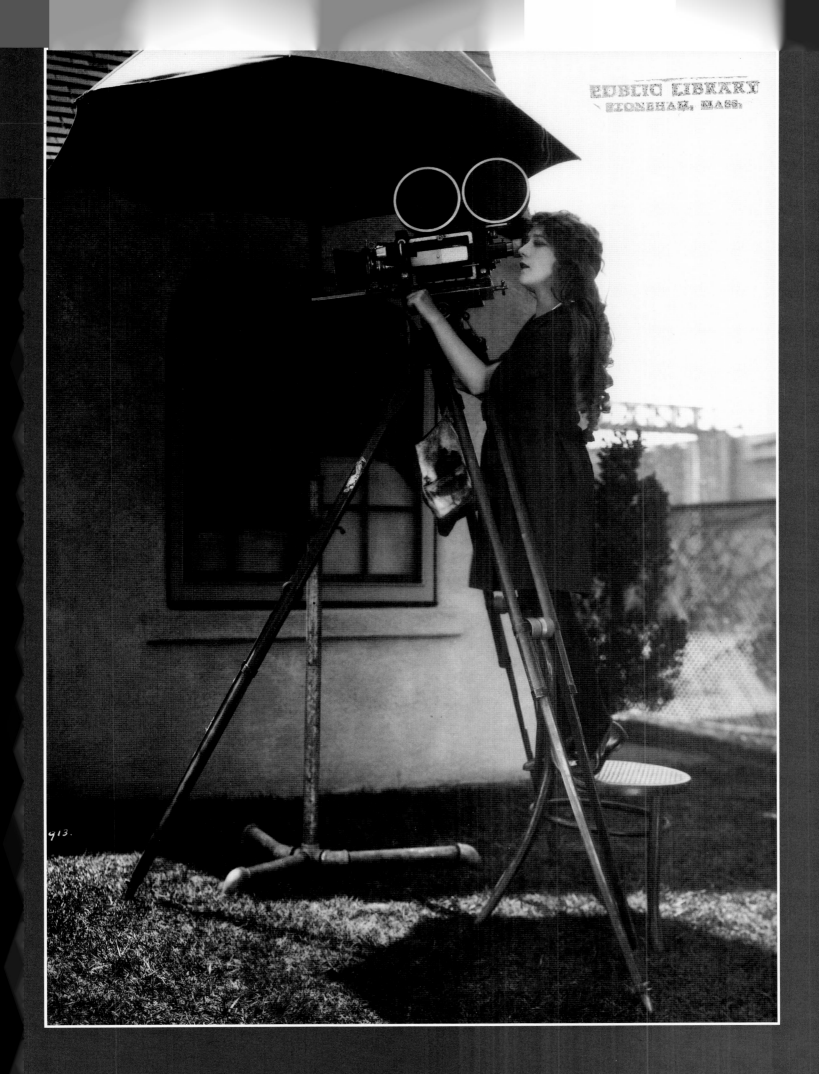

EDITOR: ELISA URBANELLI

DESIGNER: CAROL ROBSON

Library of Congress Cataloging-in-Publication Data

Brownlow, Kevin.
    Mary Pickford rediscovered : rare pictures of a Hollywood legend / Kevin Brownlow ;
Robert Cushman, general editor.
                        p.   cm.
    Includes bibliographical references and index.
    ISBN 0–8109–4374–3 (hc.)
    1. Pickford, Mary, 1892–1979.   I. Cushman, Robert, 1946–.
II. Title.
PN2287.P5B76   1999
791.43′028′092—dc21   98–41302

Printed and bound in Japan

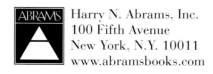

Harry N. Abrams, Inc.
100 Fifth Avenue
New York, N.Y. 10011
www.abramsbooks.com

Page 2:
Portrait by Charlotte Fairchild, 1918.

Page 5:
In costume for *Little Annie Rooney* (1925), Mary Pickford checks a camera angle for publicity footage to be taken outside her bungalow at the Pickford-Fairbanks studio.

Opposite:
Pickford as Judy Abbott in *Daddy-Long-Legs* (1919) plots the ultimate crime, stalking a doll that she plans to snatch from a spoiled rich girl and give to a deathly ill orphan at the asylum.

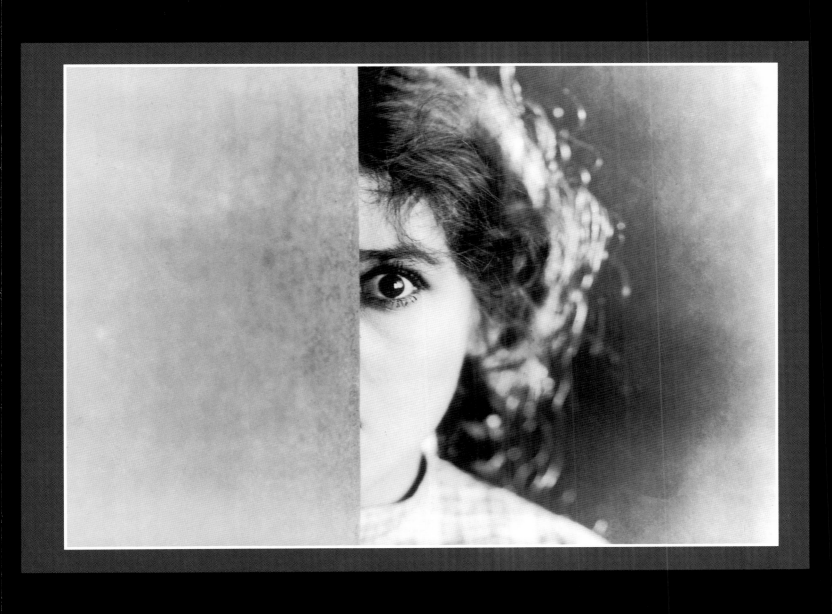

FOREWORD

The Academy of Motion Picture Arts and Sciences is famous around the world for presenting its annual Awards of Merit, more commonly known as Oscars. The same institution is equally renowned, albeit to a smaller percentage of the population, as the custodian of the history of the film industry. Since the 1930s the Academy's Margaret Herrick Library has been collecting, cataloging, and preserving the scripts, posters, personal and business correspondence, books, periodicals, newspaper and magazine clippings, sheet music, music scores, and scrapbooks that are generated by the people and companies who make movies. In the Library's Roddy McDowall Photograph Archive—which was named in honor of the actor prior to his death in 1998—over 7 million stills and negatives are given meticulous attention and care. Every year, the Library makes these materials available to tens of thousands of researchers, students, scholars, journalists, filmmakers, and others seeking a glimpse at the workings of the unique marriage of art and commerce known as the movies.

Mary Pickford Rediscovered: Rare Pictures of a Hollywood Legend is a natural outgrowth of the Academy's commitment to preserving Hollywood's history and sharing it with all who want to learn about it. The remarkable images on the following pages, accompanied by Kevin Brownlow's text, tell the story of an extraordinary woman whose rare blend of artistic talent and business acumen are perhaps unmatched in the history of twentieth-century American culture.

The photographs on these pages are also a tribute to the thousands of individuals over the years who have had the foresight to place their photographs and other documents—or those of their grandfathers, aunts, or siblings—into the hands of the Academy's library, where professional archivists can properly preserve and catalog the material and provide access to it for legitimate research purposes. Foremost among this group are Charles "Buddy" Rogers, who gave the Academy much of the Pickford Collection after Ms. Pickford's death in 1979, and the Mary Pickford Foundation, which over the years has provided considerable support so that the materials in the collection could be made available for future generations to enjoy. This book is testimony to their vision.

—The Academy of Motion Picture Arts and Sciences

Portrait by Hartsook, 1918.

INTRODUCTION

I think Oscar Wilde wrote a poem about a robin who loved a white rose. He loved it so much that he pierced his breast and let his heart's blood turn the white rose red. Maybe this sounds very sentimental, but for anybody who has loved a career as much as I've loved mine, there can be no short cuts.
—Mary Pickford to Kevin Brownlow, 1965

INTRODUCTION
ROBERT CUSHMAN

Jack, Lottie, and Gladys Smith (who became Mary Pickford the following year) at the Lansing, Michigan, Depot in 1906. The car was either hired or quickly "borrowed" for this shot.

Pickford costumed for the playlet *The Littlest Girl*, Toronto, 1900. Photo by the T. Eaton Co.

Page 10:
Portrait by Campbell Studios, c. 1916.

Opposite:
Portrait by George Hurrell, 1937.

"Open up Stage 3!" cried the night watchman at the Goldwyn studio in Hollywood around eleven o'clock one night in 1958. A large, black Rolls-Royce had just pulled up at the gate. The driver emerged and opened the door for Mary Pickford, who exited the vehicle and proceeded onto the lot, greeting the old-timers on duty, all of whom she remembered on a first-name basis. A couple of them had been there since the 1920s when the property was the Pickford-Fairbanks studio. After exchanging pleasantries, she was ushered into the stage—the same stage where she had filmed scenes from *Tess of the Storm Country* and Douglas Fairbanks had shot portions of *The Thief of Bagdad*.

She had gone through this ritual late at night for quite some time—about every two weeks. A call had been placed to Samuel Goldwyn: "Mary Pickford keeps coming to the lot at night and wants to go to Stage 3." Goldwyn's reply came swiftly: "Give her whatever she wants."

Once she was inside the stage, a chair would be brought to her if the stage was empty, and she would sit in the barren space. If the stage was rented and dressed for the next day's shooting, she would sit on one of the furnishings for whatever the film might be. Sometimes she would have a drink; sometimes she would not. Sometimes she sat and cried. Sometimes she sat rapt in deep concentration, silently reflecting on her tumultuous life, her personal relationships, and her stupendous career. Then she would be quietly driven back to Pickfair.

These sessions of intensely and deeply solitary thought were part of a lifelong pattern. At age three, she would often refuse to go to bed but rather would hide in a secluded area of the house "to think." She had a distinct memory of not liking the world at age three, and of thinking, "If only I could get back there." She had some sort of vague memory of another, previous existence. She believed that if she thought hard enough and long enough, she would discover where she came from and who she was. When found by her mother and ordered to bed, she would say, "No, Mama, I must stay here and think." In 1957 she remarked, "That's a morbid attitude for a little baby, isn't it?"

Contrary to general present-day perception, Mary Pickford was much more than "the little girl with the golden curls." She was a unique symbol of the birth and growth of the only art form that found its origins in the western hemisphere—the motion picture. She was the most popular, powerful, prominent, and influential woman in the history of the cinema. Unfortunately, not many people are aware of that fact today. Why? It is largely Pickford's own fault: she rigidly controlled and kept her films out of public view for over forty years. Why? She was afraid she would be laughed at—in the wrong way. She could not have been more mistaken.

One of the earliest of the great pioneer performers in films, she had been making movies for several years before luminaries such as Lillian Gish and Charles Chaplin ever stepped in front of a camera. Having been a stage actress since age five, Mary Pickford entered the movies in April 1909, at age seventeen; and within a few months, at a time when most "legitimate" actors looked on the "galloping tintypes" with dismissive, withering contempt, she had the vision to realize the hitherto undreamed-of potential of

the motion picture while it was still in its infancy. She stayed with this new medium that many derided as a toy and went on to build a career that was unprecedented in the annals of entertainment and eventually made her the most popular woman in the world.

She was certainly the world's first "superstar," as she was the first figure in the performing arts to achieve international fame and recognition among millions of people around the globe. There was simply no precedent for this level of fame, no concept or comprehension of just what such fame meant in terms of both professional and personal life. Mary was the first person to learn precisely what this entailed—and how to deal with it.

Pickford was the first female star to found her own corporation (in 1915), and she virtually invented the concept of the independent star/producer. To this role she added the concept of distributor, an entrepreneurial inspiration that resulted in the incorporation and co-ownership (with partners Douglas Fairbanks, Charles Chaplin, and D. W. Griffith) of United Artists early in 1919. That was a unique moment in film history; to this day no one has ever succeeded in amassing so much control. Even the likes of Steven Spielberg and Barbra Streisand do not personally own their distribution companies.

Until her retirement from acting in 1933, after more than two hundred films and twenty-five years after her motion picture debut, Pickford was never to desert the screen, save for a brief Broadway run in a David Belasco play early in 1913. She developed a deep respect for the motion picture medium at a very early stage in her career and would always take whatever steps necessary, often risking life and limb, to

Douglas Fairbanks, Mary Pickford, Charles Chaplin, and D. W. Griffith on the occasion of the founding of their new company, the United Artists Corporation, in early 1919.

Opposite:

As amused carpenters look on, Mary Pickford drives a nail during the construction of her bungalow at the Pickford-Fairbanks Studio in Hollywood, 1922.

P. 281.

achieve all effects correctly. Nothing—no job—was beneath her, even when she was her own producer and the world's biggest star. If it was for the good of the picture, she did it. She would ride a horse at full gallop atop a narrow twenty-foot wall, plunge into icy water, and pick up a five-foot snake. Reminiscing with Kevin Brownlow, she recalled, "There was always something sacred to me about that camera."[1]

The work of Mary Pickford has been in need of reevaluation for more than sixty years. A comprehensive film-by-film study of her films has never appeared in print. Film historians Kevin Brownlow, James Card, Anthony Slide, Edward Wagenknecht, and Alexander Walker have written perceptively about Pickford's career, as chapters in their books; but no one has ever undertaken a truly complete study of her films. A few other film commentators have paid brief tribute to Pickford, but their comments usually tend to discuss her personal life, her image, or her sharp business acumen, and almost never make any attempt to discuss her artistry and her films themselves. However, two recent biographies (one by Scott Eyman in 1990 and the latest by Eileen Whitfield in 1997) have discussed her work more thoroughly than anything previously published.

The space allotted Pickford in film histories has been inappropriately small, in light of her enormous importance, but some observations have been insightful. In 1915 Julian Johnson was one of the earliest to grasp her significance:

Occasionally, a science, a trade, a craft or an art produces some single exponent who stands above all other exponents; who becomes not so much a famous individual as a symbol; whose very name, in any land, is a personification of the thing itself. . . . What Edison symbolizes in electricity, what Stephenson stands for in mechanical invention or Spencer in synthetic philosophy, Mary Pickford stands for in the great new art world of living shadows.[2]

In 1931 even the severe critic C. A. Lejeune succumbed when she wrote in her *Cinema*:

. . . she is at once a myth and a surety, a legend and a pledge. . . . It is a rather curious corollary . . . that Mary Pickford, a woman of steely sense and practicality, should have become the cinema's great sentimentality, the concrete expression of our ideals and memories. . . . She sends us away from the picture-house absurdly generous, ridiculously touched, so that we want to stop the first grubby urchin in the street and surprise it with a five-pound note, buy an orphanage, adopt a township of homeless dogs, or sell all we have and give it to the poor.[3]

Pickford is dwarfed by her dog in a quiet comic moment from *Through the Back Door* (1921).

Opposite:
Portrait by Moody Studios, New York, 1915.

Iris Barry, in her *Let's Go to the Movies*, was most successful in grasping the essence of Pickford's significance:

. . . she is Everywoman: that is her strength, because she is Everywoman much more whole-heartedly than any of her lesser rivals. In so far, she is above criticism. . . . The two greatest names in the cinema are, I beg to reiterate, Mary Pickford and Charlie Chaplin . . . from an historical point of view they will always be great, as pioneers and patron saints. . . . One went, not to see "the picture," but to see Mary Pickford and Charlie Chaplin. There was in effect a revolution. Chaplin had little or no hand in bringing this off. The public took to him, his managers and friends did the rest towards creating a star out of a comedian. But Mary Pickford had a big hand in it. In one sense, she "created" stars. . . . Mary made herself a star by her own unremitting efforts: she created a character for herself on the screen, she invented a brand of girl-hood which the public responded to, and she built up this character and stabilized this brand by every effort in her power. And she succeeded magnificently.[4]

Barry concluded by pointing out that Pickford, sharing honors with Chaplin and Fairbanks,

. . . happen[s] to be wholeheartedly and absolutely interested in the cinema. . . . There is all the difference in the world between a serious artist (irrespective of fame) and a popular favorite. Fairbanks, his wife, and Chaplin are, and behave like, serious artists: in that is their great strength. They are their own raw material, and it is with the use of that that they concern themselves. . . . They are, largely, the history of the cinema . . .[5]

The experience of viewing all the extant Pickford films reveals a brilliant career almost unknown to the public today and confirms her position as a genius in the annals of motion pictures. Paris audiences made this discovery at the triumphal (and first ever) major retrospective of Mary's films—at the Cinémathèque Française in 1965. But until a retrospective series of (only) ten Pickford features was briefly issued in 1971, almost none of her films had been shown publicly in the United States since her retirement. The 1971 series was successful and well received but not widely distributed. Since then her films have rarely surfaced for screenings, save a small handful at the Silent Movie Theater in Los Angeles and an occasional screening at the George Eastman House in Rochester, New York. However, in 1997 screenings of several Pickford features at the Museum of Modern Art and the Film Forum in New York were well attended and enthusiastically received, and there have been a few Pickford screenings in other cities in the past few years. Apart from this recent exposure a vast and immensely significant part of film history has been lying dormant in vaults for most of the last six decades.

The unavailability of the Pickford films was no accident, for it was Mary herself who had been hesitant to permit screenings, fearing to suffer by comparison to the films of later generations. She did not need to fear the scrutiny of modern audiences, however, for her pictures stand the test of time as well, and in many cases better, than the complete body of work of any other silent-screen star. She has a presence and immediacy that time has not diminished, and today her films impress with their surprising range and variety. The stories, settings, and characterizations never duplicate themselves, even though she produced her pictures at an exhausting rate (in 1915 alone, she starred in eight full-length features); and she was capable of adapting herself to any kind of role.

Mary was the first great star of motion pictures, and from her phenomenal rise grew the concept of the "star system." The possibility of film performers becoming nationwide celebrities had occurred to her, however, well before Adolph Zukor established his Famous Players Film Company on that premise in 1912. As early as 1910 she had suggested to the Biograph studio's executives that her name be released to the public and the press; but, with a characteristic lack of foresight that has since become associated with many movie backers, they created one of the great blunders of film history: they refused her request and clung dogmatically to their

The most famous head of hair in the world is shampooed, c. 1920.

policy of actor anonymity, fearing that once known to the public, Mary could command a greater salary. Of course she could have, and would have—and later did—but Biograph's profits would have skyrocketed as well.

Despite Biograph's secrecy and restrictions, audiences throughout the country began recognizing "the girl with the curls" and looked for her distinctive work on their local screens without even knowing her name. Thus, with Pickford rests the distinction of having been discovered by the public. Finally, late in 1912, Mary heard of Zukor's plans for Famous Players and quickly signed a contract with the new organization, which was practically tailor-made for the development of her own ideas. At that point Zukor did not consider Pickford an especially important asset, for his concept was that his films would star famous Broadway stage players of the period. But the public was to decide that Mary was the most "famous player" of them all. Quickly, most of Zukor's stage actors, who had no grasp of the entirely different technique required for film acting, flopped in their attempts before the camera. Within two years Pickford was the best known and most popular actress in America.

Today it is difficult to comprehend the enormous popularity held by Mary Pickford at her particular time in history. In 1915 film statisticians told her that she projected a wordless story into the minds of 12,500,000 people every twenty-four hours.[6] Zukor, her mentor and employer from 1913 to 1918, wrote in retrospect:

. . . Mary's rise had been sensational—and more than a little frightening. While preaching a glowing future for motion pictures, I had never prophesied anything like this. Had so unseen a vision even come to me—at least that so popular a star would rise so soon—I doubtless would have had my head examined, as people had told me to do. . . . There has never been anything like the public adulation showered on Mary.[7]

She was universally known, in every country where films were shown, as simply "Our Mary," a remarkably warm and genuine gesture of affection. Chaplin had his comic-sadness; Theda Bara had her exotic, forbidden sexuality; and Garbo was to have her erotic mystery; but Mary Pickford was the only great film star whose popularity was based largely on spiritual love. She projected herself as the kind of person that everyone wanted to meet and fall in love with. She was vibrant; she was sincere. She was good. She was also disarmingly charming and had a wonderful sense of humor. The whole world wanted to put its arms around her and, in a way, it did. She had a definite sexuality, but of the kind that one anticipates experiencing only after having fallen deeply and idealistically in love. She was truly the ideal girl of the American Dream.

As *Photoplay* expressed it, ". . . she has in twenty years become that which ordinarily requires two hundred—a tradition . . . for she has become a symbol of love to the lonely soul of the world."[8] Pickford herself once considered the question of her hold on her audience:

People have asked why audiences have loved me, and I can only say that it must be because I love them. I always have. . . . I went on stage before I was five, but long before that I can remember praying to God to make people love me. I just had to have people's love. . . . Love seeks response in love. Nothing is more pathetic than half a love affair.[9]

In an article explaining "why the world loves Mary," Adela Rogers St. Johns concluded:

We are not a nation that as a whole cares for the arts of painting, sculpturing. Nor are we inclined to symbolism in our churches—churches filled with saints and angels which answer man's craving for spiritual beauty. But somehow we crave that something—that indefinable conviction of beauty, truth and immortality that I see in Mary's face. . . . In the mass of people is a splendid, upward surging toward good—and they have found the symbol of that goodness in Mary's face.[10]

**Portrait by Hartsook,
Los Angeles, 1918.**

People really felt that they knew her, her problems and joys. They could sympathize and identify with her because she was, symbolically, the soul and inner conscience of everyone who saw her. She could be trusted. In 1965 Pickford remarked to Kevin Brownlow, with utmost sincerity in her voice, "I am a servant of the public. I have never forgotten that."[11] So perhaps James Quirk, the editor of *Photoplay*, summed up Mary's unprecedented appeal when he said, "Mary is our queen because she is our most loyal subject."[12]

Most people who have ever heard of Mary today harbor unfortunate misconceptions about her screen personality, most of which center on the sadly misinformed assertion that she was limited to the portrayal of sweet little girls and naive romantic heroines. Nothing could be further from the truth. Such an inaccurate and simplistic appraisal not only does an injustice to Pickford but also seriously distorts film history.

Mary Pickford may have been the ingenuous and beautiful child-woman who captured the devotion of a nation for two decades, but she was also an actress of inexhaustible versatility and possessed a dynamic dramatic range surpassed by no other star of the silent screen. She probably did more for the development of screen acting than any other performer during the whole era of silent pictures. In 1909 her naturalistic approach to pantomimic acting was revolutionary. Her method was to make her characters real and believable as life. In 1917 she said,

Study human beings constantly you must, in order to do good film work. I find myself studying the policeman on the corner, even the street cleaners. You cannot work effectively into a picture where you are surrounded by all sorts of people unless you comprehend them. It is, after all is said and done, a case of living for your work, and making that work as human as possible.[13]

By 1912 she had clearly proven that a naturalistic acting style was essential to bring truth and authenticity to the screen, and she demonstrated a degree of subtlety and restraint never before seen. Mary Pickford was to acting what D. W. Griffith was to directing in that pioneering period. As the historian Leslie Wood pointed out, "Mary Pickford was the complement of Griffith's genius."[14]

The fact that many contemporary critics regarded Mary Pickford as the most accomplished of all film actresses from the beginning of her stardom and well into the 1920s has been forgotten because of the unavailability of her films and the resulting evaluation of Pickford's importance on the basis of hearsay. Her technique can be discussed in terms of what was much later referred to as "the method." The distinguished director George Cukor, in fact, once declared that Mary Pickford was the first method actress, and was also often heard to proclaim, "She *invented* screen acting."[15] Pickford once commented, "I didn't act—I *was* the characters I played on the screen. During a picture, I didn't leave the character at the studio; I took it home with me. I lived my parts."[16] The extent to which she immersed herself in her roles can often be seen in her closeups, which contributed inestimably to the quality of her pantomimic work. In a single closeup, she often expressed several distinct and separate ideas with remarkable precision and economy; in a few seconds she told a complete, self-contained little story.

Very early in her career, a few individuals began to realize that there was more to Mary Pickford than was obvious at first glance. In June 1915 this remarkably perceptive comment appeared:

It is not at the first or second viewing of a Pickford film that one comes to a full appreciation of the little woman's surprising power. You may think at first only that she is sweet and charming and unaffected. Then you begin to realize that she has a very remarkable way of saying things to you without words . . . and that you are never in doubt as to what she means. Next you find that she is expressing exactly the spirit of her character and you think, of course, "How well she is chosen for that character. It fits her perfectly." But the next time you see her she is playing a different part and

During a kids' gang fight in *Little Annie Rooney* (1925), Pickford seeks refuge from blunt flying objects, having pitched plenty of them herself.

expressing that exactly, too, and the conviction that she is versatile begins to grow on you. . . . In everything that she does there is the strange unexplainable, eerie quality, the distinction, perhaps the touch of genius that lifts her acting above the ordinary things that ordinary players do.[17]

Thus began a continuing and seemingly contagious inability among commentators to analyze the appeal of Mary Pickford. They could state only that she was "beyond analysis." They did so, unfailingly and perpetually. Dissecting the Pickford character is no easy task, for her outward appearance is deceptively simple.

The screen character of Mary Pickford has become a genuine American folk heroine and bonafide twentieth-century icon. As one observer wrote, "I think she is the first woman who received a fortune because of her *character*. That is really Mary's earning power—her character."[18] It seems very curious that until recently most commentators and historians have dismissed her personality as simple and failed to look beyond its surface, for any individual who has achieved such distinction must surely have some degree of depth and complexity. It is sad to note, as Alexander Walker pointed out in *The Celluloid Sacrifice*, that Pickford was often a victim of her simplistic, sentimentalizing legend in her own time, when people should have known better. But whenever a person becomes a leading figure of an era, he or she falls prey to inaccurate generalities. Throughout two decades of her career, critics were continually making the amazing discovery that "Mary Pickford can really act!" Although she always alternated her little-girl roles with adult portrayals, and never even played a little girl in a feature film until she had been making pictures for seven years, reviewers habitually commented that "Mary Pickford has finally grown up in her latest film."

Those who think of the Pickford character as a naive girl who knows nothing about what really goes on in the world should be reminded that she once made a film that deals precisely with this very theme: *Stella Maris* (1918), an intensely realistic drama in which Mary, as a young woman who has been carefully sheltered from life's harsh realities, is shattered by the truth and loses all faith in humanity.

Above all, critics were always quick to notice Mary's "human touches," and writer Herb Sterne commented in retrospect, "Mary is one of the few motion picture artists to succeed in humanizing the gag. With the exception of Charlie Chaplin and Mabel Normand, none have been able to shuffle so successfully antithetical emotions."[19] As Sterne intimated, the Pickford character is made fascinating by virtue of its elusive paradoxes and complexities. Most important, she is a delightful, natural woman, clever and irresistible, with the ability to communicate with anyone. She is sometimes romantic but more often realistic. On the exterior she is fun-loving, but her inner spirit gravitates to the serious. She is loving but strong, mischievous but never unkind, and optimistic but well aware of adversity (and perfectly capable of dealing with it). She is always responsible for her own destiny and has an unerring instinct for knowing what is just: she often makes her own distinction between what is legal and what is fair. If any summary is possible, it is that Mary Pickford's character is the embodiment of everything that is beautiful about youth.

To the contrary of their supposed naïveté, her characters can always grasp every situation or problem that confronts them, and, invariably, they will quickly charge off to do something about it. When menaced, Mary is more likely to get herself out of her predicament than call for the hero's help. In fact, the leading men in nearly all of Mary's films can scarcely be called heroes and usually have precious little to do with solving the conflicts of the plots.

When cornered in *Tess of the Storm Country* (1922), for example, Mary swiftly clobbers the threatening villain (who seems about three times her weight) with a huge flounder, yanked from her fish basket like a billy club, and sends him crashing against a fence—and then runs off laughing. When threatened again later in the film, she temporarily dispatches the same villain by dousing him with a kettle of

Above:
Pickford debeautifies her hair with oil prior to going before the camera as the homely cockney Amanda Afflick in *Suds* (1920).

Opposite:
As a plucky department-store clerk in the romantic comedy *My Best Girl* (1927), Pickford reveals her charm, wit, and beauty. Photograph by K. O. Rahmn.

scalding soup. When the hero bursts in, attempting to rescue her, the villain overwhelms him, and it is ultimately Mary who finishes off the villain by smashing a heavy chair over his head while he is strangling the hero.

No one ever succeeded in putting something over on her, and she never played an insipid ingenue who does nothing but bat her eyes and swoon over the latest matinee idol. The Pickford character is one of indefatigable spirit and energy. She is almost always certain that all will turn out for the best, but, as Margaret Case Harriman remarked, "that optimistic glow in her eyes is always accompanied by a glint that says, 'it damn well better.'"

Pickford's characters are girls and women of intelligence, always perceptive and sensitive. Some of them are ignorant by accepted social standards, such as Tess, the cockney Amanda Allick in *Suds* (1920), or the unschooled Mama Molly in *Sparrows* (1926); but they are never dim-witted and have an intuitive ability to outsmart the pompous, pedantic, or socially prominent, establishment-type characters with whom they are so often at odds. The Pickford character is often a crusader, rising as the courageous defender of the oppressed and the outraged challenger of the oppressors. She always comes to the aid of the underdog—the social outcast, the poor—or anyone against whom prejudice is directed. In *Rebecca of Sunnybrook Farm* (1917), she campaigns for (and obtains) social acceptance of a common-law husband and wife; and in *Little Lord Fauntleroy* (1921), she agitates for better treatment of peasants living on an earl's estate. She even assumes the role of a protestor, organizing the people against the wealthy landowner who would evict the squatters and deprive them of their livelihood in *Tess of the Storm Country* (both 1914 and 1922).

The Pickford films that involve the rich-poor class struggle (and many of them do) always show Mary championing the poor and deriding the rich—or if she *is* rich, challenging their thoughts and values and refusing to conform to their standards. From this standpoint, in *The Hoodlum* (1919), *The Poor Little Rich Girl* (1917), and *Through the Back Door* (1921), Mary belittled the upper class from within. Other Pickford characters paved the way for social comment in other areas. As a struggling factory worker, Mary protests and exposes the scandalous abuses of sweatshop labor in *The Eternal Grind* (1916). *Daddy-Long-Legs* (1919) shows her at the mercy of deplorable conditions in a prisonlike orphanage, and the practice of placing parentless children in oppressive workhouses is exposed through her portrayal of the deformed slavey Unity Blake in *Stella Maris*. *Sparrows* starkly depicts Mary and several children submitting to squalid and terrifying conditions on a southern "baby farm" located in an isolated swamp. Although these kinds of conditions may seem far removed from today, one must consider that they were all very real social problems at the time these films were produced, and that they parallel the shocking accounts of foster-home abuse we hear about frequently in today's news.

Not only did Mary play all kinds of American women and girls but she also portrayed several characters of other national origin. This was no accidental trend, for she announced her intent to appear in many international characterizations during her early days at Famous Players. At a time when the subject matter of most American films was decidedly American, she helped bring a better understanding of other cultures to the millions of Americans who flocked to her films, most of whom would never travel to foreign lands and could not learn of them through the electronic media available today.

The list of these portrayals alone is impressive: she was a Dutch immigrant in *Hulda from Holland* (1916) and a French peasant in *Fanchon the Cricket* (1915). She played a deposed Herzegovinian monarch in *Such a Little Queen* (1914) and an Alaskan Inuit in *Little Pal* (1915). She was the Japanese heroine of *Madame Butterfly* (1915), an Italian in both *Poor Little Peppina* (1916) and *The Love Light*

Jack Pickford (costumed for *Tom Sawyer*), Mary Pickford (costumed for *A Little Princess*), and William S. Hart (costumed for *The Silent Man*) clown around on the Famous Players-Lasky lot, probably during lunch hour, in late 1917.

(1921), and an Englishwoman in both *Mistress Nell* (1915) and *Dorothy Vernon of Haddon Hall* (1924). In *Kiki* (1931), she took the role of a violent French chorus girl, and she played a Belgian refugee in *Through the Back Door*. In both *Stella Maris* and *Suds* she was a cockney, and she transformed herself into a Hindustani Indian for *Less Than the Dust* (1916). She donned highland garb as a Scottish lass in *The Pride of the Clan* (1917) and cavorted in both rags and finery as a fiery Spanish street singer in *Rosita* (1923).

As both American and foreign women, Pickford often played people placed in unfamiliar environments in which they are not understood and sometimes openly derided. Her films are almost all, in some sense, pleas for tolerance and understanding among human beings. It appears that this aspect of the films was a conscious effort on Pickford's part, and she once urged the federal government to take advantage of motion pictures as a medium of international understanding and good will. On another occasion she wrote:

Because they are universal entertainment, the pictures will acquire a new world viewpoint. . . . A result of this change will be a new understanding between nations. Distrust and hate are often engendered by a lack of understanding, and through motion pictures we are all coming to understand and know each other. The films will prove a means of spreading the feeling of brotherhood throughout the world, and in time, I hope, be one of the chief factors in making even small and obscure wars impossible.[20]

Unfortunately, Pickford's optimistic hopes about war have not been fulfilled, but if there is any one theme common to all Pickford's films it is that nearly all of us are, or at least have been, idealists at heart.

Mary's disproportionately famous portrayals of little girls comprised a portion of her career that might be called a part-time specialization. The reason why so many identify her with little-girl roles probably lies in the fact that she created the illusion of childhood with a skill and convincingness that has never been surpassed by any other adult screen actress. Also adding to the confusion is the fact that her child roles are often lumped into the same category as her portrayals of adolescents (as in *Rags* [1915] and *Sparrows*). Mary certainly deserved the title "childhood's patron saint," but this referred more to her universal appeal to children than her portrayal of them. Actually, Pickford did not appear as a little girl throughout an entire film until her twenty-fourth feature, *The Poor Little Rich Girl*. Prior to that she had experimented only once in a feature film with a child role, in a brief sequence of *The Foundling* (1916). She plays a little girl in only seven of her fifty-two feature films, and in only three of these does she remain a child throughout. Ironically, at the age of seventeen in her Biograph days, Mary often played married women with children. Her portrayals of childhood were offset by the mature heroines of films such as *The Little American*, *Rosita*, and *The Love Light*. Nor are her little-girl characters stereotyped. Rebecca is very brash, precocious, and aggressive; whereas Sara Crewe of *A Little Princess* is much more timid, unassertive, and wistful.

Pickford put a great deal of thought and concentration into her portrayals of girlhood. For a twenty-five-year-old woman to convert herself into a ten-year-old girl was no small task, especially given the era's sometimes harsh lighting and lack of special effects. In 1917 she wrote an article explaining some of the mental machinations underlying her simulations of childhood:

. . . there are certain changes in the contour of the face that come with maturity. The face of a child is full and without the depressions that appear in the face of an adult. The adult who portrays a child role must resort to some method of concealing these depressions. Wearing the hair in long curls which fall over part of the cheek is one way of solving the problem. . . . There are many things to remember in impersonating a child role. For instance, the facial muscles of the grown-ups are controlled, while those of a child spontaneously reflect passing moods. A child pouts when it is displeased. When children are awed, or surprised, or frightened, their eyes open wide and their mouths droop, but their foreheads remain unwrinkled—and just there is another

Pickford, as the title character in *Kiki* (1931), wears the famous "question mark" hat.

difficulty, for when we older people are under the influence of similar emotions, our brows have a tendency to become lined. Then there are the muscles about the mouth: those of the child's, unlike the grown-up's, are relaxed. Another technical problem that is difficult to solve is that of carriage. You see, the child moves about freely, its arms swinging carelessly, its shoulders droop very slightly, the knee joints are loose, and the toes point inward. An actress can't be too careful in noting and copying such movements as these in the case of a child. It all takes time and study—more than my audiences have imagined.[21]

Thus, in her portrayals of children Pickford brought adult perceptions and sensibilities to a child's actions and likeness, but she did so in a manner that cannot be detected as adult perception. She was able to govern her actions precisely by virtue of her adult comprehension of the subtlest ramifications of a scene. We can watch a child in real life, and his actions are truly natural—if he does not realize he is being watched—but to try to get a child *actor* to duplicate a real moment of life convincingly, in a situation that he perhaps does not fully understand, can sometimes result in falseness.

The fact that Pickford was an actress of skill, superb technique, and long experience, however, coupled with her natural ability to assume the appearance of a ten- or twelve-year-old with uncanny conviction, resulted in impersonations of childhood that are unsurpassed in their credibility. But aside from her physical appearance and technical prowess, Pickford herself once explained the inner drive that really made these portrayals definitive: "When you see me in the role of a child on the screen, I am living the childhood that was denied me when I was a little girl myself. The child in me never grew up because it was never quite satisfied. So I still have the dreams and longings of childhood."[22] In 1922 she further elaborated on this subject, recalling her fifteen-year-old frame of mind:

One deep-seated grudge I held against the world. It had cheated me out of my youth. From the age of five, when the death of my father made it necessary for the rest of the family to make a living, life had been merely a procession of jobs. I had never really played; I had never been a real child, with toys and games and time to enjoy them. I knew how to make out a weekly budget that would keep just inside of a meager salary; I knew how to travel as cheaply as possible from one part of the country to another; how to talk with theatrical managers and boardinghouse keepers; but there is not much fun in any of these things. What I wanted was a real childhood with all the candy I wanted to eat and all the things that other children had. I was becoming a little bitter about it.[23]

Pickford never experienced anything that even approached a real childhood, having been a continually working professional and breadwinner for her entire family from the age of five onward. Above all these considerations, however, what really made Mary's little-girl characters so believable was the fact that she realized, as do too few people even today, that children are totally feeling, complex human beings, and she presented them as such.

Writing for *Vanity Fair*, Clare Boothe Brokaw (later Luce) found the Pickford films to contain "the wish-fulfillment dream of all democracies," and added that "there is always the element of optimism and uplift in her work, a belief in the inherent good that lies dormant in every human being."[24] She might have added that Mary's films never overlooked the fact that that "inherent good" is often decidedly difficult (and sometimes impossible) to locate. The Pickford films were generally dramas and melodramas, woven against every imaginable social context, sprinkled with comic bits and episodes. However, it would be terribly inaccurate to associate her pictures with maudlin melodrama and the Griffith films, for example, with great drama or tragedy. Griffith, in fact, tended to cling to the romantic or melodramatic conventions to a greater degree than did Pickford.

The person who goes to see a Pickford film to witness the unfolding of a great plot usually goes in vain. Fate plays a big part in many of her films: accidental

Cinematographer Charles Rosher's extraordinary lighting technique has seldom been seen to better advantage than in this exquisite study of Pickford in *Rosita* (1923). Rosher himself took many of the stills of Pickford's productions.

meetings affect the plot importantly; long-lost kinships are discovered by chance; characters gain new information essential for the advancement of the story by luck or coincidence. But these conventions pervade almost all of the films of the period and are unimportant beside the real essence of Pickford's films. Mary's message was the style and spirit of it all, and one needs to look at her films for their personal values, pictorial qualities, Pickford's pantomimic skill, and the exuberance of her personality.

Like many great creative artists, Mary Pickford did not have a happy, secure personal life in her formative years, and many years were frankly miserable. After eight years of treading the boards with second- and third-rate stock companies throughout the northeastern United States, at age thirteen she found herself no further ahead in the game than she had been at the beginning. She had always been willful and determined; but her drive and spirit slowly degenerated to a state of numbing depression. Even at thirteen she was old enough to perceive the frightening realities of the situation that surrounded her. In New York, her precarious accommodations were with a married couple who were kind enough to let her sleep in a Morris chair in the living room of their tiny tenement apartment. Mary remembered, "The chair was so narrow that it forced me to sleep with my arms stretched above my head. It was not until long after that I could sleep in any other position no matter how large the bed."[25] Around this time she was appearing in a play called *For a Human Life* and reached what must have been the lowest point of her entire professional life:

The theater was the old Thalia, in the heart of the Bowery. Yes, the Bowery at its cheap, tinsel worst. I lived in a little rooming house. The carpets were worn and threadbare. The furniture was chipped and rickety. Dust hung in the air. The windows in my room probably hadn't been washed in years. I washed them and then wished I hadn't. The view was not inviting. And the theater was even worse, but in a gaudy way. Its front was decorated with cheap lithographs of violence and crime representing scenes from the melodramas. Everything inside and out spoke of decaying grandeur: cracked marble, dulled gilt, creaking seats, raggedness, and dilapidation. When I looked at some of the women in the play my heart was filled with pity for them and

Mary Pickford surrounded by fan mail in December 1914. She was already recognized as the most famous woman in America.

Above:

Pickford and Owen Moore in 1911, during the period when they worked at Carl Laemmle's Independent Motion Picture Co. (IMP). Photograph by Frank C. Bangs, New York.

Right:

Owen Moore poses informally with Pickford in 1918. The couple was estranged, and this session was arranged for publicity purposes only.

dread for myself. They were fading so fast. Life had trampled them without mercy. The paint could not conceal the lines in their faces. Day by day their eyes became more dulled and hopeless.[26]

. . . [I]t was a great question whether the members of the cast or the audience [of For a Human Life] suffered the most during the performance. I took the part of a small boy working in a mine. I have never worked in one, but I am sure that it must be undiluted pleasure compared with my experience in this part. My make-up was hot and grimy, and I have never known a heavier sense of fatigue and depression than I felt night after night as we went through this awful play. I was pretty well used to the hardships, the sordidness, and, at times, the utter wretchedness of this sort of life. I had been on the stage almost continuously since I was five years old, traveling about the country . . . sometimes with no one to take care of me, seeking out cheap rooms in the towns where we stopped, doing my own washing and mending, and wondering if other people's lives were as miserable as mine. One learns, however, to accept these things. But there was another thing I could never learn to accept. This was the fact that the dreariness and fatigue which we felt seemed to be reflected in the audience. Night after night I watched their bored apathetic faces, their entire lack of response, and I felt I could have borne the discomfort of it all if our performance had brought some small measure of satisfaction to them. As it was, it seemed a most useless and painful business for everyone concerned.[27]

By 1907 Mary decided she had had enough. At fifteen she vowed to be in a Broadway production that season or quit show business for good and seek employment elsewhere. It was to be either the top or nothing. Luckily for Mary, and posterity, she did indeed land a part on Broadway (in the David Belasco production *The Warrens of Virginia*), and after its long run found her way into the movies.

Having done very well in Biograph films during 1909 and 1910, she secretly married fellow Biograph actor Owen Moore in early 1911, after signing a new contract at a better salary with Carl Laemmle's Independent Motion Picture (IMP) Company. Moore proved to be an abusive alcoholic and a jealous egomaniac who seldom offered Mary anything but criticism and derision. In 1915 Mary became estranged from Moore in an attempt to escape their nightmarish, crushing marriage. When Mary finally divorced him in 1920, she literally had to pay him off—in cash. During their estrangement, she fell in love with Douglas Fairbanks—a married man—with whom a future seemed impossible, if either of them were to retain their careers. Distraught by her situation, in 1917 she came within a hair's breadth of committing suicide by leaping from a window of her New York hotel suite. Yet, all this was going on during the period of Pickford's greatest popularity

and her most prolific and creative professional output. Many of her films were joyous romps, and it seems as though the happiness and personal satisfaction she never obtained until her marriage to Douglas Fairbanks in 1920 found their release and expression in her films—and only in her films.

Soon after her arrival at Famous Players (later Paramount and Artcraft), Mary Pickford became the focal point of the entire film industry and remained so for at least ten of its most important formative years. The historian Benjamin Hampton remarked:

Above:

Douglas Fairbanks with Mary, Mrs. Charlotte, Jack, Gwynne, and Lottie Pickford at the Pasadena train station in 1927. This may be the only surviving photograph of all five Pickfords together.

Pickford and Fairbanks enjoy the Pickfair pool by canoe in 1920. That they had just moved into the Beverly Hills house is evident from the newly planted landscaping and the barren hills in the background, which are now thoroughly populated.

Fairbanks and Pickford pose informally in the living room of Pickfair, 1922, when the house still retained its original Craftsman-style character. Mary extensively remodeled (both inside and out) and refurnished the home around 1930.

Opposite:
Pickford's semi-secret marriage to Douglas Fairbanks took place during the filming of *Suds* in 1920. Here the wedding party poses in front of Pickfair. Left to right are Charlie Chaplin, playwright Edward Knoblock, film actress Marjorie Daw, unidentified man, Jack Pickford, Mrs. Charlotte Pickford, Mary Pickford, Douglas Fairbanks, unidentified woman, and unidentified man.

Although theaters, studios, and exchanges in 1917–18 represented investments of several hundred million dollars, and gave employment to a hundred thousand people, Mary Pickford remained the industry's most valuable asset. . . . While [the] vast [perhaps 50,000,000] audience divided its affections among fifty to a hundred players, Mary Pickford was the outstanding favorite of very close to one hundred percent of them.[28]

She proceeded to exert an impact on the development of American filmmaking in many ways as significantly as Chaplin and Griffith. As Daniel Frohman, the great theatrical producer under whose banner Mary's early Famous Players films were made, said, "She was an expert critic."[29] Early on she demonstrated her ability to diagnose what ailed the movies. In 1917 she issued a statement that presently emerges as an amazingly topical portrait of some of the conditions that still hinder motion pictures (and television) as an industry today:

You want a truly serious interview? You shall have it. To begin with, I'm wondering just where the photoplay is drifting. Surely it isn't moving forward. It lacks leaders fearless, progressive and courageous enough to blaze the way. . . . The whole thing has become a mad race—in a circle. . . . The whole screen drama is in a complete rut of conventionality . . . producers fear originality and twist scripts into the hackneyed . . . the producer lacks aggressiveness. He will not venture. Just one man in the motion picture world will take a chance—David Griffith. He is the one man who dares risk anything to prove an idea. . . . Producers have been lax, extravagant, and impractical. . . . They have wasted thousands in the studio, in advertising and in the distribution of the photoplay. But they are standing still artistically.[30]

Pickford put these critical obervations to use once she began to exercise control over her own pictures, and the quality of her films increased notably. She did, in fact, conceive the idea of a star becoming her own independent producer; and once this concept was put into effect, she insisted on technical perfection at all levels of production. Considerations were made far beyond merely showing off the star to her best advantage. She did not fall into the trap of producing mere display vehicles for her own talents but created an impressive output of films that were also important from the standpoint of thematic content and technical innovation.

Douglas Fairbanks, Charlie Chaplin, and Mary Pickford (in costume) clown for the benefit of director Ernst Lubitsch on the set of *Rosita* (1923).

Above:
Sid Grauman with Mary Pickford and Douglas Fairbanks, placing their footprints and handprints in cement at the first ceremony in the forecourt of Grauman's Chinese Theater, April 30, 1927. Photograph by J. C. Milligan.

Left:
Fairbanks (costumed for *The Three Musketeers*) and Pickford discuss plans for the day over breakfast at Pickfair, 1921.

Fairbanks, Pickford, and Chaplin campaign during a
Liberty Loan Drive, 1917.

Mary Pickford, Honorary Colonel and "godmother"
of the U.S. 143rd Field Artillery, greets the regiment
in San Francisco upon its return from France in 1918.
She is perched on the shoulders of Private Kenneth
Harlan (a well-known leading man in silent films).

Pickford distributes signed photos and cigarettes to
sailors aboard the battleship U.S.S. *Texas* in 1918.
The Azo brand paper (detectable on the label of the
photographic paper box) is still manufactured by
the Kodak company to this day.

Opposite:
Pickford arrives to address a crowd
for the American Red Cross drive in
San Francisco, December 21, 1917.

Because of her new influence and high standards, Mary's post-1916 films reached levels of technical craftsmanship that were rarely surpassed—even though she was well aware of the fact that these efforts would go unnoticed (other than subliminally) by ninety percent of her audience. She was the biggest star, but she had artistic integrity; she knew the difference between a good film and a bad one; and hers had to be the best. As Samuel Goldwyn wrote, "Back of those lovely brown eyes, disguised by that lyric profile, is the mind of a captain of industry."[31]

Pickford's strong abilities in business and finance have become legendary. It has been said that if she had decided to become the president of General Motors instead of being a movie star, she certainly could have done so. In his autobiography, Charles Chaplin recalled a meeting between the principals of United Artists (along with their lawyers and managers) to discuss the incorporation of their new company early in 1919:

I was astonished at the legal and business acumen of Mary. She knew all the nomenclature: the amortizations and the deferred stocks, etc. She understood all the articles of incorporation, the legal discrepancy on Page 7, Paragraph A, Article 27, and coolly referred to the overlap and contradiction in Paragraph D, Article 24. On these occasions she saddened me more than amazed me, for this was an aspect of "America's Sweetheart" that I did not know.[32]

Why Chaplin was saddened only he could know, but perhaps he was expressing the prevailing attitude then that it was unthinkable for a woman (especially one of such youth and beauty) to be conversant with—much less expert on—such matters.

Mary's daughter, Roxanne, has mentioned that there was much turmoil during the transactions that resulted in the reorganization of United Artists in the early 1950s, adding that she could often hear the meetings from outside the closed doors of the boardroom at the studio. When asked if Mary raised her voice to make her ideas known, Roxanne replied, "My mother could be very forceful. She did not have to yell and scream. She had an intonation that put the fear of God into some very powerful men—or anyone else that bucked her."[33]

Edward G. Stotsenberg, Mary's accountant since the early 1950s and later a trustee of the Mary Pickford Foundation, recounted, "Mary could sit around a boardroom table with any ten men and outwit them all—as a group or on a one-to-one basis. I know this because I saw it happen."[34]

However, when an interviewer mentioned to her that she was the only woman in the history of the film industry with this sort of "preeminence" in business, and asked how she accounted for the fact that none of the other women who tried it accomplished what she did, Mary answered:

I suppose . . . it was that my pictures were my whole life, outside of my family. I never went any place. I never went to cafes, restaurants, never went dancing. I had no social life whatsoever. My whole life was wrapped up in the creative. As a mother lion or tigress, I had to assume the business role, in order to protect the thing I loved, my work. . . . It was a protective measure. . . . I run my own business; so I have to tend to these dry, dreadful meetings. . . . I never enjoyed it, to tell you the truth. . . . It's just a foreign atmosphere that I dislike. There's something about a typewriter that upsets me. It looks as if it's going to bite me—I don't know—I really detest it.[35]

Very early in her career, Mary began to keep a close eye on all facets of her productions (even before she was officially authorized to do so) and maintained a keen watchfulness for which she became noted in the industry. "I would like to concentrate on acting alone," she said, "but I realize I can't. I must be responsible for the entire production. So many things can ruin fine work. You must supervise even the printing and the developing."[36]

Although Mary never officially directed any of her films, it was often said that she directed her directors, without letting them know they were being directed—a rather neat trick, one must admit. She did, in fact, direct sections of some of her films in the absence of the director and never was at a loss to take over the reins on the spur of the moment in emergency situations. One such incident took place during the filming of *Dorothy Vernon of Haddon Hall* on location in San Francisco's Golden Gate Park, where Mary had herself, the principal cast, and scores of extras clad in full Elizabethan regalia. Director Marshall "Mickey" Neilan failed to show. As Louise Brooks related the tale:

It was nine o'clock in the morning; they had the great procession of horses, and hundreds of extras, and Mary was on her milk-white steed. They were all ready to shoot. It was a very expensive sequence, but there was no Mickey Neilan. So Mary said, "Who's in town?" "Well," somebody said, "we hear Norman [Kerry] and Jack [Pickford, Mary's brother] are in town." They scouted all the speakeasies where Mickey and Norman and Jack might be, and all the hotels, and they couldn't find them anywhere. So Mary directed the sequence. There was no trouble. She knew how to do it. Nobody thought a thing about it. Today everyone would fall apart and nobody would do anything.[37]

Apparently Mary did think something about it, however. At some point while she was absorbed with the direction, Neilan's tipsy, smiling face popped up in the crowd as he waved happily and said, "Say, you're doing pretty well," and then disappeared back into the crowd. Although he had always been Mary's favorite director and had made her most successful films, she was never to hire him again, save for the abortive first version of *Secrets* in 1930, which was only about one-third completed when Pickford abandoned the production.

Discussions with Mary's coworkers have indicated that her relationship with her directors was usually a collaborative one, each listening to the other's suggestions, but as cinematographer Hal Mohr pointed out, "Mary had a very firm way of suggesting."[38] Pickford explained, "Being the star and the producer, I simply didn't have the time to direct my pictures. That's what I hired the directors to do. That's why I paid them!"[39] However, it was no accident that, in his *The Parade's Gone By*, Kevin Brownlow slyly inserted his chapter on Pickford in the dead center of his section on directors.

Samuel Goldwyn early on noticed Mary's devotion to true craftsmanship:

In reality she made herself, for no firmament could have long resisted anyone possessing such standards of workmanship. I am aware that here I sound suspiciously like the press-agent, who invariably endows his client with a passionate devotion to her work. It is unfortunate, indeed, that the zeal of this functionary has calloused public consciousness to instances where the statement is based on fact. All screen stars are not animated by devotion to work. Mary Pickford is. To it she sacrificed pleasures, personal contacts, and all sorts of extraneous interests.[40]

She hired the best technicians in all crafts, and as a result production values in her films were far above average. She also retained Charles Rosher, surely one of the great artists among cinematographers, for twelve consecutive years; her films therefore emerged as examples of some of the finest photographic work ever seen on the screen. The special effects in the Pickford films—the superimpositions, matte shots, irises, dissolves, and double exposures—were generally much better than similar endeavors in other films. Most of the intricate double exposures (shot on one piece of negative before it was possible to combine two pieces of film)—for example, in *Stella Maris* and *Little Lord Fauntleroy*, in which Mary appears simultaneously as two different characters—could hardly be done better today.

The body of work created by Mary Pickford probably comprises the most consistent output of fine films produced by any of the superstars—any who produced as prolifically as Pickford did, at any rate. She accomplished this by surrounding herself with highly creative individuals and focusing on production values, as opposed to Chaplin, for example, whose personality and actions are really the primary creative aspect of his films. Great as his film work is, all that was inventive grew from him, which was right for his character. But Pickford's films have superior visual and technical qualities.

Mary Pickford witnessed the film industry grow from its obscure beginnings to a position of worldwide influence, and she learned all the techniques of filmmaking literally as they were discovered. As Charles Rosher recalled, "She knew everything there was to know about making a movie: she could do everything—she was a walking motion picture company." Her philosophy that a creative talent must be given a free hand in filmmaking is possibly best expressed by a statement she made to George Pratt at the George Eastman House of Photography in 1958: "No one ever worked for me, and I never worked for anyone. We always worked together."[41]

If greatness can be measured by fame, Mary Pickford has probably been the greatest star in the history of motion pictures. It is doubtful that any figure in motion pictures will ever be able to surpass the level of popularity she reached, for hers was truly a universal medium, unconstrained by any language barriers. Her pantomimic art could, and did, communicate to the people of nearly all the countries of the world, at a time when movies were a bigger part of people's everyday lives than they are today, and before the language barrier of the talkies set up national filmic boundaries. A crowd of 100,000 turned out in Moscow, of all places (in 1925, slightly after her heyday), just to see Pickford and Fairbanks arrive at the train station. Similar throngs amassed in London, Rome, Paris, Stockholm, Berlin, and Tokyo.

There is a simple phrase that explains what Mary Pickford communicated to the world. That phrase is "America's Sweetheart." Cecil B. DeMille wrote: "Scores of such phrases are born daily in Hollywood. Most of them, mercifully, die young. About once in a generation such a phrase lives on because it is more than a phrase: it is a fact."[42] The phrase may be a simple one, but it summarizes what all the complexities of Mary's onscreen image and offscreen personality meant to America and the world. It puts into words the unique spiritual message that she communicated to her audiences—a message that each individual comprehended, feeling not as if he were part of an audience to which Mary, an actress, was playing, but rather as if he were a privileged person for whom Mary, his friend, was performing as a personal favor. Once, after her retirement, a Hollywood producer made the distressingly gauche proposal to Mary that she relinquish the title "America's Sweetheart" to a promising young starlet he had under contract. She answered that the title was not hers to give; that, in fact, she had never officially accepted it, but it had been bestowed upon her by an old friend—D. J. "Pop" Grauman (father of Sid), who invented the title and put it into electric lights for the first time in 1914, when he was showing *Tess of the Storm Country*. Indeed he had, but Mary might have added that it was also bestowed upon her as a gesture of love by another old friend: the American people. The title has remained intact.

Portrait by Nelson Evans, Los Angeles, c. 1920.

PUTTING IT TOGETHER:

HOW THE MARY PICKFORD COLLECTION CAME TO THE ACADEMY LIBRARY

ROBERT CUSHMAN

Shortly after I began working at the Academy Library in 1972, I first contacted Mary Pickford (officially, in writing) about the possibility of her collection of still photographs and papers coming to the institution. She responded that, although she didn't have "very much left," she would eventually give what remained to the Academy. When the Academy held the grand opening of its new Wilshire Boulevard building in 1975, we decided to feature a huge Pickford exhibit (on two floors) to commemorate the event. Not only was she one of the great figures of film history and a founder of the Academy, it was (and is) widely believed that the concept for the Academy was originally her idea.

The Academy Library had a respectable amount of Pickford photos of its own, and I had by then personally acquired a substantial collection of Pickford stills. But, hoping to make the display as spectacular as possible, I thought of asking Mary for permission to borrow stills from her holdings, which we could copy for inclusion in the exhibit. She immediately gave her consent, and I quickly went to Pickfair to see what she had. Her husband, Buddy Rogers, friendly and hospitable as always, led me to a basement area, near the Western bar, and into a small furnace room. There, on shelves along one wall, sat a huge array of still photo albums. At this point he turned me loose and even found me a pair of pliers and a screwdriver so that I could take the books apart to access individual prints. At the end of the day, I borrowed more than 600 stills, some for inclusion in the exhibit, but most to be copied for the Library files.

Now we knew that Mary had much more material than she realized. But there was no further word from her regarding the collection coming to the Academy. When she died in 1979, I learned that her will made no mention of her collection of photographs, papers, and other memorabilia whatsoever. It was up to Buddy to decide. When I reminded him of Mary's letter about the material going to the Academy, he immediately agreed.

There was no further progress for over a year, as we awaited the sale of Pickfair. When it finally sold in 1980, the premises had to be emptied of all contents. Finally the call came, and off to Pickfair I went again, to round up the collection. This process turned into several days, as we discovered there was material scattered throughout the massive house: in various basement areas, in closets, in furniture, in Mary's room, in the attic, in her secretary's office, in cabinets in a storage area next to the porte cochere, in a storage area under the guest wing—and finally, in the enormous garage.

Portrait by Baron Adolph De Meyer, c. 1924.

I'm sure I combed every room, closet, and piece of furniture, from basement to attic, all this while witnessing the entire contents of Pickfair being dismantled and removed—an eerie, disheartening, and somewhat depressing experience. Pickfair was bare to the walls. Most of the furnishings were auctioned, with Buddy retaining pieces of his choosing, per Mary's wishes (stated in her will), for his own new house on Pickfair Way. The material I was able to piece together for the Academy—photos, papers, scrapbooks, clippings, etc.—was removed from Pickfair in scores of boxes, like a gigantic jigsaw puzzle, which became our job at the Library to assemble.

And then there was the garage! Amid piles of cast-off furniture and every other imaginable sort of flotsam were several boxes and crates containing even more stills and—incredibly—several thousand original 8x10 nitrate still negatives from Mary's film productions, some dating back to 1918. Even though they had been in the garage for decades with no temperature and humidity control, they were nearly all in perfect condition. This was an entirely unexpected bonanza. These negatives we later preserved by making archival fiber-base prints from them, with the assistance of a grant from the Mary Pickford Foundation. The prints now reside in the Pickford Collection at the Library. The garage also yielded one of the few remnants of Douglas Fairbanks found on the entire Pickfair premises: the complete still photo album for *Robin Hood* (1922).

However, the albums I had seen and accessed in 1975 were nowhere to be found. Later, to my dismay, I discovered that someone, somehow, apparently during the dismantling of Pickfair, had managed to spirit them away and sold them to various memorabilia dealers around town. I received legal advice that

Pickford and director Ernst Lubitsch consult on the set of *Rosita* (1923). The production was fraught with heated conflicts between these two iron-willed perfectionists, and they never worked together again.

Mary gently consoles a woman who has been the victim of rape at the hands of German soldiers in *The Little American* (1917).

an attempt to confiscate the photos for ultimate return to either Buddy Rogers or the Academy would be extremely difficult, would probably not succeed, and/or would result in the material being locked up for years pending a settlement of the case. At least we had already copied more than 600 of the best photos, and later, I was personally able to buy back several hundred more prints from one of the dealers who ended up with some of the booty.

In the mid-1980s, another incident occurred involving ill-gotten photos from Pickfair. Buddy had agreed to do a book on Mary with a writer whom he considered a personal friend. In his usual trusting manner, he turned over a large number of photos to this writer, who took them to his residence to "work on the book." Soon after, I was asked to review the material and identify the films and persons depicted in the photos. I gladly did so, and in return for my services asked to borrow about 200 of the prints, again to be copied for the Academy collection. I initialed the backs of all the prints borrowed so that those working on the book would know for which the Academy had copy negatives.

A few months later, a friend told me that yet another dealer suddenly had a huge new selection of Pickford stills. I quickly went to the shop without a thought that the stills I would see would be familiar and was aghast to discover that the stills in the shop came from the same body of material I had seen at the writer's house. Sure enough, my initials in my own hand were on scores of them. Mary's writing and that of her personal secretary were on many as well. File folders also bore the writing of the secretary. I was furious. This time, legal advice or not, I decided to blow the whistle. I said nothing, made a token purchase, left the shop, went home, and called Edward G. Stotsenberg, a trustee of the Pickford Foundation, about my discovery. Mr. Stotsenberg called Buddy's wife, Beverly, who in turn called the Beverly Hills Police Department, who in turn called me. Would I accompany two police detectives to the shop, my function being to identify all items bearing my writing, Mary's writing, or her secretary's writing? Of course, I consented. This was a tense and unpleasant experience but resulted in the police being able to seize all photos thus earmarked. The rest had to be left behind for the moment, and while the Rogerses thought they eventually got everything back, I'm sure there were several hundred photos (I remember them) that never surfaced again. Needless to say, that particular book project did not go forward after this turn of events.

I had personally collected over three thousand Pickford stills over the previous fifteen years. Next, I decided that these should join the Pickford Collection at the Academy, but I was in no financial position to make an outright gift of them. Moderately salaried, I had spent too much money and time to acquire them, and they were simply too valuable. I presented my case (and showed many of my photos) to Mr. Stotsenberg. On consultation with Matty Kemp, then managing director of the Mary Pickford Company, he decided to make the acquisition possible: the Pickford Foundation gave a grant to the Academy Foundation so that my photos could be added to the Library's Pickford Collection. My collection covered the 1913–18 feature films very well, whereas Mary's holdings for these years had been sparse; thus, the amalgamation of the two collections was a happy and appropriate one.

Then, more material came from Buddy and his wife, Beverly. They had retained a large quantity of Mary's memorabilia and gave the Library nearly all of it in two separate donations as additions to the Mary Pickford Collection. Around the same time, Mr. Stotsenberg also donated Mary's financial and accounting records, which he had maintained in his office.

The collection now covers photographically all of Mary's fifty-two feature films (1913–33) and most of her approximately one hundred Biograph shorts (1909–12), of which all but two were directed by D. W. Griffith. Also included are over eighty scrapbooks, script and story property material, and other papers. Unfortunately, the papers are scant for the years during which Mary was appearing in and producing her own films. Her production files and correspondence files for these years are conspicuously absent. Indeed, the extant Pickford papers primarily cover the 1940s through the 1970s, though there is a little (and some very good) material from the earlier years. For instance, among the financial records are Mary's federal income tax files, dating back to 1914—the first year in which the IRS collected income tax!

The fate of the bulk of her papers from her active years as a star and producer remains a mystery. Mary's personal secretary for over twenty years, Esther Helm, told me that when Samuel Goldwyn took full possession of the old United Artists studio (having acquired Mary's 50 percent interest) in the mid-1950s, Mary's files had been stored there for decades. As Mary was vacating her portion of the lot, Miss Helm received a call from the studio manager: Did Miss Pickford want them to throw out "all that old stuff" in her file cabinets? When Miss Helm put this query to Mary, she elicited the resounding reply, "Good God, no! Have them sent to Pickfair at once!" According to Miss Helm, the cabinets were dutifully delivered and relegated to the Pickfair garage.

Portrait of Pickford as Dearest, the mother in *Little Lord Fauntleroy* (1921), attributed to Charles Rosher.

What happened to them in the interim is unknown. Could they have been inadvertently disposed of without Mary's knowledge? I can only attest to the fact that they were not in the garage the first time I entered it in 1980. I asked the Pickford estate (Mr. Stotsenberg) if possibly this material could have been put into storage somewhere. After running a check, he relayed that they had nothing like what I was describing in storage or, as far as he knew, anywhere else. We can only hope that someday these valuable files will surface.

I can close, however, with the comforting thought that the still photographs in the Mary Pickford Collection at the Academy Library are unprecedented in their comprehensiveness and volume, and unequaled by any other archive in the world.

Isadora Duncan was one of the most important and influential figures of the dance world in the twentieth century; she looked toward classical Greece for her inspiration. Mary Pickford parodied her style in *Johanna Enlists* (1918).

Opposite:
As the title character in *M'liss* (1918), Pickford asserts her authority.

A Note on the Photography

The images contained on these pages comprise some of the finest examples in existence of still photography from the era of silent film. Indeed, today this style of photography is virtually a lost art form.

The still photographers of that period, both in the portrait galleries and on film sets and film locations, worked nearly exclusively with the 8x10-inch negative format, a practice that would be unthinkable today. The job required both artistry and considerable physical stamina. The 8x10 view camera and accompanying tripod were large, heavy, and cumbersome. So were the film holders bearing the 8x10 carriers and sheets of film. The film, incidentally, had to be loaded—individually, sheet-by-sheet—*in the dark*, before the photographer ventured out to shoot. Carrying all this paraphernalia all over the studios, around the sets, and onto locations was, quite simply, a lot of hard work. Furthermore, the film and the lenses were much slower than their counterparts of today, making the job even more exacting and time-consuming. But the pictorial results were superb.

The gloriously lit, sumptuously detailed, glittering images produced by the 8x10 nitrate film negatives of Hollywood's first decades can simply no longer be created. In the silent days, ample time was taken in the lighting, posing, and composition of the stills—a luxury which is no longer feasible given the drastic time constraints and enormous costs of modern film production.

Anyone who has ever thought that early film lighting was harsh should take a careful look at these pages. Richly toned and subtle lighting effects were the hallmarks of the industry during the early decades. In addition, the large format and slow speed of the 8x10 film allowed for exceptionally fine grain and extraordinary detail that can never be equaled by the modern smaller formats. In the silent-era stills, one can normally see the finest details—even the stitching in a costume, for example. Enlargements from the early 8x10 negatives can be blown up to six feet high with no graininess detectable to the naked eye and all the marvelous tonality intact.

About one-fourth of the photographs in this book were made from the original nitrate still negatives that I found in Pickfair's garage while gathering up the Pickford Collection for the Academy Library. The remaining stills were reproduced from original vintage prints by making 8x10 copy negatives, and from them 8x10 double-weight fiber-base custom archival prints. The copy negatives were made by Producers and Quantity Photo, and the superb prints (from both the original and copy negatives) were painstakingly produced by Manoah Bowman. The source for the frame enlargements from the Biograph films were 35mm safety fine-grain prints made by direct contact from the original nitrate Biograph camera negatives, which were donated by Mary Pickford to the Library of Congress in 1969.

The 8x10 negative format was almost totally phased out by the early 1950s, after which only special gallery settings were occasionally photographed with the 8x10 camera. Since about 1960, almost all still photography has been handled in the 35mm and 2¼ x 2¼-inch formats.

As in all other areas of her productions, Mary Pickford acquired the best still photographers available to cover her films, and the results were spectacular. She also sought the same quality for her gallery portraits, and was photographed by virtually all the best artists in the business. The work of many of the masters of the day is here on these pages: Evans, Hartsook, Abbé, Moody, Campbell, Fairchild, Hill, Rosher, Rahmn—and even Steichen and De Meyer.

Because this book deals primarily with Pickford's films, space considerations have precluded representation of many other fine portrait photographers who captured her: Witzel, Russell Ball, Melbourne Spurr, Alfred Cheney Johnston, Nickolas Muray, and so many others. But maybe that's another book!

Portrait by Edward Steichen, c. 1923.

THE SEARCH FOR MARY PICKFORD

KEVIN BROWNLOW

Portrait of Pickford by Baron Adolph De Meyer, in the dress she wore when she married Douglas Fairbanks, 1920.

Although I was born too late for the silent era, my interest in Mary Pickford goes back more than forty years. In the 1950s, silent pictures were regarded as a joke, especially in England, where I lived. You could go to London news theaters and see old movies parodied with ridiculous commentaries and whoop-de-do music. You could read patronizing comments in so-called film histories. But it was hard to see the films themselves. The British Film Institute occasionally showed silent films, but usually the prints were wretched and the films, worthy but dull, tended to be Russian or German. Even if they had had one, they would never have shown a Mary Pickford feature. There was a snobbery about film appreciation, which led to people being bored by high-minded Continental art films rather than entertained by something from much-despised Hollywood.

I became fascinated by early films when I was given a 9.5mm home-movie projector at the age of eleven; I discovered films starring Douglas Fairbanks, William S. Hart, and Bessie Love, but no Pickford pictures. Not that I cared. According to the history books, Mary Pickford seemed to have played little girls all the time, and her antics sounded juvenile and tiresome. Mind you, my parents, who grew up in the silent days and were serious film devotees, spoke of her with real affection. But she was hardly my type of actress, or so I thought.

It was not until I met a man called Bert Langdon that my outlook changed. In a sense, he was my tutor. But anyone less like an academic would be hard to find. Bert was a typical cloth-capped Cockney, an employee of a Camden Town piano factory. Unlike his colleagues, who spent their leisure time at a pub or football pitch, Langdon taught himself about music and the theater. He built up a huge collection of 78rpm gramophone records. But his passion in life was the cinema—the cinema of his youth. As a boy, he bought the rolls of 35mm film they sold for toy projectors—a minute or two of some long-lost silent feature—and quickly became a discriminating and knowledgeable collector.

There was a large circle of film collectors before World War II who would buy, sell, and exchange with each other, even though it was a dangerous business. Projecting the flammable nitrate in your home presented risk enough, but storing it could be equally dangerous if the conditions were not right. And these collectors used to circulate the films by mail and by rail. Imagine the devastation that would have been caused if a cigarette had landed on a parcel of films in a train! Worse still, what might have happened had Langdon's house been hit during the Blitz? His films were piled up in his cramped Camden Road flat, on the first floor above a greengrocer's shop, while the incendiaries rained down. The local tube station received a direct hit, and many houses nearby were blown apart, but, miraculously, Bert survived scot-free.

I first met Langdon in the early 1950s. He looked like a friendly gnome—a little man with a quizzical expression, a turned-up nose, and a high voice. But he was kindness personified. He sensed my enthusiasm and gave me an invitation to attend his soirées on Saturday evenings. The audience invariably consisted of middle-aged and elderly people who had grown up with silent pictures. They sighed over long-forgotten films that had impressed them in their youth, especially Rudolph Valentino. They must have wondered how this bespectacled boy fitted in.

These were not casual shows. Bert took great care with his presentation. Incense burned in a corner. Softly colored lights illuminated the proscenium, and the curtains were drawn electrically. He was forced to use a low-powered bulb in the projector because of the heat, but the original nitrate prints—and they were always original prints—were of such eye-popping quality that one forgave him. With one hand he cranked the ancient Powers No. 6 Cameragraph (1916 model), and with the other he changed the records on twin turntables, to provide orchestral accompaniment.

My first glimpse of Mary Pickford was as a youthful actress in Biograph films, those early American one- and two-reelers[1] made by D. W. Griffith. I could not quite share Bert's enthusiasm. Griffith was canonized by the history books as the director of the most spectacular films ever made, the man who invented all the cinematic devices ever known. And here we were, watching simple little stories of calf-love that were invariably directed in the standard fashion for 1911—one scene, one shot. If Griffith invented closeups, he appeared to have forgotten all about them. And as for spectacle, the entire casts of these films would barely have filled a touring car. But Bert made me look more closely at the performances. There was an immediate difference between the theatrical style of the older players and the delicacy of the newcomers, such as the Gish sisters and Mary Pickford. It was small wonder Griffith needed closeups;[2] he had to bring the camera closer to concentrate on the faces of these extraordinary young women. Besides being astonishingly beautiful, they had an almost electric gift of conveying emotion. They did not use their arms like the older players. They used their eyes. Eventually, I realized what attracted Bert to these pictures. The best were exquisite short stories. But the filmmaker in me recoiled from the primitive technique—the painted sets, the view from the stalls.

Bert had a rare print of the last film Pickford made for Biograph—*The New York Hat*, made in late 1912, which had been written by a young woman called Anita Loos. Charming as it was, it differed from earlier Biographs by very little. It was still minimalist. One Saturday, Bert told me he was going to show a more elaborate Pickford film, made just seven years later—one of the jewels of his collection. He begged me not to reveal its existence to anyone; collecting was then a proscribed activity, and collectors had served terms in jail. The Pickford film was entitled *The Ragamuffin*, which just made it sound another example of Victorian whimsy; it turned out to be the English release title for *The Hoodlum* (1919). That evening marked my conversion to Mary Pickford and my final surrender to the American silent film.

To think that such a technically sophisticated production could have been made just seven years after the primitive simplicity of *The New York Hat* amazed me. How had it happened? When was there ever such a rush of artistic and technical progress? (Such lightning strides certainly have not been made again—ask yourself what difference exists between the films of, say, 1990 and 1997!)

"What can one possibly find to criticize in *The Hoodlum?* I wrote in my notes:

It stands up as well today as it did when it was made. The entertainment value is as high, even though the story—of a ruthless tycoon realizing the error of his ways after a visit to the slums—may seem rather naive to present-day audiences, accustomed to somewhat different goings-on in slums! The most exciting thing about the picture is the way it is made. Charles Rosher's camerawork is superb, and in this original tinted 35mm print, some of his closeups are almost three-dimensional. *The Hoodlum* is one of those silent films that makes you wonder quite what we've achieved since. Completely satisfying entertainment, impeccably made, with a high degree of imagination and skill—obviously the work of people who *cared* about pictures.

Since the cameraman had won an Oscar for *The Yearling* (1946), I felt there was a good chance he would be still alive. (It turned out he was still working.) I sent him a fan letter in care of the American Society of Cinematographers in Hollywood. There was no reply. Why should there be? What advantage would there be in corresponding with a teenage film enthusiast miles away in England? I took the rejection as the sort of behavior only to be expected from Important People and forgot all about it.

A few weeks later, the telephone rang at my digs. "I'll bet you don't know who this is." The voice had an English accent, but with a slight American intonation. "It's Charles Rosher."

There was a momentary pause while I sank into a chair. "Did you say . . . Charles Rosher?" I asked, weakly. "Yes. Your letter was forwarded to my home in Jamaica by the ASC. I have some data that might interest you."

I managed to remain coherent enough to arrange a meeting at his hotel in Victoria. Rosher and his wife were awaiting me in the lobby. They were both short, she neat and delicate, he strongly built and assertive. He was dressed in American sports clothes, which, in the England of those days, were highly conspicuous, and he had a hail-fellow-well-met manner that fitted oddly with his English accent. He was extremely friendly and answered every question I asked him, but for some reason would not allow the use of a tape recorder; so I had to scribble down everything he said, making eating tricky. One thing struck me as odd. Rosher had no false modesty; he had no modesty at all. He took as much pleasure in his achievements as a ten-year-old, and while there was no necessity to convince me how splendid he was, he carried on as though I were a confirmed skeptic. I overlooked this for his generosity and kindness—not to mention the fact that he was one of the most brilliant craftsmen in the history of the business.

When I left him, I had been told far more in three hours than I could have picked up from a year of study. Rosher was born in England. He became a portrait photographer at Speaight of Bond Street, but an illness forced him to emigrate to Canada. He joined the fledgling motion-picture business when film developing was still carried out in bathtubs. Once he proved he could thread a camera, they made him a cameraman. He became a cameraman at the first studio to open in Hollywood, in 1911, and a year or so later he was filming Pancho Villa in Mexico for the Mutual Film Corporation. When he returned, he was taken on by the Famous Players-Lasky Company and became one of its top men. Mary Pickford poached him in 1918 when her previous cameraman—another Englishman, Walter Stradling—died suddenly of pneumonia. Rosher won worldwide fame for his lighting and special effects, and Mary occasionally lent him out to people she admired, like Norma Talmadge and John Barrymore. In 1927, he won the first Academy Award for cinematography, with his colleague Karl Struss, for F. W. Murnau's masterpiece *Sunrise*, still regarded by many as the finest silent ever made.

Photograph of Mary Pickford by James Abbé for *Suds* (1920). She is in costume but not in makeup for the homely Amanda Afflick.

The meeting was to have several momentous results. The first involved Bert Langdon. When I told Rosher about Bert's Saturday shows, he asked if he and his wife, Doris,[3] could come the following weekend. Bert was thrilled and brought out of the deepest recesses of his collection his favorite film of all—Mary Pickford and Charles "Buddy" Rogers in *My Best Girl* (1927). What an evening that was! The film was superb, and since Bert's favorite star was Mary Pickford, he and Rosher talked for hours.

Rosher became a close friend, and we saw each other every time he came to London. And when he died, in Portugal in 1974, he left me everything he had kept from his early career, including the Mary Pickford stills camera, which took so many of the photographs in this book.

By the time I had graduated in the film industry from office boy to film editor, I decided to put all I had learned about the silent era into a book. It would have been wonderful if it could have featured Mary Pickford, but by the 1960s she had become a recluse, and not even the Roshers saw her. Certainly no one had done a systematic interview with her, to my knowledge, for ages. I gave up on the idea; it was simply hopeless.

In 1964, with my co-director Andrew Mollo, I completed a feature film that was partly financed by Tony Richardson's Woodfall Films. Its pictures were distributed by United Artists. When he arranged for me to meet the head of UA, George Ornstein, in London, and he offered to distribute our film as well, I was dazzled by the name. To me, United Artists still meant Mary Pickford, D. W. Griffith, Douglas Fairbanks, and Charlie Chaplin. In the back of my mind I had heard that the company had passed into other hands, but I still imagined Mary Pickford was behind it somewhere.

As soon as George Ornstein heard that I was going to America, he offered to arrange a visit to Pickfair. He was married to Gwynne, the daughter of Lottie Pickford and the niece of Mary, whom she loved like a daughter. I explained that I could only afford to go to New York. (And I had had to sell my print of DeMille's *The King of Kings* to pay for that!) Woodfall producer Oscar Lewenstein said he would stake me the extra fare, and Ornstein promised me a trip to Pickfair and an interview with Mary Pickford.

Tom Webster, my host in Hollywood, and I had difficulty locating Pickfair. The few photos I had seen suggested a much more elaborate mansion than it turned out to be. It was a country house in the English style, rather than the over-decorated baronial hall that constituted so many Hollywood homes. We drove in to a covered entrance to be greeted by an elderly retainer. We asked, as instructed, for Miss Helm, and she informed us that—as I feared—"Miss Pickford was indisposed." Blast. But we would be shown the house and the estate by the elderly gentleman, Mr. Fenton, who turned out to be Miss Pickford's bodyguard. Our first port of call was the so-called Western bar, apparently a Pickford jest for Doug. In the days of Prohibition, this Western bar operated like a speakeasy, the door of which was set into the wall and operated by a switch. The room was equipped with an authentic bar over which "many a trial was held and many a man sentenced to be hung." Decorating the bar were paintings by Frederic Remington.

The whole house, eerily silent and incredibly neat, had the air of a museum, and it was frustrating thinking of Mary Pickford, alive, if not particularly well, in a bedroom so close above us. She was, said Mr. Fenton, "resting." Apart from a still of Mary and Buddy Rogers in Buddy's dressing room, there was no indication whatsoever of Doug's and Mary's careers. Perhaps such mementoes would have been too painful. The house seemed designed to impress others, rather than for its owners' personal tastes—hence a photo of Lord and Lady Mountbatten, who spent their honeymoon at Pickfair in 1922, was displayed in the guest suite. The only film book I spotted was Edward Wagenknecht's *The Movies in the Age of Innocence*, a study of the silent era with an impressive section on Pickford.

Outside, the grounds were of moderate size, with the statutory swimming pool. I filmed the winter roses with the 16mm movie camera I had brought in the hope of filming the elusive one. As our guide escorted us off the premises, we passed Miss Helm on the phone to Miss Pickford. I longed to grab the receiver and rattle off my questions before it was too late. What second chance would I ever have? Tom Webster and I left Pickfair, both rather sobered by the experience.

When I returned to London and reported back to George Ornstein, he was apologetic. Fortunately, I had met so many others from the silent era—from Lillian Gish to Buster Keaton—that I was in a totally bedazzled state. I gave up on Mary Pickford. It was a shame, for there was no denying her towering importance, but at least I had tried.

Thank heaven for Mary Pickford's niece! Because of the close family ties, Mary Pickford paid regular visits to Gwynne at Arlington House, the Ornsteins' home in Mayfair, London. Ornstein discussed the possibility of smuggling me into the house the next time she came. I told him that I had a copy of one of Jack Pickford's best films, *The Goose Woman* (1925), directed by Clarence Brown, and he said she would do anything to see Jack again. My diary recorded my frequent attempts to make sure this happened. Then I went to Paris, fell ill on my return, and missed a message that Mary Pickford had arrived. In desperation, I rang the Ornsteins the following day, hoping it was not too late. "M-m-m," said Gwynne. "Nothing definite. Maybe this evening."

But later that day, they were out. In an agony of suspense, I telephoned every fifteen minutes until I got Gwynne again, and she told me to come to Arlington House at eleven the following day.

I arrived to find the Ornsteins' place as unlike Pickfair as it was possible to imagine. It was in a state of chaos, with babies and nannies and deliveries. Gwynne was still in her bathrobe, her face strained. Trying to book a flight to Paris above all the noise was Charles "Buddy" Rogers, Pickford's husband. When he saw me staggering in with projector and screen, he laughed. But when things calmed down, and while I waited for Miss Pickford to appear, I was able to talk to him. Soon it was lunchtime, and Gwynne fed us. Still no sign of Mary Pickford. No one thought this unusual. Gwynne thought it would be fun if they could see *The Goose Woman*; so I set up the projector and screen and ran it. Still no Mary Pickford.

At the end of five hours, I heard footsteps on the stairs. I surreptitiously switched on the tape recorder. Beneath the screen, which I had hopefully left up, I noticed a pair of slippers, with gold tassels. A baby, one of Gwynne's grandchildren, was sitting on the carpet. As the slippers approached it, the shadow of Mary Pickford fell across the child, and I heard her voice for the first time: "Hello, man, Ah, cha-kit-kit-kit-kitty-kit!"

The baby, understanding perfectly, replied in similar vein. Miss Pickford then appeared from behind the screen. She apologized for her appearance. She was wearing a handsomely decorated dressing gown. She also apologized for not meeting me at Pickfair. "I had a very bad accident," she said. "I broke my ribs." She was seventy-two and looked her age, but the Pickford face was distinct. She turned out to be an endearing mixture of an old-fashioned fusspot, like an aunt in one of her pictures, and a highly amusing, intelligent woman.

Gwynne had found a reel of home movies which Mary had given her, showing her in the 1920s. As I began to lace these up, the talk turned to the origins of her family—with the emphasis on the Irish side. Her grandfather came from Tralee, in County Kerry, and she identified most strongly with the Irish, although she was born in Canada (in 1892).[4] I made sure she knew I was half Irish! We ran the home movie, and Mary spotted that a child with Gwynne was Charles Rosher's daughter, who took the screen name of Joan Marsh when she became an actress in the 1930s. I doubted that Mary would be able to sit through more than a brief extract from *The Goose Woman*, but to my delight, she was eager to see the whole thing: "I'd love to meet my brother again."

She watched the film with devout concentration. It looked beautiful—it was a tinted 16mm Kodascope Library print, made right from the negative. Jack Pickford's performance was very good, but oddly for someone who is said to have pursued women so relentlessly—(or perhaps not!)—he played it in a slightly effeminate way. Of course that fitted the role he was playing, of a mother's boy inadvertently identified by the doting mother (Louise Dresser) as a murder suspect.

At the end, she said, "I thought I'd be too emotional to see my brother, but I loved seeing him. Johnny would be a good actor today. Do you know, Kevin, what he is? A mood actor. He didn't act, he felt. That's a mood actor. I'm a mood actress. He is superb in this picture. I think it could be released today."

She saw me produce a notebook but luckily took no notice of the tape recorder.

Now, I don't mind if you have a notebook, because I'm used to it. I'm so pleased with you that I'm going to cooperate. Nobody follows in my footsteps today. It's too bad. Because they have a big heritage. They waste their time. Imagine that of all the children I have, Kevin, none of them have used my experience. To me, that is for me to die.

I've tried to start the museum in Hollywood and the one in Paris and the one in New York. I haven't liked the one in New York [The Museum of Modern Art]. I think they were naughty. They're not supposed to take my films and run them for money. If they make money, I want it to go to the Motion Picture Relief Fund. The museum in Hollywood has become a political issue. And I have withdrawn. I will not have anything to do with politics. The minute a politician walks into the room, I'm finished. Henri Langlois [of the Cinémathèque Française, Paris] wanted my films. I made over fifty features, and all he got was eighteen. Because we had difficulty, as you know, in finding them. They disintegrated. We had two fires—one in our office building, the other in our storage. We did everything to save them.

In 1931, Pickford was reported[5] to have added a codicil to her will ordering her films to be incinerated. I asked her about this. "Definitely. Well, frankly, I didn't want to be compared with the modern trend. If you look at the magazines of thirty or forty years ago, the writing is ridiculous. I mean, it's so sentimental."

Did she think that had happened to her films?

For a long time, I saw none of my pictures. Then a strange thing happened to me quite recently. A picture called *Suds* came out of the nowhere into the now. And she's funny! She's pathetic, too, without wanting to be. I seemed to inject into the character—what shall I say?—individuality. I was not standardized. Maybe it's a form of gratitude, I don't know, but I will not put my films on television. I will not do anything to that young girl who made everything possible for me. I will not exploit her.

I never thought, Kevin, that my films were important—I never did anything to save them. I put them in storage and when I opened several tins—just brown dust, red dust. Mr. Kemp is an ex-actor[6] who has been working on my films. He has such affection for my films that when he found two or three reels missing, he practically wept. When they burned, I called up and said, "Poor Matty!" and he started crying. I knew what time and love he'd put into them.

Mary Pickford may have been, as her biographers discovered, a heavy drinker, but there was no sign of it that I could see. While she occasionally got titles wrong and remembered things in the wrong order, I am equally guilty of

that, and I'm a teetotaler. She was fascinated by motion pictures, and when talking about them was as dogmatic as only passionate people can be. What delighted me was her sense of humor. I liked this extraordinary woman very much indeed.

I asked her about directing. Those films of hers that I had seen represented the finest qualities of the American silent film—in a sense, they were infinitely better made than they needed to have been. Her audiences would have been happy with simple sets and flat lighting so long as they had her; what she gave them was Art with a capital A. So what degree of control had she exercised over the films?

"Everything, if I wanted to use it. But I didn't use it. I would today. But you see I'm older today. As we get older, we get more positive."

I told her that one of her directors, Sidney Franklin, had told me that she was "the whole show," that she would direct if she thought it necessary. And Charles Rosher confirmed this.

I always watched rushes. My name was Retake Mary Pickford. Because I was never pleased, and that's why I'm not today. I see a picture and I say, "Well, Mary, you're pretty good in that scene," and I see others and I say, "Why, that's dreadful." I was never satisfied.

As far as directors are concerned, I rated Griffith first and Marshall Neilan second. Griffith used to say of me, "She will do anything for the camera. I could tell her to get up on a burning building and jump and she would." There is something to me so sacred about that camera.

I asked her how she would nowadays rate D. W. Griffith.

Great. Wonderful. But the parade passed him by. He was offered jobs but wouldn't accept them. He was too much of the Great Master, which, of course, I never accepted. I respected him, yes. And I even had an affection for him. But when he told me to do things I didn't believe in [at Biograph], I wouldn't do them. I would not run around like a goose with its head off, crying "Oooooh . . . the little birds! oooooh . . . look! A little bunny!" That's what he taught his ingenues, and they all did the same thing.

She clapped her hands and did a very funny imitation of Mae Marsh in *Intolerance*.

But he taught me a lot. For instance, in one picture' I was a poor little girl, and I had this miserable little coat on, with a moth-eaten fur collar, and a funny little hat with a bird on it. I came into my room, threw the hat on the bed, and threw my coat on top of it. Griffith stopped the camera.

Now to stop the camera in those days, with film costing something like two cents a foot, was unheard of. He walked over to the set and said, "Pickford, you'll never do that again. You'll never come in and throw your hat on the bed and put your coat down without shaking it. You must take care of your clothes. No heroine is untidy."

I said, "Yes, sir."

"Now, Pickford, you go back and come in again. Camera, Bitzer."

I thought, "Mr. Griffith's right." So I went outside and came back in, took my coat off, shook it, brushed the fur, fixed the little bird on the hat, put it down on the chair, and put my coat carefully on the back.

Mr Griffith said, "Very good."

That was the way he directed me. He once said that he could sit in back of the camera, think something, and I'd do it. He also said that there were only two people who ever outworked him—Lillian Gish and Mary Pickford. I think in a way he loved me, and I loved him.

I asked if she had as much creative control over her films as Douglas Fairbanks had over his.

"I'd say about the same, yes."

Gwynne interrupted. "Aunt Mary! More! More!" But Mary moved off the subject.

Portrait by Ira L. Hill, New York, 1916.

"I never had any trouble with my directors because I didn't embarrass them. If I wished to, I had the power, but I didn't believe in that. I don't believe in embarrassing people."

I mentioned that those directors made their best pictures for her because of the opportunities she gave them.

"Well, I gave them a free hand, but once in a while, off-scene, I would suggest things."

I added that she supplied the finest possible settings, from the best art directors . . .

The art directors! . . . *Rosita* and *Dorothy Vernon*—they were beautiful. But I would rather have a little shack with a beautiful story like Chaplin's *The Gold Rush*. You know he found the story at Pickfair? I gave Douglas these stereoscopic cards [of the 1898 gold rush]—three-dimensional—and Charlie was going out to luncheon with Douglas and me. He saw these cards. Douglas had a whole library of them, and he stayed the whole afternoon, and that is how *The Gold Rush* was born.

> Gwynne Ornstein interrupted. "Are you planning to go out this evening?"
> Mary Pickford replied: "Am I planning to do what?"
> "Go out this evening."
> "Well, you see, I'm a married woman and I don't say."
> "We'll have dinner sent up from downstairs."

Then we'll eat here. That is the mid-Victorian wife. And I'll never get over it. But you know, I think the girls today are no different. All we hear about are the beatniks. There are just as many nice children, nice teenagers, as there ever were. It's just like motion-picture actors. One or two misbehave themselves, then we all get a black eye. I was very strictly brought up, Kevin. You can see that by my films. I never did anything censorable. Never. Nor would I today. I don't think it's necessary. To be entertained, we don't need to descend to the garbage can. Or to hang over it and think bad things of people and situations. Look to the sky and to the stars.

She spoke of the work done by people like Debbie Reynolds for such charities as the Thalians, for retarded children. "It's too bad that more of the good things that picture people do isn't known." Mary herself did an incredible amount for charity, the full extent of which will probably never be known.

It was Gwynne who decided that Mary was getting tired. The interview had to be brought to a close. Never one to discourage enthusiasm, Mary said, "Two more questions," and she answered them fully and intelligently. We said goodbye so fondly I was convinced I would see her on my next trip to California. But although I visited Pickfair and tried to make contact I never saw Mary Pickford again.

When I had organized her interview into a chapter for my book, I sent it to Pickfair. Some months later I received it back, slightly amended. The book was published in 1968; I concluded the book with her quotation: "It would have been more logical if silent pictures had grown out of the talkie instead of the other way 'round."

The following year, I got married. My wife, who came from Ireland, reacted with enthusiasm to the early pictures I showed her—with only two exceptions. She couldn't stand the "Oirish" films of John Ford, which she described as "jigging pig," and she did not appreciate Mary Pickford. As a teacher of small children, she found the idea of an adult playing a child grotesque. Even when I arranged for her to see Pickford in an adult role, her reaction was antipathetic. She thought she overacted, or was "too cute" and unconvincing. This saddened me, but I realize it is not a lone reaction. There are plenty of otherwise sane people who find Mary Pickford irritating. Chaplin has suffered from revisionism, too. (My wife adores Chaplin.) No doubt the same thing will one day happen to Buster Keaton, who is enjoying such universal popularity at the moment. However, the fact that someone whose opinions you respect disapproves of one of your favorite personalities should not cause you to desert that personality. Opinions are not facts, after all. The facts are that millions of people have never heard of Mary Pickford, let alone seen her. But there are plenty of people curious about the past. If the films can be presented in big theaters, in prints of superb quality, tinted as they were originally, and shown at the right speed with orchestral accompaniment, they will make a huge impact. For this is what the movies once were—at their best—a past forgotten, as theaters are "multiplexed" and shrink to the size of phone booths. But public presentations, essential as they are, can only be the icing on the cake.

Pickford famously declared that she would not allow her films to be shown on television, but those were the days when films were interrupted every seven minutes for commercials. She could not have anticipated the videocassette revolution, which has largely replaced film collecting. Cassettes—and the superior-quality laser discs and DVDs—can do reasonable justice to the films, and they are far more accessible than the 16mm or 8mm prints of thirty years ago. Isn't it better that people should see the films again under these conditions than that Pickford's work should suffer the sort of neglect it has endured for the past seventy years? The Mary Pickford Foundation is making huge efforts to restore and revive the films, and they are doing film history an immense service. This book is intended primarily as a lavish kind of trailer for the films themselves. But like everything else concerned with Mary Pickford, we were given extra value. The stills taken in connection with those films were of a remarkably high standard. Many stand equal with the finest photographic work of the day, and I am sure, once seen, they will be exhibited as such. This book gives us the chance to bring from the vaults not only stills that became the most famous of their time, but also some so rare that they have never been seen in public before.

Mary Pickford, this is a salute from posterity.

MARY PICKFORD ON FILM, 1909–1933: COMMENTARIES

KEVIN BROWNLOW

During the filming of *Secrets* (1933), her last film, Pickford sits at her mirror with makeup man Roy Laidlaw, her personal maid Erna Jorgenson, and director Frank Borzage. Photograph by K. O. Rahmn.

32-424-P

AMERICAN BIOGRAPH

Mary Pickford was introduced to the movies in 1909 by a man who hated that word. If you used that vulgar term he would reprimand you.[1] D. W. Griffith, the chief director[2] of American Biograph, was an autocrat who longed to be a successful author of plays, like David Belasco, not a manufacturer of "galloping tintypes," which were still despised by those of the legitimate theater. Griffith was an ambitious man. He regarded himself as an artist, and he did what he could to turn the primitive motion picture into an art. He demanded the same respect and dedication from his players that they reserved for the theater. Since he was charismatic and distinguished, his company was mesmerized by him and became fanatically loyal.

Griffith's first encounter with Pickford, in the foyer of the Biograph studio, a converted mansion[3] at 11 East 14th Street in New York City, was not one she would remember with pleasure. He demanded to know whether she was an actress—this to a Belasco veteran! He told her she was too little and too fat. She thought him "pompous and insufferable," but as he led her unwillingly through the studio, she was awed by the ballroom, with its looming banks of Cooper-Hewitt mercury-vapor lights, the most modern form of studio illumination, giving a blue cast to everything— "sinister and uncanny" as she described them.[4] Griffith gave Pickford a test for *Pippa Passes*; she thought her makeup more appropriate for Pancho Villa than Pippa. When she was led out to work in front of the cast—no introductions, of course—she heard them using one another's Christian names. For one from the Belasco school, this was alarmingly familiar behavior. Mr. Griffith himself was always referred to as "Mr. Griffith," although he was anything but formal with Miss Pickford. One actor, "a handsome young man with a melodious Irish voice," stepped forward during the taking of a scene and enquired, "Who's the dame?" Mary was outraged, but when she stopped acting to demand why he was insulting her, Griffith was yet more outraged. "Do you know how much film costs per foot? You've ruined it. Start from the beginning."[5] Mary was surprised that Griffith invited her back for another day's work, but she quickly established her business acumen. Offered five dollars a day, she replied, "I'm a Belasco actress, and I must have ten." Griffith laughed and paid up.

The young man turned out to be Owen Moore—the Beau Brummel of Biograph—who became Pickford's first husband. It was Biograph company policy not to make public the names of their players, in the hope of discouraging the absurd (in the opinion of the producers) amounts paid to star names in the theater. Despite not being credited, Florence Lawrence had aroused such a following that she had become known as "The Biograph Girl," only to be poached by Carl Laemmle of the IMP company.[6] Mary was so full of personality and so astonishingly

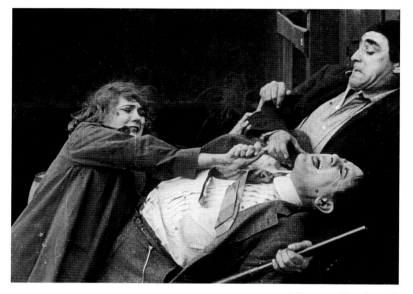

A Beast at Bay (1912).

Just Like a Woman (1912).

The Broken Locket (1909).

Ramona (1910).

When We Were in Our 'Teens (1910).

The Mender of Nets (1912).

The One She Loved (1912).

attractive that she was soon "The Biograph Girl" herself—and later was filched by Carl Laemmle as well. But not before she so impressed Griffith that he threatened to leave the company unless the Biograph management paid Mary forty dollars a week. They surrendered.

Nonetheless, her relationship with Griffith was stormy. On one occasion, when he shook her very roughly, she bit him. This, she insisted, was the only time she ever bit anyone. She shouted that she was through with pictures and left the studio in a huff. Griffith soon rushed after her and apologized on the sidewalk in front of the building. And she could inflict wounds by her choice of words—refusing to play a scene, criticizing the choice of story. "Wishy-washy" heroines and anemic stories were made a bit more believable, thanks to Pickford's frequent rebellions.

Perhaps because she was given some roles no one else wanted, she played a tremendous variety of parts—some of them, like frisky mountain girls or fishermen's daughters, excellent training for the feature films to come. Others, like *Wilful Peggy* (1910), seemed designed specifically for her boisterous and enchanting personality. In that picture, set in the eighteenth century, she is taken advantage of by a rake and turns on him with something of the fury she would display in *Tess of the Storm Country* (1914), apparently quite willing to dash the man's brains out with a stool.

Griffith hated the cold and avoided New York winters by taking the company to California. Here, he could give greater exercise to his pictorial sense, since the landscapes were so spectacular. His company worked at the old Spanish missions, in the orange groves, at the rocky seashore of Santa Monica—and in a deliciously picturesque village eight miles west of Los Angeles. One day, when Mary ruled the world, she would have her domain here. It was called Hollywood.

Despite her invaluable training at the "University of East 14th Street," Mary never lost her loyalty to David Belasco. She had told him that should he want her, she would come to him from wherever she might be. And so, late in 1912, after more than 100 films at Biograph, she joined the cast of *A Good Little Devil*. In early 1913, when she signed with Famous Players to make the film version, Griffith arranged for a "home movie" to be shot at the Biograph studio, showing Mary with Edwin S. Porter, David Belasco, and Griffith himself. It was a charming farewell gesture, and Mary's excitement can be seen in her eyes as she talks to her new director, Porter. A few frame enlargements, such as the image on page 77, are all that's left; the film itself, alas, no longer survives.

Griffith recalled in 1928:

She has tremendous driving power in her, a spiritual dynamo like Mussolini, and a most remarkable talent for self-appraisal. She never "kids" herself. The thing that most attracted me the day I first saw her was the intelligence that shone in her face. I found she was thirsty for work and information. She could not be driven from the studio while work was going on. She was—and is—a sponge for experience. Her spark burst into such a blaze that it has burned steadily for eighteen years.[7]

A frame enlargement of a private film that D. W. Griffith made for David Belasco shows Pickford with Edwin S. Porter (at left) and Belasco, in early 1913.

A Feud in the Kentucky Hills (1912).

The Informer (1912).

Won by a Fish (1912).

INDEPENDENT MOTION
PICTURE CO. (IMP)

Carl Laemmle, owner of the Independent Motion Picture Company (IMP), had already purloined the original "Biograph Girl," Florence Lawrence. It made commercial sense to steal her successor. Mary was unhappy with her salary at Biograph, and when Laemmle offered her $175 per week she accepted. For the first time in her film career, in December 1910, her full name was publicized.[8] Shortly after, in 1911, she secretly married the handsome Irish Biograph actor Owen Moore, who had also joined IMP.[9] He turned out to be one of those Jekyll-and-Hyde types, utterly charming at times and violent and unbalanced at others. Due to internecine warfare in the industry, IMP sent its company—Mary, her family, and Owen Moore—to Cuba, and it was on the voyage that Mary confessed to her mother that she was married. Charlotte cried for three days and nights, and Jack and Lottie refused to speak to their sister. They had good reason for this reaction. Owen was desperately jealous—not of other actors in the company, but of Mary's relationship with her family. He disliked the director, Thomas H. Ince, and came to blows with his assistant. Charlotte managed to get Owen and Mary off the island just as the police arrived, but the marriage—not to mention the association with IMP—was doomed.[10]

Pickford's films at IMP were not in the same class as those she had made at Biograph, but we probably owe them a lot in that they stirred Pickford's sense of dissatisfaction and determined her to attain a position where she could control her own productions. This still from *The Toss of a Coin* (1911) sums up the IMP films. Biographs were small-scale and often resorted to theatrical makeup, but they were not as cheeseparing as the IMPs. The "old" father is clearly a young man made up. The boy is Irvin Willat, who was not even an actor but was taken out of the laboratory for the occasion. Willat told me that when Mary wanted to break with IMP, one of the facts she brought up was that they had used a darkroom boy as a leading man.[11] Lottie Pickford is in the center.

Mary made about thirty-five one-reelers for IMP during 1911 and finished off the year with five more films during a short-lived stint at the Majestic company. She returned to the Biograph fold at the beginning of 1912.

In 1969, when I first met Irvin Willat—who became a director—he said the only film he had kept was this one. When he finally found it, it turned out to have deteriorated so alarmingly that the only thing to do was to bury it. So late one night, with David Shepard, then archivist for the American Film Institute, I somewhat miserably gave the last rites to one of the last surviving Pickford IMP films near a deserted highway in Culver City.

**Mary Pickford and Irvin Willat (far right)
in *The Toss of a Coin* (1911).**

IN THE BISHOP'S CARRIAGE

RELEASED: SEPTEMBER 10, 1913

This picture no longer survives. It was undoubtedly filmed in the starkly theatrical style favored by Famous Players. Its loss is a pity, because the chance of seeing another Pickford performance—whatever the drawbacks of the staging—is never less than rewarding. The *New York Dramatic Mirror* commented on Mary's "beautifully varied performance," and concluded, "An actress who can suggest feeling with so little apparent effort is indeed a rarity."[12] And *Bioscope* proclaimed, "We have rarely seen a character stand out on the screen with so much real distinction."[13]

I had always discounted this film because its title suggested a religious subject, and I imagined it highly sentimental. Far from it. Mary played a thief in the story—Nance, a girl on the run from a charity home, who forms a team with a crook, Tom Dorgan (David Wall). In the scene shown in this still, she is seeking refuge in his apartment. Their heists are successful until they stage a jewel robbery, and in fleeing the police she jumps into a bishop's carriage. This changes her life. She goes straight, embarks on a stage career, and switches her loyalty to a theatrical agent (House Peters). Dorgan escapes from Sing Sing and tries to take Nance with him, but the agent defeats him.[14]

H. Lyman Broening was cameraman:

We made one picture with Mary Pickford called *Caprice*. It wasn't anything to set the world on fire, but they figured Mary Pickford would carry it by her personality. The next picture was *In the Bishop's Carriage*—that was a cute little story and a better picture than *Caprice*. They decided to release it first.[15]

The picture was co-directed by Edwin S. Porter and J. Searle Dawley. Porter had made *The Great Train Robbery* in 1903, and in a scene in a freight car had included an impressive moving background. He suggested that Broening do the same in the interiors of the carriage.

"So we just held an old black velvet thing out the window so it wouldn't expose, and then I matted it all off except where the window was." He then photographed the scenery from a moving car.

"We had to make tests—they sometimes took longer than the actual scene. But that's how we got moving backgrounds—by doubling them in. It made the cameraman an awfully important person."[16]

This was the first and last Pickford picture to be seen by her English grandmother, who had assumed it to be a religious story before entering the theater. Not only did Mary play a thief, in an era when some people covered the legs of furniture, Mary appeared in a ballet costume, and Mrs. Smith was shocked to see her legs so shamelessly displayed. Her shock was doubled when she heard that Mary was earning $500 a week. "She's not worth it," she declared bluntly. And when Mary repeated the story in later years, she added, "I think she was right."

Pickford and David Wall.

CAPRICE

The makers of *Caprice*, Edwin S. Porter and J. Searle Dawley, considered this a pretty weak effort for Mary's first feature from Famous Players, and they released their next production, *In the Bishop's Carriage*, ahead of it.[17]

Based on a play, *Caprice* told the story of Jack Henderson (Owen Moore), a wealthy but disillusioned young man, who accidentally shoots a mountain girl while hunting. Mercy Baxter (Mary Pickford) impresses him so much that he falls in love with her, convinced he can transform her, à la Pygmalion, into a graceful and refined wife. He proceeds with the marriage, against his father's objections, but Mercy's attempts to educate herself are ludicrous. Embarrassed once too often, Jack admits his mistake and sends Mercy back to the mountains. After a while, he begins to hear about a Miss Wheeler, a friend of his sister's at boarding school. She sounds graceful and charming enough for anyone's wife, and Jack investigates. He is overjoyed to find that Miss Wheeler is actually Mercy and that he is married to her already.[18]

For one scene, Mary had to carry a fellow schoolgirl out of a burning building. Mary was only five feet tall, the girl was heavy, and Mary severely strained herself. She became violently ill and was taken to a hospital with internal injuries. There was talk of a ruptured appendix. Some historians have assumed that this event was a bungled abortion, heavily disguised. But whatever happened, when she emerged from the hospital, she could no longer have children.

Caprice may be lost, but the fan magazine *Picture Play* considered it had a lot to do with making Pickford a star: "It was received royally wherever shown."[19] Pickford had been signed by Famous Players at $500 a week; they now realized that she was undeniably worth it.

This photo shows Mary as Mercy Baxter in a lush bucolic setting, at odds with a review in *Bioscope*, which stated, "The Famous Players Company always seem a trifle eager to turn possible exteriors into studio scenes—using painted scenery—when Nature might have been made to provide a setting."[20] However, regarding Mary's performance, *Bioscope* continued, "Miss Pickford, like all other really fine artistes, is quite inimitable. There is no one who can even approach her. She stands alone."[21] This sort of praise seems extraordinary, considering that *Caprice* was only the second Pickford feature to be released.

HEARTS ADRIFT

RELEASED: FEBRUARY 10, 1914

Audiences were evidently shocked by the ending of this shipwreck drama. "It shows some pretty outdoor scenes on the Pacific Coast," reported *Variety*, "with a burning volcano the main scenic thriller, and Miss Pickford doing a Brodie into the seething sulphur with her island baby clasped in her arms. That's a gruesome enough ending for any ordinary picture actress, let alone one of Miss Pickford's reputation."[22]

The film was based on a magazine story that Mary had read, but she could not remember when or where, author, or title. The company wanted to do it anyway. "I told them it wasn't original and the author would come after us," Mary said, but Edwin S. Porter insisted and paid her $100. The author did come after them, and Famous Players paid up—even though he had, in his turn, plagiarized the climax of the 1912 play by Richard Walton Tully, *Bird of Paradise*.[23]

This was Famous Players' first production on the West Coast, and it was shot in December 1913, about the same time as Cecil B. DeMille's *The Squaw Man*, the first feature to be filmed in the town of Hollywood.

The film was such a success that Mary was encouraged by her mother (and manager), Charlotte, to approach Adolph Zukor and ask for a raise. Zukor took her to tea to discuss it at the Hotel Breslin in New York, just across the street from the Hamilton Theater.

"Mary," said Zukor,

I want you to know that your happiness means everything, not only to me personally, but to my pictures and to my company as a whole. You asked me for more money. How would you like to have your salary doubled?[24]

Mary said she must have beamed unashamedly at the prospect of one thousand dollars a week. Every so often her eyes flicked across the street, noticing the title of the film; it should have been *Hearts Aflame*. It was February and getting dark, and the lights of Broadway were coming on.

"Suddenly I saw it," wrote Mary.

One of the most thrilling sights of my whole career: my name blazing on the marquee. That was the first time I saw my name in electric lights. That dear, sweet man had planned his surprise with such loving care, and I had repaid him by asking him for a raise![25]

A GOOD LITTLE DEVIL

RELEASED: MARCH 1, 1914

A Good Little Devil was Mary Pickford's first feature-length production, although the fourth to be released. It was produced by arrangement with David Belasco, the leading impresario of the time, and a great character in his own right. He carried himself with such dignity, always wearing a clerical collar, that he was known as The Bishop and was regarded with awe. Critic Gilbert Seldes thought he gave himself "insufferable airs." But if anyone fulfilled the American dream, it was Belasco. Who could have guessed he had been a poor Jewish boy from the Lower East Side? His greatest contribution was the illusion of realism on stage; so it was only to be expected that he would display an interest in the motion picture.

The play of *A Good Little Devil*—a fairy tale along Peter Pan lines—was written by Rosemonde Gerard and her son Maurice Rostand and adapted for Belasco by Austin Strong. Belasco felt that the part of the blind girl would be ideal for Mary, with whom he had had such rapport during *The Warrens of Virginia* in 1907. After that success, Mary had said, "Mr. Belasco, remember, no matter where I am or what I am doing, when you want me, just let me know and I'll come." Mary was doing splendidly at Biograph with Griffith, but when the call came, she obeyed.

Mary's presence in the play brought her motion-picture fans and the publicity cameras out in force. This film version was a literal filming of the play. Mary later called it "one of the worst pictures, if not the worst picture I ever made."[26] She wrote in 1923:

It was not a good picture, largely because stage technique was followed too closely. The stage manager held the book of the play, and we all went through our lines just as on the stage. It was not according to Griffith's methods, and I feared that it would not turn out well. I had been in about one hundred and fifty pictures and written about thirty, and I felt I knew something about pictures.[27]

It was shot in May 1913 at the Famous Players New York studio on 26th Street. The idea that the players must religiously speak their lines was J. Searle Dawley's. Porter's associate, Dawley became a director and made the first two Pickford features to be released, *In the Bishop's Carriage* and *Caprice* (both lost), and many films with Marguerite Clark, a Pickford rival. Although Mary was apprehensive about the outcome of the film, audiences of the time responded with enthusiasm. *Bioscope* declared, "Miss Pickford plays the blind girl with a beauty and pathos that no other actress one knows of could have managed."[28]

At an exhibitor's convention, Mary and the cast played the prologue as if for the camera, and the celluloid version was then projected—to tremendous applause. As *Variety* put it, "Here's one film on which the movie exhibitors of the country can't go wrong."[29]

The opening of *A Good Little Devil*—it was Zukor's idea to show Belasco in his study, while the wraiths of the characters float past. Mary is double-exposed on the right. The other players are (left to right) Edward Connelly, William Norris (as the old woman), Wilda Bennett, and Ernest Truex.

TESS OF THE STORM COUNTRY

RELEASED: MARCH 20, 1914

When I interviewed Adolph Zukor in the 1960s. I was in my twenties. and he was in his nineties. He was the oldest person I had ever met. In his oak-paneled office in the Paramount building in New York. where he was still chairman of the board. he spoke of his pioneering days with reluctance. as if a trifle embarrassed to have lasted so long. But when I asked him which films he recalled with most affection. he was unambiguous. "I am most proud of *Tess of the Storm Country*, *The Covered Wagon*, and *The Ten Commandments*. I've made other pictures of importance. but nothing that gave me the thrill of those pictures."[30]

Although quite primitive. even for the time. one can understand audiences going mad over *Tess*. It consists of a series of surefire situations: the tyrannical rich man. the Deacon. who tries to evict the poor squatters. and the tough little spitfire who resists him. yet who saves the rich man's daughter from disgrace by taking charge of her illegitimate baby. Of course. the rich man's son is in love with her. and since he's a theological student. she obligingly steals a Bible to understand him better. But when he sees "her" baby. he abandons her. The climax (shown in the photograph below) comes with the imminent death of the baby. Tess

ELDER GRAVES DENOUNCES TESS AND THE FATHERLESS BABE.

MARY PICKFORD IN "TESS OF THE STORM COUNTRY"

PRODUCED BY THE FAMOUS PLAYERS FILM Co.

believes that if he is not "sprinkled"—i.e., baptized—he will never get to heaven. So she scandalizes the congregation by marching up to the font with the infant. The Deacon prevents the vicar from baptizing the godless child; so she does the job herself. And then the Deacon's daughter steps forward and claims the baby as her own—a tremendous moment in the history of melodrama.

B. P. Schulberg wrote the scenario, based on the hugely successful Grace Miller White novel that had been adapted for the stage by Rupert Hughes in 1912. It is difficult to believe he failed to introduce any of the characters apart from Mary, but if the surviving version is anything to go by, he abbreviates the plot so willfully he must have expected everyone in the audience to be as familiar with the story as he was. Edwin S. Porter shows talent in his camera setups; there are some marvelous exteriors in what would now be called "deep focus," characters appearing in the far distance while the viewer is concentrating on the foreground. The exteriors are the best part of the picture, shot in Del Mar and at the Japanese fishing village in Santa Monica. The interiors, shot at the old Bradbury Mansion on Bunker Hill, Los Angeles,[31] are as stagey as one would expect for a picture of this age. It is a ragbag of acting styles; the direction simply lets everyone get on with it. Thus Harold Lockwood, who a year or two later was playing comedy leads superbly for director Fred Balshofer, presents here a parody of the stock-company juvenile. Whereas Mary is brilliant; her character, incredibly strong, frenetically angry, bursts from the screen. You wonder how anyone so small can be so powerful; it is perhaps the most violent performance she ever gave.

Mary Pickford summed up Porter thus: "He made the Simplex projection machine. He owned part of Famous Players. He knew nothing about directing. Nothing."

"So was the film a poor one?" I asked.

No. It saved the company. They thought I was just another actress, but when I made *Tess of the Storm Country*, that was really the beginning of my career. Mr. Zukor told me he had found a wonderful story. I said I didn't want to read it. He used to call me "sweetheart honey." He said, "Sweetheart honey, read it." So I read it. I couldn't wait to call him in the morning. I said, "Mr. Zukor, this is the most wonderful story. I'd be happy to do it. I can't wait to start."[32]

Mr. Zukor told me later that he had taken his wife's necklace and his own insurance to pay salaries. Never once did he complain. Our salaries were there every Saturday. But it was such a surprise for everybody, myself included, because we didn't see any rushes. They had no means in Hollywood to develop the film. The negative was sent to New York, which was very dangerous; so none of us knew what the picture was going to be like.[33]

The heart of the story is Tess's selflessness in taking Teola's baby and pretending it's her own. When *Motion Picture Magazine* chose its first group of classics in 1916, *Tess* was described as Mary's most sympathetic role. "Runs the gamut of her emotions, from childish appeal and spritely comedy to fine pathos and rugged dramatics."[34]

This scene shows Tess clambering down from a jailhouse window, where she has been talking to her beloved father. *Tess of the Storm Country* would be the only one of her pictures that Mary Pickford would remake. It was the film that sent her career into orbit and made her the most popular actress in America, if not the world.

Mary Pickford may have stood up against some of D. W. Griffith's direction and avoided the most cloying of his portrayals of young girls, but his influence is apparent in much of her work. *The Eagle's Mate*, directed by James Kirkwood, was a story of moonshining in the mountains of West Virginia. In the introduction, we see Mary, playing Anemone Breckenridge, chatting to a bird, which shows its affection by clambering onto her face. This was a characteristic Griffith touch. He takes it back again in *The Birth of a Nation*, released the following year, in which Lillian Gish kisses a dove. Such extreme sentiment belonged to Valentine cards and song slides and would almost vanish from the movies by the 1920s.

But *The Eagle's Mate*—and *The Birth of a Nation*—were both produced in 1914, when features were a mere two years old. No one could be certain that features would last, and while Griffith was determined his pictures should play in the most prestigious theaters in the world, Mary knew that her films would be shown in every kind of theater imaginable. To every kind of audience. Such devices were an essential part of the campaign to "sell" a star. Fortunately, the picture had more sophisticated aspects.

Historians talk of how deep focus was introduced by Gregg Toland in *Citizen Kane* (1941). Photographed by the long-forgotten cameraman Emmett A. Williams, *The Eagle's Mate* contained an astonishing shot, during a big shootout, in which the camera looks over Mary's shoulder at a battle raging in the distant valley. Thomas H. Ince had shown distant battles, but never in so striking a setup. The films of the 1910s may not be as advanced technically as those of the 1920s, but they often contained more surprises.

This was Mary's first collaboration with fellow Canadian James Kirkwood. There was a great deal of pressure on Kirkwood, who also played the lead, as the film had to follow the staggering success of *Tess of the Storm Country*. In this gorgeously backlit photograph of Mary as Anenome and Kirkwood as Lancer Morne, the use of a reflector illuminates Mary but not Kirkwood.

Variety's editor was puzzled by the strength of Pickford's appeal and became philosophical in his notice:

Mary Pickford is one of the few actresses who can interject personality into a negative. She breathes the role taken and it fits her up, down and all around. Peculiar hold a picture will take. Here is this slip of a girl carrying the admiration of millions, and millions of those who would never have seen her if she had become the greatest of $2 stars on the footlighted stage. *The Eagle's Mate* is a lively feature without real kick—but it has Mary Pickford, better than the best kick or punch that could have been put in.[35]

Pickford and James Kirkwood in *The Eagle's Mate*.

SUCH A LITTLE QUEEN

RELEASED: SEPTEMBER 21, 1914

This quaint title conceals a fascinating plot, and the recent situation in the Balkans has made it topical again. The film was set in Bosnia and Herzegovina. By the time it was released, this part of the world had already sparked off the Great War, but the story was set earlier in the Balkan conflict. The powers behind the thrones decide on an alliance between the Queen of Herzegovina (Mary Pickford) and the King of Bosnia (Carlyle Blackwell). The monarchs detest the idea but are persuaded into marriage by the prime minister. In the middle of the ceremony, an uprising breaks out, and the royal families have to flee. With the help of a young American, Robert Trainor (Harold Lockwood), the queen and her retinue arrive in New York closely followed by the Bosnian king. The only work the heads of state can get is in a meat-packing plant.

The trade press thought these American scenes very funny:

The deposed queen, seen in the kitchen of her Harlem flat in her coronation robe, in order that her only street dress may retain its usefulness, mashing potatoes with her scepter, jumping with fright at every blast of the dumb-waiter whistle, and putting her shoes in the ice-box, provide many of the humorous moments of the film.[36]

Their only criticism lay in the Bosnian mob scenes, which they felt had not used enough extras. Hugh Ford, who co-directed with Edwin S. Porter, made up for this when he went to Italy later in the year to make *The Eternal City* (1915) and staged crowd scenes that, thanks to official cooperation, were monumental.

Julian Johnson, *Photoplay*'s critic, thought the story an absolutely irresistible idea, "but somehow it missed fire in the vocal play and it missed fire again on the screen."[37]

These photographs show Mary as the queen, in regal glory before the coup, and later, after her flight to America.

BEHIND THE SCENES
RELEASED: OCTOBER 26, 1914

*B*ehind the Scenes will soon be rescued from oblivion by the George
Eastman House, with funding from the Mary Pickford Foundation
and other donors. Its advertising slogan was "a fascinating play that
contrasts the drama of life with the glamor of the footlights."

Audiences of the silent days craved the glamor that was missing from
their own lives. They loved stories that showed someone as ordinary as
they were catapulted to the heights. Such stories may have been variations
on Cinderella, but only the superior critics made the connection. A hefty
dose of temptation helped to bring in the public, and Mary is saved from
it here by her husband, Steve (James Kirkwood), who takes her from the
stage to a farm out west, and orders her to stay put. Dutiful she might be,
but she is quickly bored, and an offer from impresario Joe Canby (Russell
Bassett) is irresistible. She sweeps to stardom, and Canby comes to her
dressing room one night to reap his reward. She is rescued by Steve and
returns meekly to the same world to which the audience will also return,
their morale boosted by the confirmation that theirs is the only worthwhile life.

The film is highly unusual in that it portrays a wife who refuses to
honor and obey, however much she loves. There is a wonderful moment
when Kirkwood comes in from the fields and slumps down to eat a meal,
staring all the while at a paper. Mary stares at him, unable to believe any
man could behave so churlishly. Marriage or no marriage, she is going to
do what she damn well wants—and leaves him, not for another man, but
for the work she loves. The picture was made by people intimate with the
theater, so it has remarkable authenticity. The attempted seduction by the
impresario is intelligently handled and contains a twist: Canby's advances
are interrupted by Steve and his pal Teddy (Lowell Sherman). Mary, not
wanting him to be beaten up, pushes Canby out of sight. But Steve discovers him and, profoundly shocked, walks straight out.

Behind the Scenes contains Mary's most sympathetic performance
from these early days—it is such confident cinema that it is hard to believe that it comes from the same year as *Tess*. Both the film and Pickford's
performance elicited raves from the critics. *Motion Picture News* declared,

To say that she acts the part to life would no doubt sound trite and unconvincing, and yet in no other way can we express our unbounded admiration. It really seems uncanny to sit and watch the different emotions . . . depicted on her
face, and then come back to earth . . . with the realization that it is only acting
. . . the smoothness with which the scenes follow one another, the special attention which has been given the smallest detail . . . all this taken with the wonderful acting of Miss Pickford makes *Behind the Scenes* a masterpiece.[38]

It was generally believed in the industry that James Kirkwood
and Mary were lovers, a discomfiting thought considering the fact
that he frequently directed Owen Moore. But according to a similar
rumor, Charlotte once dispatched an employee to raid his apartment
at 3:00 A.M. in order to remove Mary. It sounds like the plot of this film,
but this incident was said to be the reason the Pickford company later
ended his unique nine-picture run. He continued to direct Jack, however. And he was subsequently signed to direct Mary Miles Minter,
one of Mary Pickford's strongest rivals.

Mary, her mother (right), and director
James Kirkwood at the premiere.

Opposite:
Pickford and James Kirkwood
in *Behind the Scenes.*

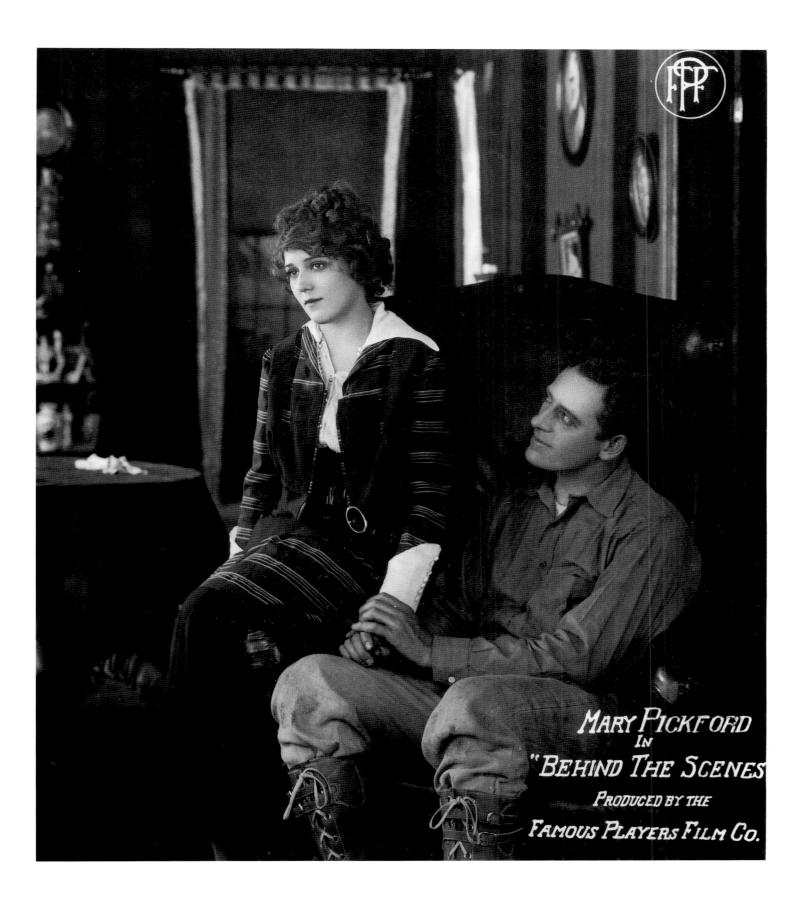

MARY PICKFORD
IN
"BEHIND THE SCENES
PRODUCED BY THE
FAMOUS PLAYERS FILM CO.

CINDERELLA

RELEASED: DECEMBER 28, 1914

Famous Players evidently decided not to meddle with this fairy tale but to give it a straightforward treatment. Hoping it would appeal as much to adults as to children, they cast Mary Pickford in the title role with her husband, Owen Moore, as Prince Charming. They planned it for release at Christmas 1914. It was an appropriately featherweight production, but director James Kirkwood chose impressive locations in Greenwich, Connecticut, for the royal palace and its grounds. The cameraman (undocumented, but almost certainly Emmett Williams) went to great pains to achieve multiple superimpositions of the fairies in the forest glades. The interiors were solidly built, to Belasco standards. So it is surprising that *Variety* greeted it with thinly disguised contempt:

In these days of feature film making, one naturally expects a lot for his money, particularly when comparison is invariably drawn with previous productions. When the Famous Players announced a feature production of *Cinderella* it would be expected it would be something out of the ordinary. . . . The photography is bad. The picture from every standpoint, and especially what was expected of it, is a disappointment. Much of it gives the impression that the camera had been placed a long way from the actors. *Cinderella* may please the kids, but the adults will likely have a different opinion.[39]

This still of Mary as Cinderella and Owen Moore as Prince Charming shows the lushness of the forest location and the intricate detail of the beautifully designed costumes.

Long considered lost, the film was discovered in the Nederlands Film Museum. *Variety*'s review proves to be uncharacteristically harsh, written as though from a much later date. Keeping the camera a long way from the actors was standard in 1914, even though closeups had been seen for years, and Kirkwood uses them here when the story calls for them—as in the cut-in to the shoes being fitted in the court. There is no hint of "dim" photography—that must have been due to poor projection, still occasionally a problem in 1914. Much of the photography is "bright"—filming in sylvan glades in filtered sunlight gives it the look of a Victorian watercolor. Admittedly, however, the picture lacks imagination. Kirkwood obtained permission to shoot in some wealthy homes, and he clearly felt that was enough. The trick photography is very straightforward and does not compare to that of French filmmaker Georges Méliès. Nonetheless, it is quite proficient for an American film of the time, and there is nothing like it in any other of Mary's early Famous Players films. Cinderella fetches a pumpkin from the garden and places it in a courtyard and sure enough—slow dissolve—we see a fairy coach. There is no attempt to make the pumpkin turn into the coach without a dissolve, as in Herbert Brenon's *A Kiss for Cinderella* (1926). But there is an effective dream sequence in which Cinderella is tormented by the palace clock, and there was much to appeal to audiences for whom feature films were still a novelty.

THE KING PROFESSES HIS LOVE FOR NELL.

Mistress Nell was based on the George C. Hazelton play, and perhaps the theatrical origins of the film made *Variety* expect something special in the way of acting. As it was, none of the performances—not even Owen Moore as King Charles II—were spared the critic's knife except Mary Pickford's, as Nell Gwynne, about whom it was said, "England would be worse than a Puritan funeral without her."[40]

Charles II is caught in the intrigues of Louise, the Duchess of Portsmouth (Ruby Hoffman), who tries to steal his heart from Nell as well as his kingdom. Louise is a spy for the King of France and, in league with the Duke of Buckingham, plans to hand over papers that would place England in the power of France. It is Nell who, putting on her boldest performance, disguises herself as a fashionable young blade and wins the confidence of the duchess. She is even entrusted with the delivery of the documents, but she makes sure they go to the King of England rather than the King of France.[41]

This photograph, taken on location in the Connecticut countryside, shows Mary as Nell and Owen Moore as the king.

FANCHON THE CRICKET

RELEASED: MAY 10, 1915

Above:

**Mary confronts, startles, and charms
Jack Standing as Landry.**

Opposite:

Pickford as Fanchon.

*F*anchon the Cricket, directed by James Kirkwood, has just been rediscovered in the National Film and Television Archive in England. It is not complete, but from the three and a half reels (out of five) that survive one can appreciate that, despite a slender story, it has exquisite photography (by Ed Wynard) and such ravishing locations (the Delaware Water Gap) that it is essential viewing for Pickford enthusiasts. It opens with Mary rolling down a hill in her most tomboyish fashion. She is extraordinarily beautiful; the first closeup of her face among the glistening leaves comes as an almost physical shock. *Variety*, however, was not impressed: "Barring the usual Mary Pickford personality, and that only visible in spots, there is very little about *Fanchon the Cricket* to justify its presence in a market consisting of first-class contenders exclusively."[42] They thought the story could have been told better in one reel. (Universal obliged the following month.)

The *Moving Picture World* reviewer, however, was in total disagreement:

I would be willing to take out every title. There are not many titles, but the picture runs so naturally, the development of the plot there is comes with the convincing simplicity of a fairy tale. . . . We must remember that color and voice played an integral part of the drama as we saw it years ago, and here the director had neither color nor voice to depend on, in spite of which he has given us a visualization of which the conventional stage is quite incapable. . . . There was never a Fanchon like Mary Pickford. Yes, I know that the greatest of the French and the English and the American stars have attempted and have successfully rendered Fanchon, but I stick to my belief that none ever surpassed and few ever approached the work of Mary Pickford."[43]

The film was based on a novel by George Sand, the only American silent feature to be made from her works. Kirkwood wrote the scenario with Mary's friend Frances Marion. Set in the eighteenth century, it was about a wild girl who lives in the forest with a crazy grandmother whom the villagers consider a witch. Fanchon is so unkempt she suffers from her grandmother's reputation. Pickford plays the role not so much as a woodland nymph, but more as a rural hooligan, using a surprising degree of violence on the boy she loves. They fall for each other after she rescues him from drowning, but she is too proud; she won't agree to marry him unless his father asks her. Not until a year later, after he has fallen ill and her presence is the only thing that helps him, do his parents beg her to marry him.[44]

Fanchon is notable as the first and only full-length film to feature all three Pickford siblings—Mary, Lottie, and Jack. The cast may also have included Fred Astaire, then sixteen, and his sister Adele. There is no proof of this, and they do not surface in the surviving reels. When asked about it, Astaire said he did not remember.[45] Neither name appears on the cast list, and there is no sign of them in any of the surviving stills. But it is a persistent and intriguing rumor, and only the appearance of a complete copy of the film could lay it to rest.

Mary Pickford, Forrest Robinson,
and players share a tense moment as
the police search their tenement flat.

THE DAWN OF A TOMORROW

RELEASED: JUNE 7, 1915

"It can almost be said that this is a picture without a flaw," declared the Famous Players publicity. "A picture so super-excellent in every phase that even the disgruntled critic is forced to become enthusiastic."[46]

Variety agreed. "First grade photography . . . plenty of interest in theme . . . among the top-notch list of current releases. Pickford is given full reign [*sic*] with her tattered garments and Pickford in rags can do considerable before a camera."[47]

The picture, directed by James Kirkwood from a script by the prolific Eve Unsell, was played for realism. "It was so well done," said the *New York Dramatic Mirror*, "we were under the impression the picture was produced in England . . . [N]ever in our experience has there been a five-reel feature in which every foot of film was photographically perfect. This is indeed an unusual and remarkable achievement."[48]

Pickford took the role of Glad (short for Gladys), a waif of the London slums, who loves Dandy (David Powell),[49] the cleverest and most daring crook in the city. She persuades him to go straight. An eccentric millionaire, Sir Oliver Holt (Forrest Robinson), is given a diagnosis of senile dementia by three distinguished specialists. Preferring suicide to madness, he decides to take his own life. He wanders the slums in the guise of a tramp, trying to summon up courage enough to shoot himself. Glad comes across him and argues him out of it. Her childlike faith and innate cheerfulness rejuvenate him, and his outlook is changed to such an extent that recovery is possible. Meanwhile, Dandy is accused of murder, and only Holt's licentious nephew (Robert Cain) can give him an alibi. The nephew will do it only if he can possess Glad. It is left to Sir Oliver to sort out the complications.[50]

Unsell's scenario was taken from a 1906 novel and a 1909 play by Frances Hodgson Burnett, whose works figure prominently in Pickford's career. It was rereleased in 1919. *Photoplay's* critic Julian Johnson wrote, "What a photoplay! What a characterization was Miss Pickford's Glad. Here was luminous tenderness in a steel band of gutter ferocity."[51]

LITTLE PAL

RELEASED: JULY 1, 1915

At last Famous Players entrusted Mary Pickford with a story not based on a play, but written by Marshall Neilan, who was diametrically opposed to the theatrical approach.

Mary played a half-breed Inuit girl. Set in Alaska, the picture owed something to *The Great Divide*. It also anticipated a film Cecil B. DeMille would make with Mary, *A Romance of the Redwoods* (1917). A saloon keeper loses his daughter, Little Pal, in a dice game to the brutal Black Brand (Joseph Manning). In the fight that follows, the father is killed, and Little Pal seeks refuge with John Grandon (George Anderson), an Easterner who has come to work his dead brother's claim. Little Pal falls in love with him, and when illness strikes, she nurses him back to health. At the same time, she and her friend Cultus (Bert Hadley) continue to work the mine. Her hard work is in vain; Grandon has neglected to inform Little Pal that he is married. His wife follows him out and wants to take him back to civilization. Grandon would like to go, too. In fact, he is warned that he will die if he remains in the harsh climate. So while she realizes she will lose him forever, Little Pal steals gold dust from a rival claim in order to provide him with the money. Black Brand, suspected of the crime, is shot. Watching the man she loves depart with his wife, Little Pal decides to commit suicide. A happy ending appears to have been added, in which she finds comfort in Cultus's love.[52]

The difficulty of showing man and woman—and a half-breed Inuit at that!—living together was solved by the stress the titles placed on the love being purely platonic. "Anyone who could place a platonic relationship," said *Variety*, "in a country almost barren of women, has an imagination previously sharpened that might conceive anything."[53]

Robert Cushman feels that every aspect of Pickford's normal personality was suppressed in this film, and as a result, her character is unappealing and rather dull. The film looks more primitive than the other films she did in 1915, such as *Rags*, although the use of locations is excellent. Cushman wrote, "It is a uniquely lifeless portrayal, with an almost total lack of animation. It might have been an interesting experiment, if the film itself had been more interesting in its subject matter and technique."[54]

The *Moving Picture World* critic found this characterization more intriguing: "Miss Pickford is most appealing in indicating the suppressed misery of a taciturn girl, to whom the relief of emotional outbursts is unknown."[55] The *New York Dramatic Mirror*, however, concurred with Cushman: "It was a part calling for the utmost suppression of all emotion and that is not the kind of part for the irrepressible and spontaneous Mary Pickford."[56]

'MARY PICKFORD
IN
"LITTLE PAL"
PRODUCED BY
FAMOUS PLAYERS FILM CO.
ADOLPH ZUKOR PRES.
1915

OVERHEARD.

Mary appears in one of the most atypical characterizations of her career, with her famous curls hidden under a dark brown wig.

RAGS DEFENCE.

DANIEL FROHMAN
PRESENTS
MARY PICKFORD
IN
"RAGS"
PRODUCED BY
FAMOUS PLAYERS FILM CO
ADOLPH ZUKOR, PRES.

RAGS

RELEASED: AUGUST 2, 1915

Marshall Neilan, who wrote *Little Pal*, played the lead in this film, making himself indispensable to Mary. But James Kirkwood still directed. The story and the scenario were written by Edith Barnard Delano, who would write Mary's picture *Hulda from Holland* the following year.

J. Farrell MacDonald, an Irish actor who had been with Mary at IMP and who became a favorite of John Ford,[57] plays Ferguson, a bank cashier. He no sooner proposes to Alice McCloud (Mary Pickford) than Hardesty, his employer (Joseph Manning), finds he has been cooking the books. For the sake of Alice, Hardesty allows him to leave town scot-free. Two years later, we find Ferguson in a Western mining camp, derided as the town drunk. Alice has died in childbirth. The baby grows up to be Rags, the terror of the camp. Her father mistreats her, but she remains loyal and defends him (as shown above) whenever she has cause to do so. She falls for a wealthy mining engineer, Keith Duncan (Neilan), who is Hardesty's nephew. Duncan seems merely to pity her, and Rags realizes that marriage is a hopeless proposition because of her inferior social position. When she hears that her father plans to rob Duncan, she betrays him to the sheriff. Her father is shot in the battle, but before he expires he writes to his old employer to take care of Rags. She travels back East, learns to live like a woman of substance, and Hardesty sends for his nephew.[58]

RAGS AND HER NEW FRIEND...RAGS.

DANIEL FROHMAN
PRESENTS
MARY PICKFORD
IN
"RAGS"
PRODUCED BY
FAMOUS PLAYERS FILM CO.
ADOLPH ZUKOR, PRES

Rags has trounced a gang of boys who were maltreating this dog, which she adopts.

Film historian James Card pointed to a remarkable moment in this film; he compares the scene in which Rags invites the mining engineer to lunch to the famous Chaplin party sequence in *The Gold Rush* (1925). She makes loving preparations in her father's poverty-stricken hut, fixing a meal, setting a table with flowers.

Rags steps out of her shack to fetch something to complete the decor. She is gone just long enough for her father to come lurching in with a drunken companion. They eat most of the food, mess up the rest and leave her pretty table in a shambles. Rags returns to see the destruction and then beholds her sweetheart on the way up the path for their first date.

Instead of feeling sorry for herself, Mary slams the door shut and goes to work. With lightning efficiency, she cleans the mess and distributes the few remaining crumbs of the luncheon onto her guest's plate, then opens the door to him. When he looks at the fantastically sparse meal and at her empty plate, she smiles at him. "Y'see, I was so hungry I jes' couldn't wait for you."[59]

Mary liked this picture so much that it was officially rereleased in 1919.[60] "One thing about Miss Pickford," said *Variety*, "and that is she and her bag of tricks are so well established in the minds of the film followers no matter what she does in a picture they are sure to term it 'cute,' and in the current offering are many little scenes that call for that expression."[61]

Rags played a significant role in the relationship between Mary and her mentor, Adolph Zukor. On her way home from the studio, driving up Broadway, she saw the theater showing *Rags*, with lines extending from both sides of the box office. The following week another Famous Players production was showing—without Mary Pickford and without the lines.

She interrogated Zukor, and he reluctantly admitted that they rented her films for a higher fee. This was the second time, according to historian Booton Herndon, that Mary suspected Zukor was not treating her with complete honesty. The year before, Charlotte had overheard a couple of film salesmen talking in the Famous Players office. One had referred to a film as "a dog." The other replied, "That's okay, we'll wrap it 'round Mary's neck and sell it like all the others." [62]

Mary and Charlotte decided that her films should be sold separately and not packaged with other Famous Players films. Rival companies were making enormous offers to Mary—Universal alone guaranteed $10,000 a week. [63]

"I still wonder whether after all it wasn't a dream," wrote Mary. "I'm afraid it was more like a nightmare to that sweet and gentle soul, Adolph Zukor."

"'Mary, sweetheart,' he used to say. 'I don't have to diet. Every time I talk over a new contract with you and your mother I lose ten pounds.'" [64]

The idea of Zukor being a "sweet and gentle soul" is hilarious, in the light of the ruthless methods he employed. The hard-hitting salesmen he used to capture theaters were known as "the wrecking crew." Not for nothing was Zukor the last survivor of the pioneer producers, remaining chairman of the board emeritus of Paramount Pictures until his death in 1976 at 103.

In this scene from *Rags*, a forlorn Mary prepares for her journey from the wild Western town of her upbringing to the East, where she will have to face both an education and a "civilized" society.

Mary with Fuller Mellish and Ida Waterman.

The trade press was harsh on this film, complaining that when it was first exhibited at New York's Strand Theater, it looked as though it had left the Famous Players studio unfinished.

"It may have been a wise selection to have 'Mary Pickford' on the sheet against competition for the first Paramount release of the season," commented *Variety*, "but *Esmeralda* wasn't a suitable selection from any angle."[65] *Photoplay* concurred as to the quality of the subject, but still had praise for Mary:

Miss Pickford is enshrined in the hearts of all the people, not because she is the sweetest of the limpid non-entities, but because she is a young woman of powerful personality and extraordinary dramatic talent. Hers is the art which conceals itself. Such hen-yard drama as *Esmeralda* is as unworthy of criticism as it is unworthy of Mary Pickford.[66]

The film was adapted from an 1881 play by Frances Hodgson Burnett and William Gillette.[67] It centered around the Rogers family, owners of a small farm. The daughter, Esmeralda (Mary Pickford), is in love with a country boy, David (Charles Waldron), but her mother (Ida Waterman) yearns for high society. A miracle happens; ore is discovered on their land, and the money rolls in. The mother forces her unwilling family to leave for the city. Esmeralda longs for her sweetheart, but her mother confronts her with a string of eligible bachelors. When she refuses to break her engagement with David, her mother tells her he is dead. Esmeralda is so heartbroken she falls ill, and her mother is able to announce her engagement to a Count de Montessin. When David hears the news he decides life is not worth living. But he appears outside the church, and, on seeing him, Esmeralda faints. In a final twist, the Rogers' ore is soon exhausted, and a fresh vein is found on David's land—thus the mother has to agree to the marriage she had opposed for so long.[68]

The critics were not impressed by James Kirkwood's direction, nor by Emmett Williams's camerawork. The film, shot at Englewood, New Jersey, was dismissed as "about the poorest picture the Famous Players could have made for a Labor Day showing, unless Mary Pickford can still hold them."

This was one of the films Mary Pickford donated to Eastman House but, according to James Card, who ran Eastman House, when they finally got around to printing it, they found cans full of sticky film and nitrate dust.

A GIRL OF YESTERDAY

Mary with her brother, Jack, and director Marshall Neilan (left).

What a tragedy that this film no longer survives! It was directed by Allan Dwan, who was one of the most entertaining of the silent directors. Mary starred in it with her brother Jack—the first in which they appeared as brother and sister. Biograph veteran Donald Crisp also appeared in it and, cast as a city vamp, Frances Marion. Marion did not write the story; it was credited to Mary Pickford herself, one of only two features she wrote.[69] *Wid's*, a trade paper, thought the story "terrible."[70] But it was a good idea; Jane and John Stuart (Mary and Jack Pickford) are both orphans, brought up by a hopelessly old-fashioned aunt and kept ignorant of what is going on in the world.[71] A wall—both physical and mental—exists between them and the up-to-date family next door. When Jane inherits a large sum of money, she and her brother break out of their ivory tower and link up with their wild neighbors. The script gave Mary the chance to display the latest fashions and to demonstrate her skills at golf, at sailing, and, more excitingly, at flying.[72]

The picture featured a pioneer aviator, Glenn Martin, later the designer of the Martin bomber. He answered Famous Players' ad by saying he could appear in the picture with a plane he had built himself. Frances Marion, expecting a tough, self-reliant flyer—the cowboy of those days—was startled to meet a gangling, nervous youth with eyes that appeared to be popping out of their sockets, thanks to the curious spectacles he wore. And her eyes popped when she saw his string-and-canvas plane, resembling a giant dragonfly. Once before the camera, Martin refused to kiss Marion "because my mother wouldn't like it." Adolph Zukor had to be brought out to the location to argue with this exhibition of self-restraint, an event perhaps unique in the annals of Hollywood. He had to resort to honeyed phrases and sharp words from the contract. "We finished the scene with Glenn Martin kissing me much in the fashion of a hen pecking corn," wrote Marion.[73]

For most of the aerial scenes, production manager Al Kaufman, wearing a blonde wig, doubled for Mary. But a shot was needed to establish Mary in the aircraft. According to Allan Dwan, her mother Charlotte would allow Mary to go up in Martin's plane only if it flew no higher than 100 feet from the ground. This was more dangerous than flying at a regular altitude, but Dwan promised. As an engineer, he had a solution in mind. He instructed the camera car to drive to the crest of the foothills in Griffith Park, and while the plane followed the topography of the winding road, the car would keep pace with the plane. "We had to go like hell to keep up with it, really give it the gun, but we did. It was a great shot."[74]

Actor Douglas Gerard was also to be in the plane. According to Adolph Zukor, they later discovered just how dangerous Gerard had thought this stunt: "Later Al [Kaufman] discovered, to his dismay, that Doug Gerard had been more concerned about the flight than he supposed. The night before, Gerard had written out a will by hand. In it he had left a diamond stickpin to Al."[75]

MADAME BUTTERFLY

RELEASED: NOVEMBER 8, 1915

*M*adame Butterfly was a good box office title. Even if it was not based on the Puccini opera, plenty of people thought it was. In any case, it told much the same story. And it gave Mary Pickford the chance to prove her versatility. For years it had been said that she was fine with parts as young girls and abandoned waifs but that strong dramatic roles were beyond her. As *Variety* wrote:

Well, you "Doubting Thomases," go to the Strand this week and disabuse your minds of any such idea once and for all. See her play the simple-minded, simpering, giggling little Japanese girl and the transition when she becomes the cast-off of the American lieutenant. . . . If she doesn't raise a lump in your respective throats when she learns the truth about her husband, nothing will.[76]

One may not agree with this verdict now. Seen with the benefit of more than eighty years, Mary does not look sufficiently Asian. Although her performance is usually well controlled, on occasion she is too unrestrained in her expressions. And certainly the players that surround her are obviously not Japanese. But resist her as you may, by the time Pinkerton returns, having married his American fiancée, you cannot avoid feeling terribly sad for poor Cio Cio San.

Mary quarreled with director Sidney Olcott. "I didn't like him," she told me. "I should never have used him. . . . My brother called him Old Flat-Tire. He was a little bit lame, and my brother disliked him because he was mean to me. I didn't rate him highly as a director." Olcott wanted her to play the role with Japanese reserve, and when she put too much American pep into it, a row developed, and Olcott walked off the set. At this point, Mary announced that she would take over the direction, which prompted Olcott to dash back to the set. Then it was Mary's turn to walk off.

She conspired with Marshall Neilan, who played Pinkerton, to put some comedy into it, but the only sign of their work remaining is Mary giggling as she mixes a knockout cocktail to repel an unwanted suitor. It jars with the Japanese atmosphere, which, for a film of 1915, is carefully evoked. (The film was to have been shot in Japan during a Pickford world tour, but World War I dashed the plans.)

In a striking sequence of Griffith-like intercutting, Mary endures the slimy suitor at the same time that Pinkerton enjoys a lavish wedding in the States. Hal Young's camerawork is full of silhouettes and glowing moonlight scenes, but these no longer carry the impact they once did because the surviving print is not tinted. The film stays faithful to the story as Cio Cio San walks slowly into the lake outside her home, which provided a picturesque background. (The film was shot at Plainfield and Bernardsville, New Jersey.) A synopsis in the *Moving Picture World* described what must have been an alternative ending, with Cio Cio San blindfolding the baby and stabbing herself in the throat. When Pinkerton arrives she clasps the child to her breast and dies in his arms, her face glowing with happiness.[77] In *The Forbidden City*, the 1918 remake with Norma Talmadge, the suicide was eliminated—for by that time a happy ending was mandatory.

This beautifully lit and composed photograph provides a delicate character study of Mary as the melancholy Cio Cio San.

SWEET MEMORIES,

Molly O (Pickford) prepares to run away (above) and contemplates how a new hat might detract from the sadly tattered appearance of her scullery maid's dress (right).

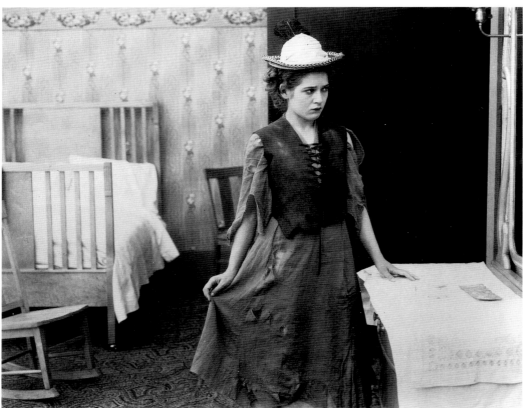

*T*he *Foundling* should have been remarkable, for it had the benefit of a scenario by Frances Marion, who would write some of the greatest scenarios of the entire silent period: *Stella Dallas* (1925), *The Scarlet Letter* (1926), *The Wind* (1928). But in the hands of John O'Brien it proved to be just another orphan melodrama, not without charm, but without the "class," as *Variety* squarely put it, that would make it last.

Mary Pickford liked Marion's original story, and when Adolph Zukor paid her $125, Marion said, "I ceased walking on this earth."[78]

It was a Dickensian tale, in which Molly O's mother dies in childbirth and her father, David King (Edward Martindale) rejects her, regarding her as the direct cause. He goes to Italy to paint his wife as the Madonna. We find the twelve-year-old living in an orphanage, the favorite of all the other kids, although badly treated by the matron's niece, Jennie (Mildred Morris). Molly O is adopted by a boardinghouse keeper, Mrs. Grimes (Maggie Weston), who tells her, "I didn't bring you here to mother you. I brought you here to work." Overworked and ill-used, Molly O runs away, taking her pet dog and puppies.

David King returns, wealthy and famous, but longing for his long-lost daughter. He visits the orphanage and is given Jennie instead. One day, King sees a girl struggling with a dogcatcher and lends his assistance. The child so endears herself to him that he installs her as a maid. The confrontation between Jennie, masquerading as the daughter, and Molly O was a high point of the film, although it takes several dramatic incidents to make King realize who Molly O is.

Pickford biographer Eileen Whitfield[79] has pointed out the Chaplinesque aspect of this film. When the dogcatcher threatens her "family," Mary crouches over the dog, and the net ensnares them both. These scenes are suggestive of *A Dog's Life*, which Chaplin would make in 1918. But in 1915, when *The Foundling* was shot, he was only beginning to investigate how pathos could be transferred to film, and such scenes were already associated with Mary Pickford.

The picture was made first by Pickford earlier in 1915 and directed by Allan Dwan, but the negative was burned in a fire that destroyed the Famous Players studio in New York. The second version might have benefitted from his sense of fun. With its echoes of *A Little Princess* and *Daddy-Long-Legs*, the Dwan version of *The Foundling* was probably the most fascinating of the lost Pickford films.

During the making of the film, Pickford discovered the Los Angeles Orphan Asylum and quietly supported it with large donations. It was not just a matter of mailing regular checks. When the press finally got wind of what she had been doing, in 1920, the Mother Superior said, "How much money in a year? I have never counted it in that way. We do not think of Mary Pickford in terms of figures, but in terms of the love she brings. If some great misfortune should remove her from us, we would miss her splendid benefactions, of course, but we would miss still more—infinitely more—herself."[80]

The asylum appeared in other Pickford films, *Stella Maris* and *Daddy-Long-Legs*, but it was nowhere near as forbidding as Mary made it look; it was enlightened in the way it preserved children's individuality, and, as they took Mary's money, so they undoubtedly took her advice about how the children should be treated.

When Lillian Gish saw *The Foundling*, she suggested that Mary play a small girl throughout an entire film.

"The public would never be interested in a story without a love theme," replied Pickford.

Gish said she liked the child incident better then anything she had seen Mary do.

"I am really indebted to her for this suggestion," said Mary, "which I followed some years later with considerable success."[81]

POOR LITTLE PEPPINA

RELEASED: FEBRUARY 20, 1916

After a prologue in which the only child of an American millionaire living in Italy is kidnapped and is thought to have drowned, this story leaps fifteen years to Mary as an Italian peasant girl, nicknamed Peppina. When her adopted family tries to force her to marry a brutal padrone, she runs away. She disguises herself as a boy and stows away aboard a steamship bound for New York. An American district attorney, Hugh Carroll (Eugene O'Brien) finds the "boy" stealing his leftovers and decides to help him. But once ashore, Peppina is put to work by the Italian criminals who had kidnapped her as a baby. They have no idea who "he" is and send her out to cash their counterfeit bills. This leads to her arrest, and she is brought before the district attorney—meeting her American benefactor once more. The kidnappers are given the third degree, and in a climactic, moving scene, she is reunited with her parents.

The film could have been merely a lachrymose melodrama, directed by Sidney Olcott, one of the dullest of the silent directors. But what a surprise! A bald storyline can only hint at the richness of the treatment. Italian actors were used, and although the gesturing is overdone, the film has the right look to it. The Italian atmosphere was cleverly caught through locations and set design: a hilltop estate[82] overlooking a picturesque river, a deserted ruin where Peppina hides, the crowded streets of Naples. But even more interesting today is the filming on the streets of New York, where the crew simply set up and shot what they needed. They generally got the shot before people fully realized what was going on. Booton Herndon recorded that as Mary's fans recognized her and spread the word a crowd gathered. Mary had to take refuge in a gro-

Mary's brother, Jack, played her foster brother in *Poor Little Peppina.* In this scene he cuts off her curls so that she can assume her disguise as a boy.

cery store, talking with the owner and his family, who were delighted at their good fortune, until the excitement had died down.[83]

Mary's brother Jack plays her foster brother. It is a pity that Mary featured him so seldom, as he is such a sympathetic and charming actor. (He had his own pictures to make, of course.) He had to perform one startling act in this picture: when Mary disguises herself as a boy, Jack cuts her hair. Although the cut curls were false, the act brought a gasp of horror from the audience.

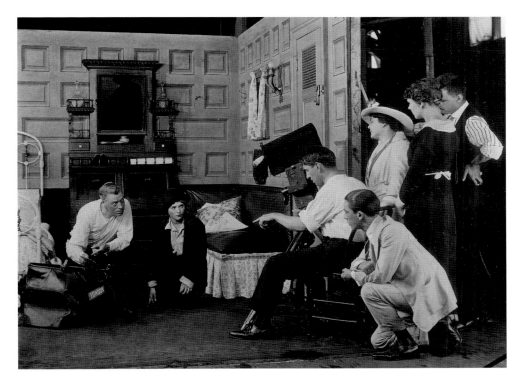

This was the first six-reeler that Mary made, and the first film in which Mary had a half interest. (Unfortunately, the available version of the film has been abridged to four reels.) Released in February 1916, it was shot during the summer of 1915. The advance in technique from a film such as *Cinderella*, which was made a year earlier, is extraordinary; it is as though twenty years had elapsed.

Variety reported that the first public presentation at the Broadway Theater did record business. At the last showing, the audience broke into spontaneous and prolonged applause.[84]

According to the *Moving Picture World*, "The reserves from two police precincts were called to handle the crowds which stormed the theatre in their efforts to see Mary Pickford in her longest picture. Never in the history of the Broadway Theatre has any film approached the record made by *Peppina*."[85]

From the evidence of the production shot above, there is a case to be made for the argument that Pickford's films were directed by the Pickford family. The set is Hugh Carroll's stateroom aboard the steamship, which was staged at the Famous Players New York studio. Sidney Olcott is directing Mary, who is in costume as a boy. Despite her trying experience with Olcott on *Madame Butterfly*, Mary agreed to work again with him only because Zukor asked her to. "We got through *Poor Little Peppina* all right, but only because I bit my lip and did as I was told. Zukor would pat me on my back and mollify me, but I resolved I would never again work with Olcott."[86]

The cameraman is Emmett Williams.[87] Jack Pickford kneels in the foreground with mother Charlotte standing behind him. The camera is a Pathé studio model. This is the earliest photograph in the Pickford Collection that shows Mary working with her director.

Such stills were carefully posed, however, and while Jack and Charlotte were often present when scenes were shot, and even more often present at rushes, they could not be classified as filmmakers. Their roles were closer to the modern category of associate producer. They both contributed a great deal to Mary's pictures—we shall never know how much we owe them, for no record was made of their ideas or suggestions. And while Jack was present less and less, Charlotte seems to have devoted her life to her daughter's career and was practically omnipresent. She was among the most powerful people in the silent film industry and deserves a great deal of credit for her remarkable managerial skill. Mary learned so much from her that she became one of the most successful businesswomen in American history.

103-39

THE ETERNAL GRIND
RELEASED: APRIL 17, 1916

A girl in a sweatshop earned $8.76 a week.[88] Mary Pickford, when she played such a girl in *The Eternal Grind*, earned $2,000 a week. "Mary Pickford has that rare art of shedding her monstrous salary when she steps before the camera," said *Motion Picture News*.[89] Illusion was all, and, as the photograph above demonstrates, the illusion was of a high order.

This film is lost. Historian Edward Wagenknecht remembers it as a somewhat depressing yarn, as indeed it should have been. But the subject of sweatshop poverty was not trivialized; the Chicago censor board "pink-slipped" it, which meant it could be shown only to adults.[90] However, on an old envelope containing stills from the film, which Robert Cushman found at Pickfair, Mary had written: "one of my *worst* pictures."

"*The Eternal Grind* started out as a good, strong sociological drama," said the *New York Dramatic Mirror*, "but lost most of its steam about the half way point and slumped into conventional class melodrama. The audience at the Strand punctured its approval of the star's excellent acting with howls of derision at the absurdity of the plot.[91] *Variety*[92] pointed out that Mary's periodic threats to leave Famous Players were due to what she considered a poor choice of scenarios, and this was perfect ammunition. It was considered nothing more than a nickelodeon scenario. Certainly it was full of the coincidences and improbabilities of "ten-twent-thirt" melodrama.

Even though the film's plotline was not generally well received by the critics, they had universal praise for Mary's performance, as this reviewer's comment from *Everybody's Magazine* attests:

A coldly threatening Mary brandishes a revolver to force a man to marry her sister.

Then comes villainy. She looks into his eyes. And, really she is a magnificent actress, and that is the sort of moment when she is at her best. Her face can change from happy innocence to suspicion, to dread, to flaming hate, while still retaining its innocence and still letting you feel that the girl never did, after all, understand what the man really meant, but only understood that somehow it was vile.[93]

We cannot judge the film now, but the Lasky press book and the Pickford Collection contain stills that suggest a production much more interesting to us today—with its images of factory conditions and tenement life—than in 1916, when the subject reflected the deadly routine for so many thousands of girls. In those days, there was no dearth of films about social problems; they disappeared only during the twenties, when the Hays office encouraged pictures that presented a rosier view of America.

Pickford with director John O'Brien.

Critics condemned this film with faint praise, using that most demeaning term *acceptable*.[94] It was directed by John O'Brien and written by Edith Barnard Delano, who was responsible for *Rags*. The working title was *Miss Jinny*.[95] Until recently, this film was thought to be lost, but new information indicates that there are original nitrate prints of *Hulda* residing in the Polish film archive in Warsaw and the Bulgarian film archive in Sofia. These are not yet transferred to safety film, and therefore I have not seen them.

The reviewers thought the opening sequences, set in Holland, were the best, with their dykes and dunes. The majority of the picture, however, took place in America. The film shows Hulda's valiant efforts to bring up her three orphaned brothers. Her Uncle Peter, a wealthy Pennsylvania farmer, brings them all to America. He goes to meet them in New York but, confused by the city, is knocked down by a car and carted off to a hospital, suffering from amnesia. Hulda and the children are abandoned on the pier, where they spend the night. In the morning, a kindly Dutch landlady takes them to her home.

Uncle Peter's disappearance causes equal anxiety to Mr. Walton (Frank Losee), the president of the New York Central Railroad. He has been trying to purchase a right of way through the property of the stubborn old man, who will not sell. He has three days to close the deal—or lose the backing of heavy financial interests.

In one of the most memorable scenes of the picture, Hulda is exploring the roof of her landlady's building when she crashes through the skylight onto the bed of Allan Walton, an artist. He doesn't object to this startling method of entry once he examines the new arrival—indeed, he insists on painting her. His picture, reproduced on a magazine cover, serves to reunite Hulda with her uncle. And since the artist is the son of the railroad president, two new contracts are drawn up, one of them marital.[96]

"Mr. Zukor always insisted that I wear my curls," recalled Pickford. "It was ridiculous to have them in the picture. So I didn't." "You'll be sorry," warned Mr. Zukor. When I went to see the picture, I sat behind two women. One had brought the other to see me for the first time. She spent the whole time apologizing to the other woman for me. "You really mustn't judge her by this picture," she'd say. "You must come and see Mary in another picture where she's herself."[97]

Hulda from Holland was the last film to be photographed by Emmett Williams. He died suddenly, on April 28, 1916, in New Rochelle, New York, a couple of months before the film's release.[98]

LESS THAN THE DUST

RELEASED: NOVEMBER 6, 1916

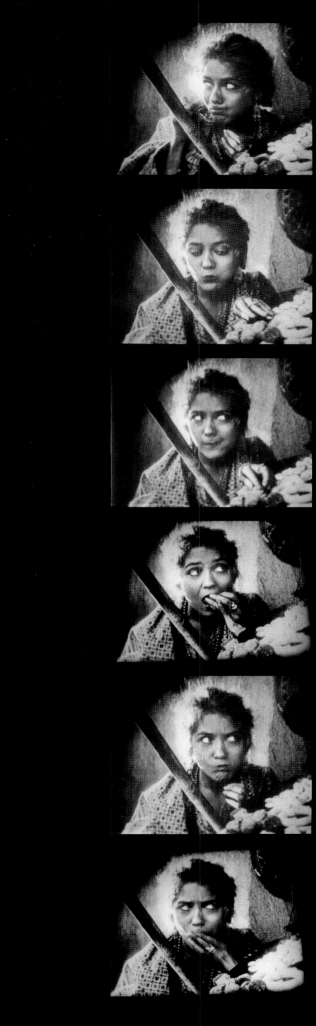

Mary Pickford always claimed that this film was one of her worst. "I remember how heartily I agreed with a woman who once walked up to me in the street and said, 'Oh, Miss Pickford, I loved you in the picture *Cheaper Than the Dirt*.'" [99]

The film, in which Mary plays an Indian, was nowhere near as poor as she made out. It got good reviews and was well received by the public. Pickford retains enough Western expressiveness not to alienate her fans, and yet she is more convincing in an Indian costume than as the Japanese woman in *Madame Butterfly* (1915). This series of frame enlargements shows her stealing food from a local bazaar.

Famous Players had recently combined with the Jesse L. Lasky Feature Play Co. and formed the Art-craft Pictures Corp. to distribute Pickford's films. This was the first Artcraft release. It was directed by John Emerson. His assistant was Erich von Stroheim, [100] who was the technical adviser on the unusually effective military scenes. Another assistant was Emmett Flynn, who would become an important director at Fox. Even the cameraman, George Hill, would become a leading director (and would marry Frances Marion).

Hector Turnbull's scenario gave Mary the chance to extend her range and to play a Hindu, Rahda, who becomes friendly with a British officer, Captain Townsend (David Powell). The Indian who raised Rahda is arrested for his part in an anti-British rebellion; once in jail, he tells Mary that she is really the daughter of a British officer who died of a drug overdose. It would have been impossible for her to cross racial barriers without this feeble plot device, a feature of virtually all the American silent films in which the heroine is of another race. It enables her to go to England to seek her inheritance and to marry Captain Townsend. [101] The last reel is missing; in any case, the English scenes are an anticlimax after all the effort expended on re-creating the Raj.

It was made in Whitestone, Queens, on Long Island. Mary had never been happier. Emerson [102] treated her royally, and among the theatrical people vacationing nearby was Douglas Fairbanks, already a famous film actor.

The campaign for the film was massive. It opened, in modern style, at eighty theaters simultaneously. [103] A third of a million people saw it on the first day.

THE PRIDE OF THE CLAN

RELEASED: JANUARY 8, 1917

Never the most reliable judge of her own films, Mary Pickford dismisses this picture in her book as a disastrous failure. Artistically, it was anything but. Shot on location in Marblehead, Massachusetts, it was infused with the tang of seaspray by Maurice Tourneur and his remarkable company. Apparently, Mary had forgotten one review, which stated, "There is every possibility that the versatility she exhibits throughout the production will cause it to be listed by critics as the best film in which she has appeared during her extraordinarily successful career as a star of the silent drama."[104]

Originally entitled *The Lass of Killean*, it was the first of two productions for Mary Pickford that Maurice Tourneur was obliged to make when he signed with Artcraft. Tourneur and screenwriter Frances Marion had worked well together at World, but Tourneur was a director in the Griffith style—he accepted no interference. The story of Scottish fisherfolk provided him with his favorite elements—sea, storms, birds, boats—and he made a richly atmospheric production.

Tourneur was a Frenchman, trained as an artist, who had shown such promise in France that he was sent by the Eclair company to take command of its studio in Fort Lee, New Jersey. He brought to his pictures a sense of composition and lighting so striking that you can recognize a Tourneur film from a single frame. His technique was light years away from the flat, stagey direction of Edwin S. Porter of just three years before. The

Above:

Shot on location in Marblehead, Massachusetts, this film had a remarkably authentic atmosphere. Had the camera pointed in the opposite direction, however, this is what it would have filmed. Pickford and the cast had to endure an enormous crowd of spectators.

Opposite:

This still of Mary is a fine example of director Maurice Tourneur's fine pictorial sense.

approach and editing of the opening storm sequence, oddly suggestive of Flaherty's *Man of Aran* (1934), is very advanced for its date. It anticipates Russian montage of a decade later. The wind whips through the tall grass and flattens it. The roof of a sheep shelter is blown off. Breakers crash against towering cliffs. Fishermen force their way into the very teeth of the gale, their wives gather pathetically at the clifftop, shawls shuddering. On the horizon, a fishing boat carrying the Clan's chieftain, Mary's father, founders and sinks. Tourneur makes no attempt to glamorize the characters with makeup or lighting. The little community, with its low thatched cabins, the pigs and geese wandering in the street, has a documentary reality.

Following an unveiling of the film in 1969, Richard Koszarski wrote:

Tourneur's eye for composition is flawless, equalling or surpassing Griffith's work of the same period, and the performances are more restrained than in much of *Intolerance*. *Pride of the Clan* also exhibits an editorial skill not generally attributed to Tourneur; a scene where Mary is herself trapped in a sinking ship is cut so rapidly and effectively as to be almost a match for the best work of the Master [D. W. Griffith] himself. Clearly this film was ten years ahead of its time.[105]

Tourneur had a distinguished group of technicians: John van den Broek, a cameraman of Dutch descent, was among the most talented in America at the time, along with Billy Bitzer and Walter Stradling.[106] Clarence Brown was assistant director and film editor and, as a director himself, would carry Tourneur's ideas through to the 1930s and 1940s. The art director was Ben Carré, another French émigré, whose attitude toward his

Maurice Tourneur was more interested in atmosphere than drama. But Pickford thought a moving picture had to move and felt this one lacked action. Therein lay the root of the reported antagonism between him and his star, which they seem to be referring to in this gag picture.

craft was revolutionary. Long before *The Cabinet of Dr. Caligari* (1920), he and Tourneur were using stylized scenery. Not in this one, though—*The Pride of the Clan* looks so authentic it might have been made in Scotland.

At the climax of the film, Mary is in a sinking fishing boat. Two cameras covered the scene, operated by John van den Broek and Lucien Andriot, who recalled that some barrels gradually shifted as the scene was shot, and the boat began to fill with water. Tourneur called out for everyone to abandon ship. This was in a wintry November—those who could leaped over the side and swam to shore, about 300 yards away. The women were lowered into a dinghy. Mary remembered she had left her makeup kit in the cabin and went back for it. She wrote:

The odd thing about it is that no one noticed me heading back into the boat. . . . Midway to the cabin a voice stopped me. It came from inside of me, the same voice I have heard time and again in my life. I heard it say very clearly, "Don't you go there!"

I rushed back just as Mr. Tourneur was about to step over the edge. We were in water up to our knees. Startled to find me still aboard, he grasped my hand and helped me into the lifeboat. Then he plunged in and swam to safety. But for that mysterious command I would have lost my life.[107]

Some sources say that the entire scene was shot in a tank at the Fort Lee studio, making nonsense of this story. But Andriot confirmed that the incident happened as Mary remembered it.[108] The story was also reported in the trade magazines.[109] The company lost the boat, the two cameras, and the film, and had to return to Marblehead for retakes in December 1916. And as final proof, Robert Cushman found a photo album in the early 1970s in which this remarkable snapshot of the boat actually sinking appeared.

Pickford appears on the deck of her docked fishing boat in the upper photograph. The snapshot below it captures the boat's accidental sinking.

MARY PICKFORD
IN
"POOR LITTLE RICH GIRL"

"I WISH I COULD GO OUT AND PLAY"

THE POOR LITTLE RICH GIRL

RELEASED: MARCH 5, 1917

Mary had played an Indian girl, a Scottish girl, a Dutch girl—her fans wanted her to play a proper *little* girl. By early 1917 there had been a slight drop in her popularity. *The Pride of the Clan* had done nothing to improve it. At Mary's insistence, Zukor asked William Brady to release Frances Marion long enough to write the script for *The Poor Little Rich Girl*. It was based on a popular play in which Viola Dana had starred.

While making it, wrote Marion, she and Mary would gang up on the director, "poor, serious Mr. Tourneur," and sweet-talk him into letting them include some wild comedy scenes that were not in the play or the script. "These could have been called spontaneous combustions, and Mr. Tourneur went home many a night with an aching head."[110]

I was a little skeptical when I read this, because "poor, serious Mr. Tourneur" had always incorporated comedy into his pictures, sometimes to their detriment. Maxine Elliot Hicks, who played Susie May Scroggs, saw only civilized differences and courtesy.[111] But there is evidence that the mud fight was shot under protest, because art director Ben Carré recalled a glimpse of Maurice Tourneur gesturing helplessly at him as if to say, "What can I do?" or "It has to be."[112]

The Poor Little Rich Girl was the first film in which Mary played a substantial role as a little girl, from start to finish—the whole thing revolves around Gwendolyn's eleventh birthday—and it was the first time, after twenty-three features, that she had played a girl so young. Indeed, one reviewer realized that this was "an entirely new Mary Pickford."[113] The film was a fascinating study of a child so protected by her wealthy parents (whom she hardly ever sees) that she has no idea of what is going on in the world. (A similar theme pervades *Stella Maris* [1918]).

Carré asked director Tourneur if he should build everything larger than normal and was told "No, I'm certain Miss Pickford will make herself fit the scene."[114] For the stair-case, he merely put in tall windows to make Mary seem smaller as she descended. Two footmen stood at attention as she appeared; a couple of bricks made them seem taller, and the film was cast with tall people.

Pickford recalled the day she showed this film to Zukor and the Paramount exec-utives as one of the blackest of her life: "All the things Frances and I had thought so funny on the set fell absolutely flat in the projection room. I went home to bed without dinner and quietly cried myself to sleep. Frances took it even harder."[115]

Zukor and his executives thought it best not to release the film and risk damaging Pickford's reputation. But it did go out, and it was an unqualified smash hit—the biggest success of her career up to that time.[116] It is often impossible to judge a comedy in a cold projection room; a sympathetic audience is the most essential ingredient.

Reviews such as this one effectively deflated the initial negative reaction of the Paramount executives:

Little Mary has been uniformly great from the inception of her brilliant career as a moving pic-ture star, but if she continues to eclipse her former notable achievements as she does in *A* [sic] *Poor Little Rich Girl*, she is destined to win recognition in the super-superlative. . . . It is pretty well agreed among the erudite that this is the best part she ever created before the camera.[117]

In addition to having stills taken with an 8x10 plate camera, the Artcraft company employed a photographer with a Graflex to capture pictures of the film in production. These shots were not posed but were taken while the motion-picture camera was running and as the scene was played out—hence, their greater immediacy. Over a thousand of these shots were taken on a typical Artcraft production. The Graflex was a hand-held camera with a reflex view finder, loaded with film producing 5x7 negatives. Here are examples from *A Romance of the Redwoods:*

1. Jenny Lawrence (Pickford) after a rough night in the barn (opposite).
2. Jenny aims her ridiculous handbag pistol at "Black" Brown (right).
3. Her tongue is a far more effective weapon (below).

Mary plays Jenny Lawrence, who goes West in search of an uncle. He has been killed by Indians, and a stagecoach robber, "Black" Brown (Elliott Dexter), has assumed his identity. Jenny faces accepting protection from him or from the local dance-hall madam—and she chooses Brown. She begs him to reform, for she quickly falls in love with him. Brown decides to rob one final stagecoach, but he is caught by vigilantes and sentenced to hang. In a daring scene, Jenny produces doll's clothing and pretends that she is soon to give birth to Brown's child. The vigilantes give in, and the two are married by the sheriff.

Any similarities to David Belasco's *The Girl of the Golden West* would not have bothered *Redwoods*'s director Cecil B. DeMille, since he had made *The Girl* a couple of years earlier. DeMille was another Belasco veteran. He and Mary had appeared together in Belasco's production *The Warrens of Virginia* (1907), written by his older brother, William.

The exteriors were shot in northern California near Boulder Creek, in Santa Cruz County, on sets built by the California Motion Picture Corporation for its productions *Salomy Jane* (1914) and *The Lily of Poverty Flat* (1915).[118]

The film turned out magnificently and survives in a superb 35mm print made directly from the negative. The drama is offset by a number of moments that are as funny and surprising as they were in 1917. Pickford's playing is absolutely naturalistic; she is convincing and amusing, a vivid personality who dominates the film and makes it unforgettable.

These three photographs show Pickford with director Cecil B. DeMille.

The year 1917 was Mary Pickford's *annus mirabilis*. Just after this film came out, Mary won a popularity contest in the *Ladies' World* with 1,147,550 votes—half a million more than her nearest competitor.[119] As they used to say in those days, "you could take 1,000 feet of Mary Pickford sitting in an armchair and they'd flock to see it." So one might imagine that Pickford was at the peak of her career. According to DeMille, Zukor asked him to make two films with Pickford to put an end to a slump they were both experiencing at the box office.[120] The grosses on the two Pickford/DeMille films—*A Romance of the Redwoods* and *The Little American*—were far higher than for any earlier DeMille film, suggesting that Pickford, despite Zukor's pessimism, was then more of an attraction than DeMille was.

Vachel Lindsay reviewed the film in *The New Republic* under the caption "Queen of My People." "To reject this girl in haste," he wrote, "is high treason to the national heart."[121] Yet Mary loathed making it. "I don't remember having a happy moment during the entire filming."[122] Her misery began with a telegram that Zukor had forced her to send DeMille agreeing to obey him without question. "It was as if I were living in an iron girdle during those weeks."[123] Yet Lindsay, in his review, quoted William Butler Yeats, "'Rhetoric is heard, poetry overheard.' For the first time in my knowledge, the acting of Mary Pickford is permitted by her director to have a divine accident in it, poetry overheard."[124] And the *Picture Play* critic proclaimed that her performance "leads one to wonder if there is anything beyond Miss Pickford's power to create."[125]

DeMille recorded that when Mary arrived, she was clearly terrified of him and so went on the offensive. And DeMille was alarmed by her, for he sent a telegram to Lasky: "If she refuses to work we are convinced we have a perfect law suit against her for heavy damages, etc. We will instantly stop paying her immense weekly stipend, which will be a relief."[126]

DeMille respected her dedication, however, and despite disagreements, they ended up firm friends, as two of these three pictures suggest.

One would think she was far too well established in the business for these sort of first-night nerves. She came to California (which she never left for another production) with the highest possible reputation, and if she felt indentured to a new master, at least DeMille was familiar with her style. He gives her—or was perhaps persuaded to give her—a large number of bold closeups, uncharacteristic of DeMille, and his cameraman Alvin Wyckoff lit the interiors with more atmosphere than usual. However, DeMille drily noted that when the two films were finished and she had her freedom again, she chose not DeMille and his writer, Jeanie Macpherson, but Marshall Neilan and Frances Marion.[127]

THE LITTLE AMERICAN

RELEASED: JULY 2, 1917

Imagine the outcry if Mary Pickford had been aboard the *Lusitania!*[128] What better wartime propaganda than to restage the event with Mary at its center? This sequence from *The Little American*, directed by Cecil B. DeMille, was shot in San Pedro Bay and at the Famous Players-Lasky studios in Hollywood, with a set built on rockers.

DeMille was a far better director at this period than he was in later years, and this is a classic of its kind. The film compresses all the anti-German sentiment and xenophobia in America into a tale of spectacular improbability. It was done with such panache, however, that one watches it with fascination, as if it were a first-class newsreel. For what it does is reveal what Americans *thought* was happening at the front. DeMille had proposed a film about occupied Belgium in January 1917, but the studio did not want to upset its Central European market. Nonetheless, it was planned as war clouds thickened, and with DeMille's usual luck, it was ready to go into production just after America declared war on Germany.

Angela Moore (Mary Pickford) has a birthday on July 4, 1914. Two suitors call with gifts, one a Frenchman (Raymond Hatton) and the other a German-American, Karl (Jack Holt), a thoroughly decent young man. Once in uniform—

and both answer the call to the colors—the German becomes just another well-drilled beast. Rescued from the torpedoed liner, Angela arrives in France to find her aunt dead and her château occupied by the Germans and converted into a hospital.[129] Angela sends messages to the French. Karl does his best to rape her—in darkness, not realizing her identity—but when she is sentenced to be shot, Karl denounces the Kaiser and joins her before the firing squad. A French shell eliminates the squad and buries them all under debris. Angela and Karl struggle to a church. After a night bombardment,[130] a French patrol rescues them, and Karl is incarcerated in a prison camp. Angela is permitted a U.S. visa for him in recognition of her service to France. She kisses him through the wire fence. By the time the film came out, America was in the war, and this ending was too much for many audiences. The end had to be reshot with Mary awaiting the Frenchman, played almost as a parody by Raymond Hatton.[131] However, in the surviving print, Mary ends up with the German.

In my book *The War, the West and the Wilderness*, based on Frances Marion's account,[132] I stated that this had been a box-office failure. However, according to Bob Birchard's research through the papers of the DeMille Estate, it now appears that the film was a success.[133] It had a negative cost of $166,949 (including Mary's salary of $86,666.66) and brought a worldwide gross of $446,236.88.[134] The net profits have been calculated at $130,000 to $150,000. Everything about *The Little American* was carefully calculated. The titles were designed to attract storms of applause. Even the names of the characters were of a nationalistic nature. The girl, representative of all that is good in America (and played by the most popular actress in the world), is called Angela. The German-American who loves her and who is brutalized by the military machine is called Karl von Austreim (Jack Holt), suggesting that as an Austrian aristocrat he is not entirely to blame for Germany's misdeeds. The rival for Angela's hand, Count Jules de Destin (Raymond Hatton), is equally aristocratic, his name positively mystical; but he is decadent and slightly comic.[135]

Despite Mary's negative memory of her two films with DeMille, they both received excellent reviews. "*The Little American* put Mary Pickford in a completely new light," said DeMille.[136] Of her performance in *The Little American*, Harvey O'Higgins wrote in *The New Republic*, "you might go a long way and see a great deal of famous acting without meeting the expression of an emotion so true, so poignant, and so beautiful."[137] In *Photoplay Journal* Bert D. Essex commented,

Miss Pickford reveals a new side to her versatility by developing some dramatic power which would do justice to a Bernhardt for its emotionalism. . . . It would not be at all surprising if when the record of her cinema achievements is completed down to finis, *The Little American* will stand out as one of her greatest triumphs."[138]

The humiliations to which the Little American was subjected went far beyond the (symbolic) removal of mud-covered jackboots, as depicted in this photograph.

Mary Pickford, symbol to the world of all-American womanhood, in *The Little American.*

Mary is splattered with mud by the property man in preparation for a scene in which she must look appropriately weather-beaten.

REBECCA OF SUNNYBROOK FARM
RELEASED: SEPTEMBER 22, 1917

"The best Mary Pickford ever," proclaimed a trade paper.[139] Robert Cushman considers it "probably the definitive Mary Pickford film." He has written that *Rebecca of Sunnybrook Farm* is

a perfect combination of all the interdependent elements of a picture, each functioning so well and harmoniously as to enhance Pickford's flawless performance. . . . [Marshall Neilan's] inventive genius produced a barrage of brilliant scenes, images, gags, and distinctive directorial touches. The economy of the structure of the film is quite astounding; it is packed with tiny details, brief events, and minute expressions—shots which may last only five or six seconds, but which add worlds of meaning. Having seen the film, one reels at how much has been packed into its fast-moving seventy minutes.[140]

Rebecca certainly set a new standard. Recovering from her feeling of enslavement on her two (albeit excellent) films with DeMille and buttressed by the staggering success of *The Poor Little Rich Girl*, Mary recalled:

With this spectacular turn of affairs I again mounted my high horse, and as Stephen Leacock once said, rode off in all four directions. Once more I demanded to have Frances Marion work with me, and this time Marshall "Mickey" Neilan to direct. Our first picture together was *Rebecca of Sunnybrook Farm*. And that, together with *Poor Little Rich Girl*, gained back the ground I had lost.[141]

Rebecca threatens to run through the unctuous Minnie Smellie with her parasol in swordsmanlike fashion. Violet Wilkey, who played Minnie, had played Mae Marsh as a child in *The Birth of a Nation* three years earlier.

Mary Pickford was a dedicated actress. Like her friend Lillian Gish, there was nothing she would refuse to do if it helped the picture. In this scene, which looks apparently simple to stage—Rebecca holding a circus in a barn—Mary was suspended by a wire so that she could comically ride bareback on a horse. The scene took hours longer to shoot than anyone had anticipated, and Mary had to wear a harness. "The harness made me so sore on the first night that I couldn't sleep, move, or breathe," she recalled.[143]

The story of Rebecca, by Kate Douglas Wiggin, was published in 1903. The film is set in that period, before the age of the automobile—the world in which Neilan, Pickford, and Marion grew up. Thus it evoked childhood for the parents in the audience while entrancing the kids.

Rebecca's sunny disposition is clouded by the aunts who have adopted her. Aunt Miranda (Josephine Crowell) cannot stand children and is irritated out of all proportion by Rebecca's pranks. Things get so bad, what with Minnie Smellie and her cohorts at school, that Rebecca decides to run away. She does so—naturally—at night at the height of a furious storm, sneaking out of her window and down the trellis. When lightning strikes the church tower, Rebecca is hit by a piece of timber and is rescued by Mr. Ladd (Eugene O'Brien). Horrified by all this, Aunt Miranda reforms her ways, which entails sending Rebecca to boarding school. When Rebecca returns (Mary having made an uncanny transformation from little girl to young woman), an academic success, Aunt Miranda is dying. There is a poignant scene in which Rebecca manages to convey the fact that she loves her.

According to her biographer, Cari Beauchamp, Frances Marion was able to see the effect that a lack of a childhood had on Mary. "She revelled in clowning in the circus scenes, not reliving past adventures, but experiencing them for the first time." Mary once confessed to her that she had been "the most miserable kid in the world."[142]

With Mary Pickford remembered for her performances as little girls, it is remarkable to see how mature she could look when playing adults. Left, Rebecca, as a child, is scolded by Aunt Miranda Sawyer (Josephine Crowell) after the circus sequence. Below, Rebecca returns from college, looking as though many years had passed (Mayme Kelso, at left, plays Aunt Jane Sawyer).

Opposite:
Mary as Rebecca Rowena Randall, formerly of Sunnybrook Farm, having been sent off to live with her crotchety aunts, feels alone and unwanted upon her arrival on their doorstep.

A LITTLE PRINCESS
RELEASED: NOVEMBER 5, 1917

Pickford with ZaSu Pitts.

Look at the girl on the left in this photo. Is that face familiar? You may have seen her in many comedy roles—as a waitress or a frantically inefficient maid. Yet Erich von Stroheim saw in her the makings of a tragedienne and coaxed from her an extraordinary performance in *Greed* (1924). It was during the production of *Rebecca of Sunnybrook Farm*—while Frances Marion was writing the script for *A Little Princess*—that a boy from the casting office announced he was bringing in "a dazzler"; he returned with a gawky teenager with enormous eyes. "Beauty like this," the boy said sarcastically, "should not go unnoticed."[144]

The girl's eyes filled with tears. Frances kicked the boy out. Named after two aunts, ZaSu Pitts had come to California with her family as a child, following the death of her father. She visited Los Angeles looking for extra work. D. W. Griffith said she looked too much like Lillian Gish to be in his pictures ("the nicest thing anyone had ever said to me"). She was an extra in *Rebecca of Sunnybrook Farm*, and Frances Marion saw in her the ideal actress to play the role of the slavey, Becky, in *A Little Princess*. She had a quality about her, a poignancy, that was perfect. And when she mentioned the way the boy had treated her, Mary wanted to champion her. She got the part.

A Little Princess was remade in 1939 with Shirley Temple and again, with tremendous artistic success, in 1995. Pickford's version stuck to the Frances Hodgson Burnett original, *Sara Crewe*. At Miss Minchin's school Sara (Mary Pickford) is known as "The Little Princess" because of her father's vast wealth. When he dies and his fortune is lost, Sara is ill-treated by Miss Minchin and reduced to the level of scullery maid. She entertains her companion in distress, Becky, with fairy tales.

An old friend of her father's from India, Carrisford, comes to live in the house next door. Not knowing anything about Sara's identity, he takes pity on the two girls and arranges for them a sumptuous Christmas treat—but Miss Minchin discovers the meal and punishes the girls. Carrisford intervenes, discovers Sara's identity, and tells Miss Minchin that her inheritance can be restored. He takes charge of the girls.

Nothing could surpass the most recent (1995) version of *A Little Princess*, but Neilan's film stands up extremely well. It has a similar emotional quality, keeping many in the audience on the edge of tears up to the final fadeout. Frances Marion was exceptionally talented at adapting this sort of story, as she proved with classics such as *Stella Dallas* (1925). But Neilan runs away with one sequence; Sara tells the children the story of Ali Baba, and the room dissolves away, leaving the children silhouetted against an Arabian pool. A few minutes of this would have been enchanting, but Neilan runs it for a reel or so. It is not particularly entertaining in itself, and Mary appears only on the periphery, albeit dispatching the villain with a dagger after performing a rather polite "cooch dance." *Variety*[145] was concerned that Neilan spent too much time (and money) on this one episode when it had so little bearing on the main story. They were right.

Otherwise, the film is almost perfect. Walter Stradling's lighting is of a remarkably high standard, as are the sets. Neilan uses bold close-ups and extreme long shots to drive home the loneliness of the small girl. The furniture is built slightly larger than normal to emphasize her diminutive height, and the camera is kept low to make teachers loom over their charges. This is so much better than other films of the period, many of which have been acclaimed as classics, that it must have escaped that description only as a result of its lack of availability.

Above:

Mary as Morgiana, the harem girl, in the "Ali Baba" sequence of *A Little Princess*. Behind her is Marcia Manon (then known as Camille Ankewich) as an extra. In Mary's next film, *Stella Maris*, Manon would have a major role as the hate-filled alcoholic Mrs. Risca.

Left:

In these two Graflex gag stills shot between takes, Mary flicks director Marshall Neilan's nose and is consequently "strangled" by him.

MARY PICKFORD IN "STELLA MARIS"

STELLA'S KINDLY WORDS DEEPLY TOUCHED UNITY BLAKE.

STELLA MARIS

RELEASED: JANUARY 21, 1918

Confined to bed by a crippling illness, Stella Maris (Mary Pickford) is sheltered to the point that all bad news is kept from her; she looks out on peaceful scenes and is visited by pet animals, charming children, and John Risca (Conway Tearle). Urbane and handsome, Risca is a journalist with a secret—his wife, Louise (Marcia Manon), is an alcoholic and drug addict. One day, Louise visits an orphanage, wanting not so much a foster child as a free servant. She treats the homely girl, Unity Blake (also played by Mary Pickford), so abominably that eventually the neighbors burst in, find the girl has been beaten unconscious, and call the police. When Louise begins her term of imprisonment for the assault, Unity is set free. She is adopted by John after he sees her in the hospital and is appalled by the savagery of the beating inflicted by his wife. John continues to pay visits to Stella Maris and is overjoyed when she has an operation that enables her to walk. Unity comes to stay at Stella's house, and the two meet momentarily. Stella falls in love with John, and hearing so much about his "castle," as he terms his house, determines to visit it. Here she receives the double shock of discovering not only that John is mar-

Pickford as both Unity Blake and Stella Maris in a double-exposure still.

Opposite:
Stella Maris must have upset some Pickford fans, for in the Unity role she looked as unattractive as she could manage, as these six frame enlargements show.

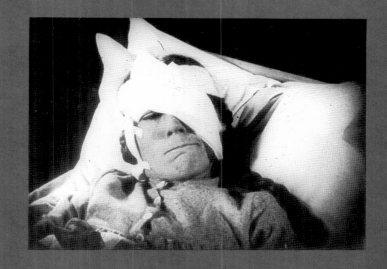

ried, but married to a woman just out of jail. Unity has also fallen in love with John, from afar, for he is the first person to have treated her kindly. When she realizes that his wife is making John's life a living hell, Unity pays her a visit. She kills Louise with a pistol; the police inform John that she also shot herself. John and Stella can be united. A happy ending is achieved at the cost of two lives.

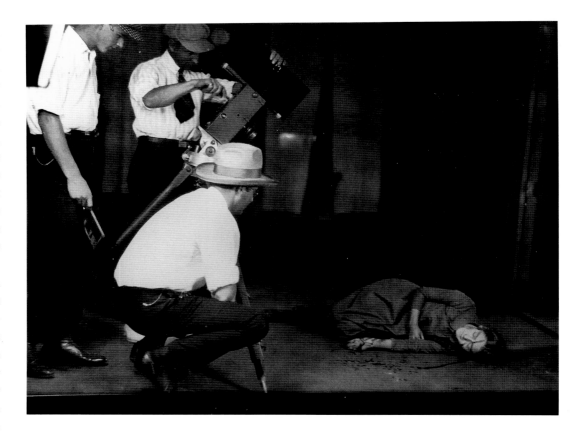

This Graflex shot records the filming of the unconscious Unity, who has been savagely beaten with a poker by Mrs. Risca.

The film is undoubtedly a classic. It could be regarded as a sincere and successful attempt to break through the shackles of melodrama. The fact that it was made as early as 1917 (released in January 1918) is a tribute to everyone associated with it. The scenario is intelligent, and although the picture has too many titles, they are all worthwhile. Marshall Neilan's direction is of a high order. He kept his skittish instincts under control, and there is a sober intensity to the narrative. For years the only surviving print had been a wretched 16mm dupe in which nearly all the quality of Walter Stradling's photography was lost. Fortunately, the Mary Pickford Foundation has restored the film from 35mm materials, and one can now be stunned by ravishing closeups of Stella Maris, contrasted with the pathetic, distorted face of Unity Blake. There are sad little moments when Unity stares at herself in the mirror, tearfully comparing herself to a picture of Stella. This creates an odd confusion: Mary Pickford in disguise, weeping because she is not as beautiful as the real Mary Pickford.

Although Marcia Manon[146] overplays the role of Louise Risca, all other parts are acted naturalistically. The Dickensian atmosphere is conjured up by the art director, Englishman Wilfred Buckland,[147] not with big sets but through small details—the street bollards, so typical of old London, the crowded shop windows, and the tall Georgian windows. This is not a spectacular picture; it is an intimate drama, and while one of the most interesting of the early Pickford films, it is far from being the most cinematic or even the most picturesque. Nevertheless, this picture was considered, by many critics, the high point of Pickford's career.

As Unity Blake, Pickford was photographed from her "wrong" side to emphasize any bad features she had. When Mary first tested the Unity make-up, which she created herself, she wandered the studio pretending to be looking for work as a cleaning lady. Nobody recognized her, not even Neilan himself. Mary was then satisfied that her disguise would work—and work it did. One critic observed that the opening titles clearly indicate that "Miss Pickford is assuming two roles, but if this were not the case there is not the slightest doubt that nine-tenths of her audience would never believe that Stella Maris and her poverty stricken double were enacted by the same person."[148] *Movie Weekly* later reported, "At the finish of viewing *Stella Maris* without having arrived in time to see the titles, an exhibitor remarked, 'Mary's Pickford's great, but she'd better watch out for the one who plays the slavey.'"[149]

Marshall Neilan directs Pickford as Unity Blake, on location at the Los Angeles Orphans' Asylum, which she had discovered during the making of *The Foundling* in 1915. The extras are orphans.

Fortunately, the dual role allowed the authentic Mary to be visible for much of the time. Her bravery won her almost universal praise from the critics. It might well have encouraged Griffith to make *Broken Blossoms* (1919), although he was not daring enough to mar Lillian Gish's beauty, even as he filmed the most vicious scene thus far put on film: her beating at the hands of her father.

Stella Maris came about in an intriguing way. Mary had grown close to Frances Marion, and when she sighed for her lack of education, Frances gave her a crash course in literature. One of the novels they discussed was William J. Locke's *Stella Maris*.[150] It was not unusual for actors to play two parts in this period, giving cameramen a chance to show how clever they were by disguising the double exposures. But for the most beautiful star in the world to play such an ugly character was an act of courage unprecedented in the cinema, and Frances Marion was amazed when Mary said she was determined to do it.[151] Mary made herself up to produce a lopsided look, her face compressed into a shapeless form. She pasted her hair down with Vaseline, which not only took out the curls but made it dark and straggly. She made her eyes smaller with white paint, and used rouge—which photographed dark on orthochromatic film—to provide the hollows in her cheeks.[152] She narrowed her nose by putting black paint on her nostrils and darkened her teeth.

Adolph Zukor had been unaware of what was going on, and when he visited the set he was visibly shocked to see Mary resembling Lon Chaney. "The look of dismay on the poor man's face was something to see," wrote Mary. "I had to pacify him that I died early in the picture." Zukor replied, "The sooner the better."[153] Even Zukor eventually had to admit that *Stella Maris* was "the most remarkable thing which Mary Pickford has ever done for the screen."[154]

AMARILLY OF CLOTHES-LINE ALLEY

RELEASED: MARCH 11, 1918

*A*marilly of Clothes-Line Alley is a champagne glass of exuberance—if that is the way to describe such an emphatically plebeian comedy. Full of typical Marshall Neilan clowning, enriching the Frances Marion script, it has an exceptionally charming performance by Mary Pickford. She plays Amarilly Jenkins, a cigarette girl at the Cyclone Cafe, in love with a bartender, Terry (William Scott). When Gordon Phillips, a wealthy sculptor (Norman Kerry), is injured in a brawl, she takes him home to her mother (Kate Price), an Irish laundrywoman. This brings Amarilly in contact with the upper class. Gordon's mother, intrigued by this working-class girl, makes her the center of a social experiment and invites her to live at her palatial residence. She is alarmed to find Gordon falling for Amarilly. But the two soon realize they are not right for each other. When Amarilly's mother, invited to tea with the Phillips family, dances a jig with the butler, Gordon's mother realizes her mistake, and Amarilly returns to her bartender.

Amarilly (Pickford), selling cigarettes in the Cyclone Cafe, eyes a dollar bill as Gordon (Norman Kerry) is about to hand it to her. Though this scene remains in the film, this particular shot, caught by the Graflex camera, does not survive in the existing print. It was probably taken during a rehearsal or a take that was later cut.

Opposite:

This photo shows the enchanting way in which Pickford introduces herself—cleaning the soap from a window to reveal her grin.

Social satire aside, the film is valuable for the light it throws on the behavior of the time. The scenes in the Cyclone Cafe show it to be the New York equivalent of an Alaskan dance hall, with cigarette girls, prostitutes, and uninhibited dancing. In one remarkable scene, a group of men troop into a brothel, but Terry leaves them at the door, where he is congratulated by a priest lurking in the shadows. This is the sort of scene that would not appear on the American screen again for a decade, and then only fleetingly.[155]

Although *Amarilly of Clothes-Line Alley* has been rarely screened since its original release, it stands as one of the most brilliantly made films of its time. Over the years, a few historians have drawn attention to it. Scott Eyman pointed out an homage to Chaplin, when Amarilly, fired from a job in a theater, seems defeated: "But then, in long shot, back to camera, she pauses, throws her shoulders back and moves briskly off into the horizon, full of new never-say-die resolve in precisely the manner that Chaplin had already patented."[156] This startling silhouette, the tiny figure dwarfed by the height of the theater, is but one of the flourishes with which this film is packed. Edward Wagenknecht praised the scene in which Neilan dissolved from three overdressed and gossipy women at afternoon tea to three Persian cats: "This was the cinematic way of doing the thing, which was right, as contrasted with the literary, which would have been wrong."[157] As a film about class consciousness, Arthur Lennig compared it to D. W. Griffith's *The Mother and the Law*, the modern story in *Intolerance* (1916): "Griffith played his film for sentiment and tragedy and drama, and saw social issues in more serious terms; uplifters encroaching upon the downtrodden. But *Amarilly*, although it deals with reformers, sees the conflict in terms of light comedy and satire." And yet the film did not betray its subject by providing the usual Cinderella ending, with the girl marrying the prince. "Instead, it disposes of him and has her marry Terry."[158]

The picture delighted most of the original reviewers.

At last we have the joy of a different ending. The story of a poor girl who, although offered all the advantages of a fine education and a wealthy marriage, has the good sense to realize that she will be a deal sight happier in her own middle class, married to the Irish lad she loves. One of the happiest bits from a director's ingenious brain is the final closeup of the happy Irish family off for a Sunday outing in the motor-cycle sidecar.[159]

M'LISS

RELEASED: MAY 13, 1918

M'liss, based on a Bret Harte novel, was made to exploit the success of *A Romance of the Redwoods*,[160] but a more diametric approach would be hard to imagine. It is an eccentric and hilarious spoof on Westerns. M'liss is an adolescent hoodlum, holding up stagecoaches with a slingshot (as shown in the above still) and charging around the countryside like a wildcat. Her father, Bummer Smith (Theodore Roberts), is a drunken reprobate whose sole asset is a chicken—he gets his whiskey in exchange for fresh eggs.

On one of her mock stage-robbing excursions, M'liss is handed a doll by the stage driver (Charles Ogle), who loves her dearly. She carries it to town in a perambulator made from a barrel, and when the kids grab it to tease her, she opens fire with her slingshot and shatters the doll's head. M'liss regards this as the end of childhood. In a mock-sentimental scene, the doll is laid in its coffin and Bummer Smith bursts into tears. M'liss is startled at this unexpected display of emotion, but as he explains: "It's the only chance I ever had of being a grandfather."

A handsome schoolteacher (Thomas Meighan) calms M'liss down and makes her keen to learn, but when her father is stabbed in the back the schoolteacher is arrested. The mood ought to change at this point, but the courtroom scene is anar-

Pickford and Thomas Meighan in *M'liss*.

chic and hilarious. Dramatic moments, however, are not skimped: a potentially nasty lynching of the real culprits is played by director Marshall Neilan on the face of a bystander (Charles Stevens), conveying the horror without forcing us to witness it.

The precious combination of Neilan, Frances Marion, cinematographer Walter Stradling, and Pickford—not to forget art director Wilfred Buckland—results in a film of unparalleled beauty. Because it is such a knockabout farce, it does not need such loveliness. Yet all the exterior scenes were on location near Boulder Creek, in Northern California, and sometimes one suspects a shot exists simply because they all fell in love with the effect of backlight on the trees and mountains.

This photograph, taken on location for *M'liss*, sums up the almost carefree atmosphere of making pictures in the heyday of silent film. In this Western farce Mary worked with one of the best leading men in American films, Irish actor Thomas Meighan (standing right behind Mary). Her director is her old friend Marshall Neilan. Walter Stradling was Mary Pickford's cameraman; he stands behind the Pathé camera, on the right. Charles Ogle holds the reins.

Neilan was admittedly an alcoholic. He had the ability to charm anyone into doing anything, but it all came too easily for him: lacking a challenge, he tended to lose interest before the picture was finished. More and more frequently, his name appeared with a co-director—Frank Urson or Frank O'Connor, his assistants—who had to help out when Mickey took the day off. He was a drinking companion of Jack Pickford and his cronies. He had been on the stage—he had even worked for Belasco as a child—but he had contempt for the all-pervasive influence of the theater on the movies. He believed in the motion picture but lacked the discipline it demanded.

"Irishmen like Mickey had a great deal of ham in them," said actress Lina Basquette. "With them talking you through a scene, and with the music playing in the background, why, they could get a performance out of a turnip."[161]

English cameraman Walter Stradling, the uncle of Harry Stradling, a more famous cinematographer of a later era, started with the industry itself, entering laboratories in the 1890s. He began as a cameraman with Edison and worked at Biograph, which may have been why Pickford selected him. In a period of outstanding cinematographers, he stood supreme. There have been few films with exteriors more exquisite than *M'liss*. The extreme closeups of Pickford and Meighan at the jail belong in a motion-picture hall of fame.

On the final day of shooting, Mary Pickford said to the script girl, Lucita Squier (who appears at left in the group shot). "Remember. Lucita, we're friends for life." One would expect the promise to be forgotten in minutes, but Mary kept her word. She and Squier always kept in touch, and Mary signed off her letters with "Friend for life, Mary."[102]

"Mickey was one of the most delightful, aggravating, gifted and charming human beings I have ever known," wrote Mary Pickford about director Marshall Neilan.

There were times when I could cheerfully have throttled him—especially at his frequent failures to make an appearance on the set until after luncheon, keeping a large company waiting at considerable expense.

I would use the most insulting Irish language I could think of, telling him he was nothing but a bog-trotter, far-down Shanty Irish and a dirty scut! Mickey, who was a good actor, pretended to be shocked and, to shame me, said "Tad" (the endearing Irish name he always called me) "what would the public think of their darling using such language?" And then he would pacify me with one of his creative gags that my fans still remember forty years later.

Pickford reluctantly accepts a snake from director Marshall Neilan.

The candid Graflex still above captures one of those legendary moments: Mickey promised a surprise one morning, and Mary noticed a large wooden box.

Knowing what a prankster he was, I watched suspiciously as he lifted the lid of the box. To my horror, a five-foot snake raised its head and looked me straight in the eye.

"Mickey, you're mad!" I cried, backing away.

"Easy, easy, Tad," he said. "It's not poisonous. I want you to pick it up."

She refused to cooperate until she saw an amused grin on the face of a carpenter and realized she would have to. "So without a whimper, I allowed Mickey to put my index finger on the snake, and gradually I had all five fingers around its body. I remember how surprised I was that it didn't feel slimy. It was just cold in a smooth, uniform way, and I was amazed at the muscular reaction of the body."[163]

There is a scene in the film in which Pickford carries the snake into a schoolroom, causing great pandemonium. She found out later that the scene—which was not in the script—was the result of a bet. Mickey had the idea overnight to work the snake into the story; the crew told him Mary would never agree. He laid a bet, and he won.

Photoplay admitted the story was inconsequential, but added, "we got the very ecstasy of laughter because of the utter gravity of the performers—and the super-gravity of the director himself!"[164]

Director William Desmond Taylor assists Mary on the set. He wears dark glasses as protection against "Klieg Eyes," a painful affliction caused by the use of open arc lights. Stills of Taylor directing are exceptionally rare.

HOW COULD YOU, JEAN?

RELEASED: JUNE 23, 1918

Even those unfamiliar with silent films might have heard of William Desmond Taylor, the director of *How Could You, Jean?*, for in February 1922 he was the victim of Hollywood's most celebrated unsolved murder. He was well liked, generous, and courteous—the sort of man Hollywood was proud to produce when public-relations events were staged, and the last person one would expect to meet such an end.

An Anglo-Irishman from Cappoquin, County Waterford, young William Deane-Tanner became what was known as a remittance man—shipped off by his wealthy family to a ranch in Kansas and given a small remittance on which to survive. He had a colorful life: he joined the Alaskan Gold Rush, taking nine months to reach Dawson City, although never striking gold. He appeared in vaudeville and straight plays, after which he moved into the antiques business and in 1901 settled down to married life in New York.

He walked out on his family in 1908 and returned to the stage, as William Desmond Taylor. When he could get no work as an actor, he worked on the railroads and in hotels. At one point he shared a hut in Nome with the famous poet Robert W. ("The Shooting of Dan McGrew") Service. It was when he fell ill and was sent to Los Angeles to recuperate that he began his motion-picture career.

For an expensive serial, *The Diamond from the Sky* (1915), Mary Pickford was offered a huge sum to play the lead, but she turned it down. Charlotte Pickford suggested Mary's sister Lottie, forgetting to inform the producers that Lottie was pregnant. The original director gave up in disgust, but the gentlemanly Taylor took over. The experience probably encouraged Mary to hire him, and he made three pictures for her. "I particularly remember Bill Taylor's beautiful manners," recalled Mary Pickford. "They were so natural and unaffected. He was a quiet, cultured man who read a lot—he'd bring books to the set and sometimes read aloud the passages that interested him."[165]

This film benefited from a Frances Marion scenario, yet was written off sarcastically by *Variety*: "On Thursday afternoons, when the cooks have their half holidays, the picture should please in the popular priced houses."[166] In fact, Mary played a cook—actually, a young woman who discovers she has lost her fortune and pretends to be Swedish in order to snare a job as a cook—with whom the hired hand, Oscar, falls in love. So does Ted Burton (Casson Ferguson), the son of a millionaire (Herbert Standing). He persuades Oscar to resign and takes his job. When Mary saves the millionaire's life, the old man is only too happy to allow Ted to marry the "Swedish cook."

The film had the distinction of being the first Pickford picture to be photographed by Charles Rosher. Walter Stradling, who had worked on previous productions, had contracted pneumonia and died earlier in the year. Rosher, who was also English, would be Mary's chief cameraman for seventeen consecutive productions.

Lottie was Mary's kid sister, though only a year younger. She had little of Mary's personality or beauty, although she used to understudy her in their theatrical days and was expected to help Mary dress. Lottie reacted by becoming the family rebel. She shared a predilection for alcohol with Jack (whom she worshiped), and her parties were notorious. Lottie was probably an amusing and loyal companion, with something of the Pickford charm, but while men could get away with being drunk every night, and even be respected for it, when a woman did it she was dismissed as a tramp. And if that woman had a child, such behavior was seen as criminally irresponsible.

The baby was christened Mary Pickford Rupp, but her name was eventually changed to Gwynne. After Lottie was divorced, in 1920, the baby was handed over to her grandmother Charlotte. Mary had a good deal to do with her upbringing, too. Gwynne grew up, surprisingly well adjusted, and married George Ornstein, who was head of United Artists in London. (It was through the Ornsteins that I met Mary Pickford when, in 1965, she came to stay with Gwynne in London.)

Mary demonstrates her dexterity for eating peas off a knife while Casson Ferguson looks on in consternation in *How Could You, Jean?*

JOHANNA ENLISTS
RELEASED: SEPTEMBER 29, 1918

Director William Desmond Taylor's best picture for Mary was probably *Johanna Enlists*. It was adapted from a Rupert Hughes story by Frances Marion and told of a girl who is bored to death with life in the country. She prays for romance, for thrills, and for a beau. God sends her an entire regiment.

The government wanted a propaganda picture from Mary, but she had had enough of anti-German sentiment. It so happened that Mary was Honorary Colonel to the 143rd Field Artillery, and it was arranged that its members would appear in this picture. It was to be indirect propaganda, so subtle that not until the end would the audience realize its intent.

Pickford asked Marion to write the scenario, forgetting that her friend was about to leave for Washington to see George Creel, of the Committee on Public Information, in the hope of becom-

The World's
Greatest –

"The World's Greatest" was proudly written on this photograph by Lewis William O'Connell, second cameraman on many of Pickford's films,[172] who is standing next to Charlotte Pickford. Mary stands next to Colonel Ralph J. Faneuf, commander of the 143rd Field Artillery, which cooperated in the making of *Johanna Enlists*. They appeared together in the last shot of the film.

ing an officially sanctioned war correspondent in France. Mary asked her not to leave until the script was finished, and Frances agreed—reluctantly. But even when the script was handed in and approved, and Frances was packed and ready to leave, Mary asked her to drive out to Santa Ana, where the 143rd Field Artillery was camped.[167] Marion never regretted the trip, for she met a remarkable man, Fred Thomson, chaplain of the regiment and a world-champion athlete. She later married him, and he abandoned the church to become, of all things, a major star of Westerns. "No one has written more satirically about love at first sight than I," Frances admitted, but it had happened to her.

The film was rushed. *Picture Play* reported that Taylor and Pickford were working on it at the same time as *Captain Kidd, Jr.* (1919).[168] But the film showed no sign of haste.

Mary took the war seriously. She lent her support to the Lasky Home Guard, but of far greater importance was her participation in the Third Liberty Loan campaign. It began on April 6, 1918—the first anniversary of America's entry—and involved such stars as William S. Hart, Douglas Fairbanks, and Charlie Chaplin. Mary rallied from coast to coast and raised millions of dollars for the war effort.

To their delight, the government made it possible for Douglas Fairbanks and Mary to travel together legitimately for five days to New York, then for three more to Washington. In front of the Capitol, Mary yelled into her megaphone, "I'm only five feet tall but every inch of me is a fighting American."[169] As a direct result of the bond campaigns, U.S. Secretary of the Treasury William Gibbs McAdoo, President Wilson's son-in-law, became involved in the formation of United Artists.

In addition to the rallies, Mary acted as godmother and Honorary Colonel to the 600 soldiers in the 143rd Field Artillery and 144 in the Aviation Corps. She made dozens of personal appearances for war charities and involved herself in a Red Cross fund-raising scheme, requesting a day's pay from every contributor and writing a personal letter of thanks. On top of this, she accepted the position of superintendent of the studio salvage department of the Red Cross, presenting them with two ambulances. When, at the end of the war, the Ambulance Fund was underspent, Mary suggested the surplus ($27,000)[170] be used to form the basis of the Motion Picture Relief Fund.[171] This proved to be perhaps her most important contribution of all.

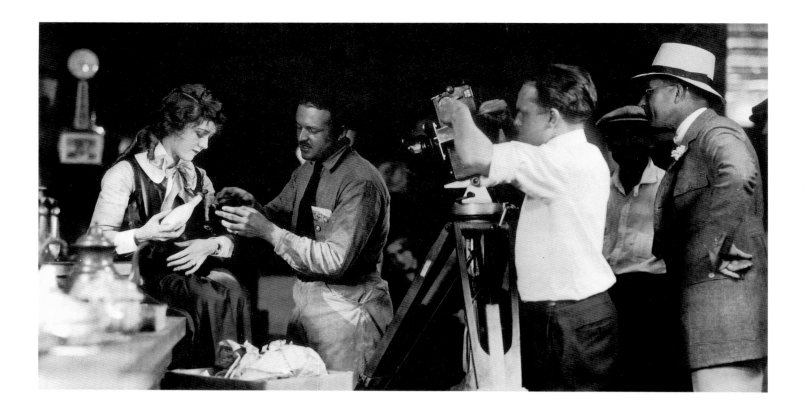

CAPTAIN KIDD, JR.

RELEASED: APRIL 6, 1919

Only two reels of this film survive. in a private collection. It had a scenario by Frances Marion, which suggests it might have been an above-average Pickford film. *Variety*[173] did not think so. The critic considered the production cheap, the only amusing touch being a parrot that shrieked curses at everybody. Judging from the surviving still photos, one could conclude that the production was relatively weak.

The story centered on a hoax that an aged recluse plays on his grandson. In the old man's will, a chart showing buried treasure is hidden in a book that is accidentally sold to a second-hand bookstore, where Mary discovers it. She and her boyfriend, Jim (Douglas MacLean), a young author, meet the grandson, Willie (Robert Gordon), and he agrees to share the treasure. Pretending to be geologists, they dig it up. The "treasure" proves to be a box containing nothing more exciting than a note saying "good health." Fortunately, the grandson discovers that the hunt was only a test, and a genuine fortune is held in trust. The critics praised Douglas MacLean, who would have a huge hit that same year: Henry King's *23½ Hours' Leave.*

Captain Kidd, Jr. was the last Pickford film released by Artcraft under the Paramount umbrella. It was held back for months until April 1919, just four weeks prior to Mary's release of *Daddy-Long-Legs* in May, which in retrospect seems a rather calculated and cutthroat act on the part of Paramount.

In 1917, two exhibitors, Thomas Tally and J. D. Williams, had organized a distribution concern, First National, designed to cut out the middleman. They were fed up with Paramount and decided to release directly to the exhibitor films they had contracted for themselves. They signed Chaplin at a tremendous price, and they finally tore Mary away from Adolph Zukor. "Let her go," Zukor was told. "It'll serve two purposes. It'll cure her swelled head and it'll ruin First National."[174]

Other companies had been offering Mary huge sums to go with them, and leaving Zukor after five years with Paramount was a tough decision, but the aims of First National seemed praiseworthy. She signed a contract for $675,000 a year plus a percentage of the profits. First National gave her total independence. from the selection of the story to the final cut. Mary Pickford was now her own independent producer.

Mary is about to feed a lamb that its handler has put in her arms, while Charles Rosher lines up the camera, and director William Desmond Taylor looks on from behind.

DADDY-LONG-LEGS

*D*addy-Long-Legs was the archetypal Mary Pickford film. It had all the elements an audience could hope for: a baby rescued from an ashcan, an orphanage run like a penitentiary, hilarious and touching comedy, much pathos, and a lover waiting in the wings for Pickford's character to grow up.

Jerusha Abbott—known as Judy—is a bright but mischievous child constantly at loggerheads with the prickly matron, Miss Lippett (Milla Davenport). One of the trustees takes an interest in her and persuades another to sponsor her college education. The agreement is that the sponsor shall remain an anonymous "John Smith." He does not want to see her and merely asks for a letter once a month about her progress in college. While in college, she attracts two men, one a shallow college freshman, Jimmy McBride (Marshall Neilan), the other Jarvis Pendleton (Mahlon Hamilton), an older man who invites her down to the farm where he grew up. There she sets about writing a novel to help pay back her benefactor. The novel is turned down, but a subsequent story, about her life in the orphanage, is a huge success, and she is able to send her benefactor a check for $1,000. Her graduation (staged at the Busch Gardens in Pasadena) is a lonely affair—in the photograph on page 160 she approaches a spectator, imagining he might be Daddy-Long-Legs. But even when Jarvis Pendleton proposes, she turns him down, remaining loyal to Daddy-Long-Legs. "I love somebody even more than you," she writes, "but I've refused to marry him. He comes from a family full of ancestors. I haven't the courage to tell him about the John Grier Home." Hearing nothing, she takes matters into her own hands and visits the mysterious Daddy-Long-Legs. Judy finds that he is Jarvis Pendleton.

Mary herself adapted the story with Agnes Christine Johnston from the children's classic during a four-hour train journey in November 1918, during which the Armistice was signed. (Johnston wrote many of the Charles Ray films about rural boyhood.) Charlotte Pickford had acquired it for Mary, along with *Pollyanna*, paying stage producers Klaw and Erlanger $40,000, an immense sum for those days. Mary gave the direction to Neilan, who imbued the film with the lovable side of his personality. He even played the role of Jimmy McBride, Judy's egotistical suitor. (These scenes were directed by Sidney Franklin.) There is hardly a thing that one could criticize about the film. Yet Mary is on record as saying that she disliked it.[175]

The craftsmanship of the film shines through even the limitations of a VHS cassette, and as a human document it is, quite simply, adorable. The orphanage scenes are so vivid and poignant you cannot imagine anyone trying to copy them. Yet they did. It is instructive to compare *Daddy-Long-Legs* with a film designed for a similar audience, *Nobody's Kid* (1921). It was produced by Robertson-Cole in an attempt to cash in on the Pickford success with a picture made on a minuscule budget—most of the money going to the star, Mae Marsh. It has often been suggested that Mae Marsh was a finer actress than Mary Pickford—they both started with Griffith—but fine acting often depends on sensitive direction. *Nobody's Kid* was given to an untalented director who turned out what the trade papers dismissed as "a weak sister—puny, ineffective, leave it alone."[176] "Faintly amusing" would be overpraising it. Comparing the two shows is the difference between painting, as in fine art, and painting, as in house.

Opposite, top:

Judy Abbott's talent for singing, intended to lighten the burden for her fellow orphans at the John Grier Home, is strangled by the jealous Pansy Gumph.

Opposite, bottom:

The Great Prune Strike. "Three times a day, the orphans faced their common enemy, the prune." Judy makes a speech about the much-hated fruit, supported by Wesley Barry. They break into what would later be called a protest song when the matron and Pansy Gumph (standing at left) burst in and haul them out.

Left:

Mary and Wesley Barry vow "to stick" and not succumb to the abuse of the tyrannical matron, Miss Lippett. Charles Rosher's glorious backlighting that gives Mary's hair a halolike glow was no accident.

Below:

Mary wreaks havoc at the orphanage—unfortunately on the day of the visit of all the trustees.

In one of the most enchanting sequences in all of Pickford's pictures, Judy and the boy are placed, in disgrace, on a bench on the grounds. We are introduced to "a gentleman who takes things easily." From a cart outside a backstreet store, the robber steals some promising looking sacks. Judy and the kid are hungry. "Please God, we want food." The robber finds in the sacks not the money-producing objects he had expected but the remains of someone's lunch, including a jug of hard cider. He hurls the stuff over a wall, and it lands on top of the kids. "I didn't know He was so close," remarks the boy. The jug of applejack soon affects their vision, and the orphanage sways before them.

"What's the matter with that building?" asks Judy.

"Which one?"

At her graduation, Mary wonders if an elderly gentleman is her "Daddy-Long-Legs."

Judy cavorts on the swings and knocks Pansy Gumph down the well. When they hear her shrieks, they haul her up, Wesley on one handle and Judy on the other. But it is hard work, and when Judy lets go of the handle Pansy's weight takes her down like a stone. As the handle revolves, Wesley is whirled around until he is hurled aside like a rag doll. The orphanage dog has been licking the cider jug, and he staggers toward them on his hind legs, occasionally leaning for support against the wall.

It was bitterly ironic that Neilan should find such humor in alcohol, for it was the scourge of Hollywood, and he was addicted to it. Script girl Lucita Squier recalled that he often came to work without having been to bed—and it was not long before he went to bed without turning up for work.[177] On one occasion when Neilan failed to arrive by lunchtime, Mary announced that she was closing the production down. On her way out, she met Neilan coming in.

"Go away," she said. "You ought to be ashamed of yourself. I've made up my mind to call off the picture."

"Oh, come on, Tad," said Neilan. "Just wait until you hear my story." He put his hands firmly around her neck and guided her back into the studio. Within minutes, Mary had burst into laughter.

The financial success of the picture was Mary's biggest so far, spectacularly refuting Zukor's advisers, who predicted she would fall on her face with her first independent production and come crawling back to Paramount. *Daddy-Long-Legs* grossed $1.3 million and became one of the best loved of all Pickford's films. To many the film brought forth this sort of praise:

Audiences . . . yesterday were laughing as hard at Mary as ever they laughed at Charlie Chaplin, and they were as near tears, too, as ever they were at *The Birth of a Nation*. . . . For once movies eclipse written and spoken art . . . it is the only thing on the screen that ever had the greatness that makes *Huckleberry Finn* the masterpiece of American writing. . . . [Pickford performs] every whit as comically as could Charlie Chaplin.[178]

In this gag shot Mary directs Marshall Neilan. Pickford was perfectly capable of directing, and she occasionally had to, when Neilan was off on a bender. But she preferred to work with a trusted eye watching her performance. Neilan was her favorite, and he certainly directed her best films. He is wearing the makeup of an actor in this still because he played the second lead, replacing Albert Ray (cousin of Charles), who had fallen ill.

In the silent days, studios had to allow for distribution abroad. They needed a domestic negative—here, the responsibility of Charles Rosher, behind the Bell and Howell 2709 camera, at left in the photograph below. Duplicating the results of one camera produced a poor-quality image, so a second original negative was sent abroad. Henry Cronjager shot the foreign negative for this picture with his Wilart camera, an American copy of the famous French Pathé. Sometimes, alternative takes were used to save a second cameraman. But how simple it all looks compared to the complex system involved today. In 1919, the biggest star in the business could make a film with seven people—modern features sometimes have seven producers, and their crews generally number 150.

"There is no man working in the sunlight medium," wrote Julian Johnson,

who has a greater mastery of human touches—whimsical, gay, tender or eye-filling—than Marshall Neilan. . . . The gift of holding a mirror up to nature, which is Mickey's, is heaven-sent; I am confident he will acquire the upper mathematics of his profession. . . . Pathos and laughter are near allies, but it takes genius to interweave them as deftly and inextricably as they are interwoven here.[179]

THE HOODLUM

RELEASED: SEPTEMBER 1, 1919

Mary Pickford contributed so much to her films—and so much was expected from them—that a director's reputation was always enhanced by working with her. Some, after all, made their best pictures for her. Sidney Franklin had worked for Griffith, and he and his brother Chester had made a series of children's pictures for Fox. (The script for this film was written by their regular collaborator, Bernard McConville.) More important perhaps, he had directed Norma Talmadge, whom Mary regarded with some awe. Not as a rival, for Talmadge did not make comedies, but as perhaps America's finest screen actress.

The Hoodlum, Pickford's second wholly independent production, was hailed as "the best Mary Pickford ever."[180] Mary played Amy Burke, who lives in a Fifth Avenue mansion with her wealthy grandfather (Ralph Lewis). When her father returns from a trip to Europe, she chooses to live with him in a slum, for he is a sociologist. At first an insufferable snob, Amy is transformed by life in the poor quarter. She revels in dancing the shimmy, shooting craps, and fleeing the cops. She falls for a young man (Kenneth Harlan) who had been jailed because of her grandfather's dishonest and brutal business practices; she creeps back to the mansion in the dead of night to steal papers proving the boy's innocence and is caught red-handed by her grandfather.

"Whatever others may hand First National," said *Variety*, "with the idea of slipping the same to the public, Mary Pickford gives that organization the real goods . . . she gives the very best photography, direction, scenarios, lighting effects and attention to detail."[181] And

In this scene, Mary and her gang have been disturbed by a cop while shooting craps. After a chase, Mary dives down a coal chute into a cloud of dust, and we cut to a rat, on its hind legs, watching her with amazement. Above, director Sidney Franklin adjusts her makeup. The closeup at right shows the final result.

the elusive charm of Mary Pickford continued to bewilder them. "After six years she is still queen of the screen. In no sense conventionally pretty, for the surface of her cheeks are [*sic*] too flat for that, she has perhaps something better, a mastery of pantomime that is unique, a charm of manner and personality that cannot be escaped and is past defining."

"I can scarcely believe that the slum scenes of *The Hoodlum* were taken in California," wrote Hazel Simpson Naylor in *Motion Picture Magazine*. "They are a true slice of New York's East Side."[182]

And here is how they were done. Art director Max Parker built a splendidly convincing section of New York at the Brunton Studios (later Paramount). His work was so extraordinary that he ought to be better known. He changed his style radically in the 1920s and became the designer for the frothy and glamorous pictures made for Cecil B. DeMille's company, Producers Distributing Corporation.

The musicians add a surreal touch to the photograph below. But they were becoming a standard feature in Hollywood studios. When you had carpenters banging nails into the set next door, you needed some way of soothing the star and of keeping the players in the right mood. One observer saw a Western being shot on a Hollywood street, the camera chasing after the horses in an automobile and the musicians following in a car behind!

Mary had been struck by the 1918 influenza epidemic, an illness that killed more people than the war itself. In the spring of 1919, she was out of action for four weeks, then returned to work on *The Hoodlum* against the doctor's advice.

The doctor told me I was crazy, and that he wouldn't be responsible for the consequences. But I don't think any outsider realizes the sense of obligation which motion picture stars feel in regard to their work. If the star is laid up, the whole picture stops. Dozens, perhaps hundreds of people have to be idle. So you take your life in your hands, if necessary, to let the picture go on.[183]

A New York slum was re-created by art director Max Parker. Charles Rosher is the chief cameraman, crouching behind the Bell and Howell camera in this photograph. Sidney Franklin is seated next to him.

THE HEART O' THE HILLS

RELEASED: DECEMBER 1, 1919

In contrast to her urban comedy, *The Hoodlum*, Mary followed with a picture set in the Kentucky mountains, using the same team. If critics were startled that New York could be built so convincingly in California, this one—made in the San Bernardino Mountains near Redlands, California—was so authentic it would later resemble the famous drama-documentary *Stark Love* (1926), shot in the Old Smokies of North Carolina.

One critic wrote, "It has been my privilege at one time in life to study these people and I wish to congratulate Miss Pickford here and now upon the faithfulness with which the characters of the play have been assembled and presented."[184]

The film was adapted from a story by John Fox, Jr. (The leading character was originally a boy: in 1924, Jack Pickford remade it as *The Hill-Billy*.) Mary, as Mavis Hawn, is a wild mountain girl fighting big businessmen from the city who are trying to seize her family's land for coal after her father has been shot. She joins the Night Riders—dressed like the Ku Klux Klan—and leads a ride to scare the "furriners" away. Mavis is accused of killing the leading capitalist, but the case collapses when the entire jury and most of the spectators plead guilty!

When a bluegrass aristocrat seizes Mavis (Pickford) at a clog dance and whirls her into an energetic waltz, she tears herself free, pummels his chest, and yells, "I air a lady!" The bluegrass aristocrat is played by John Gilbert, the "great lover" of a few years later. He is on the right. Betty Bouton, playing his sister, is at left.

Mavis practices for the day she
can confront the man who shot
her father.

Although the film has enormous charm, it is entirely without sentiment. Characters no sooner look at each other than they are exchanging blows. Mary, far from whimpering on the sidelines, is more likely to wade in and thump everyone concerned. The clog dance is a classic sequence—or would be, if anyone had ever seen this film since its release. It is played for the rivalry between the two admirers, the rhythm of the dance increasing in pace, with frequent cuts to the fiddler and foot-tapping spectators, until a white-bearded ancient throws his arms in the air and cries, "Hold on thar! I done lost me teeth."

Despite the revenge motif, the picture is lighthearted and sunny. Mostly shot out-of-doors, the entire film has a feeling of warm sun and fresh air—you can practically smell the pine needles. And when Charles Rosher photographs Mary, her golden hair bathed in the late afternoon light that causes insects to flit across the lens, one feels quite awestruck. Here is a first-rate story, handled with the highest level of artistry.

If anyone needs to be converted to Pickford, this picture should do the trick. *Photoplay* said of her performance, "Mary Pickford . . . once more enters her physical descriptions with the fury of a novice who has everything to gain and nothing to lose—and the painstaking care and cunning detail of the celebrated performer who has everything to lose and very little to gain."[185]

When I interviewed director Sidney Franklin, he recalled this film with affection. He had made a number of pictures with children—the "Fox Kiddies"—and these proved ideal preparation for Pickford.

There was that same fresh quality—the same spontaneity—that our children displayed. And directing her was equally enjoyable. Working with Mary was unusually simple. She was a pro in every sense of the word: no nonsense, no temperament. Mary was the boss; she was her own producer. And this led to the only argument we had.

Franklin preferred to watch his rushes alone with the cutter. But Mary came, too.

Whenever she saw herself on the screen, she would mutter in the dark, "I look terrible in this scene" or "I don't like my hair" or "I think I did that badly." It became obvious that Mary was only looking at herself, which is quite normal for any star. But a director must look at a scene for the overall effect. Most of the time, I didn't agree with Mary, who was naturally supercritical about her performance and the way she looked. After three or four sessions, I waited until everyone had left the projection room, and I asked Mary to stay behind. I told her I couldn't agree with her criticisms. "At this rate," I said, "We'll be reshooting everything."

Mary realized this was hardly a constructive way for our association to proceed—she graciously backed down and allowed me to screen my rushes on my own. She knew how to run a motion picture company and, although the producer, seldom argued with the director. But if she saw something that was critical and needed discussion, of course she would take it up with the director—and if need be have it taken over. This was her prerogative—and she wasn't afraid to use it.[186]

Mary Pickford was harsher on her own films than most critics. She disliked *Pollyanna*, her first production for United Artists, for its saccharine qualities. Perhaps she was influenced by screenwriter Frances Marion. They both thought it nauseating. "I hated writing it, Mary hated playing it, yet we managed to edge in some funny little scenes in spite of our indifference."[187] Burns Mantle had this to say in *Photoplay*: "It reeks with the sentimentalism of the theater at its baldest. But during its performance . . . it is a good game, and a cheering one. A week of it and you might strangle Pollyanna. For one afternoon or evening she is an inspiration."[188]

I am sure the dislike was retrospective. Frances Marion's memoir appeared in the 1970s, when sentimentality of any sort was treated with derision. In 1928, Pickford had picked it as one of her films she liked best.[189] By the 1950s she had altered her opinion, perhaps to protect a film she cared for so that people would not be taken aback by the Victorian ideals it espoused.

Pollyanna was a well-loved story, and millions would have been drawn to it because of its fame as a novel and a play. Pickford could hardly sabotage their expectations by departing radically from the original. It is an unabashedly sentimental story, and it is to the credit of everyone concerned that one can still watch it with enjoyment. Marion was praised for her skill in *Cinema Craftsmanship*, one of the first books to offer serious analysis of motion pictures: "She veiled her titles so ingeniously that those who did not believe in the rather tiresome philosophy of Pollyanna might detect a gleam of bantering humor in the titles, and those who liked bathos and a bit of super-sentimentality could swallow them whole upon their face value."[190]

An example occurs at the opening, when Pollyanna attends her dying father, a minister. "Oh, Daddy, you must not leave me—I love you so," she says. He addresses a comforting remark to her and expires. How does Pollyanna take it? Weeping lamentations? Does she hurl herself around the room? Not at all. She says to the doctor, "I'm glad he's gone to Heaven. I—I'm sure it's an improvement over missionarying in the Ozark mountains."

What a hit *Pollyanna* was at the time! The National Board of Review, the group responsible for censorship, fell on it with gratitude. There had been a lot of films regarded as immoral, and industry scandals were beginning to hit the tabloids. It was also highly praised by clergymen for its positive, wholesome message.[191] *Variety*'s review was endearing:

It is perfect technically, ably directed, charmingly acted, touches and stirs the heart, brightens the eyes with tears and is full of that amazing optimism so typically American and yet so utterly ridiculous. With considerable force, it asserts that the world is a nice place to live in. A fat lie this, but it helps to believe it, and so anything able to make us believe it is as valuable as a blue river diamond mine.[192]

The film was directed by Paul Powell, a journeyman director who had worked for D. W. Griffith. As one of the founders of United Artists, it might have been expected that were he to comment on the film, Griffith himself would do so with tact and discretion. Instead, he described it as "the most immoral story" ever put on the screen: "It takes a fake philosophy of gilded bunkum. Its reasoning, if applied to actual life conditions, will handicap its believers and leave them actually menaced."[193] Mary herself described it as "a sweet little picture, made with sincerity."[194]

The comic appeal of Pollyanna, who brings both her optimistic philosophy and havoc to Aunt Polly's household, presided over by Katherine Griffith[195] as Aunt

Polly, rides over the sentimentality for much of the film, making it almost as enjoyable as *Rebecca of Sunnybrook Farm*. "Miss Pickford's exuberance was never more in evidence," wrote Edward Wagenknecht, "and even if one gets tired of 'The Glad Game,' it takes a pretty hard heart not to be moved by her gallantry in the final reels."[196] Following a scene in which she is run over by a car, the final reel is as housebound as Pollyanna herself. Scene after scene takes place in her bedroom. Then we see her in a wheelchair, from which she rises in an attempt to walk with crutches. Eventually, there is an inserted closeup in which Pollyanna raises her eyes heavenward for strength and, throwing her crutches aside, staggers forward in a scene reminiscent of *The Miracle Man*, the smash hit of the previous year. *Pollyanna* grossed more than a million dollars.[197]

Even the usually Pickford-resistant *London Times* succumbed to Mary as Pollyanna:

She is still without question the best comedy actress that the screen world possesses . . . she shows herself to be a perfect screen actress. . . . She can convey every possible emotion with the same ease and there is never a suggestion of overacting. When England can discover a Mary Pickford we shall be in the position to challenge the supremacy of the United States.[198]

Aunt Polly (Katherine Griffith) collapses in fright when she mistakes Pollyanna for a burglar. Helen Jerome Eddy, as the Aunt's maid, Nancy, is at left.

Opposite:

This portrait reveals how astoundingly childlike Mary could still appear at age twenty-seven.

In this melodramatic moment, Pollyanna walks again.

Below:
When Pollyanna first meets Jimmie Bean (Howard Ralston), she perceives him as a potential nemesis. But they quickly become close friends, help one another through several crises, and ultimately become husband and wife.

SUDS

RELEASED: JUNE 27, 1920

If Chaplin and Pickford influenced each other, then *Suds* is Pickford's most Chaplinesque film. She plays a Cockney laundress, and much of the film is slapstick. She even cast a veteran of Chaplin's stock company, ex-Karno comedian Albert Austin, as the man she loves.

Once again, Mary took a minor talent, director John Francis Dillon, and encouraged him to produce remarkable results. Not that *Suds* is a complete success—some of the comedy falls flat nowadays, and Mary's performance is a little too broad to be as emotionally effective as it might be. But it has many strengths. Mary plays a role similar to Unity Blake of *Stella Maris*, although this time the slavey is brighter and more feisty. And accepting that Charles Rosher's atmospheric shots of London's dockland are only to be expected in the period immediately after *Broken Blossoms*, what comes as a surprise is the bold, almost expressionistic lighting in the laundry and particularly the abbatoir interiors, as the above photograph illustrates. Germanic as it may appear to us, the Germans had not yet shown many signs of understanding the art of lighting for films. *The Cabinet of Dr. Caligari*, released the same year as *Suds*,[199] was content with its novel idea of expressionistic shadows painted on the wall, and showed little interest in creative lighting. But Rosher and his associate Lewis William O'Connell lit these interiors like a von Sternberg film

of the late 1920s. (There can be no higher praise.) And one must not forget the immense contribution of Max Parker, who continued to prove himself perhaps the industry's finest art director.

    Suds was originally called *The Duchess of Suds* and was adapted from an English one-act play of 1905 that had brought Maude Adams international fame.[200] Amanda Afflick is a plain little slavey working in a laundry, so plain she must have dismayed her audience. She even asks, "Who could love me? Who could? Nobody never won't." The only creature who will share her loneliness is a horse called Lavender that she saves from the glue factory. She is so sorry for the horse that when it rains she brings it up the outside stairway into her tenement. This is an unforgettable sequence. It opens with a closeup iris on what appear to be Pickford's curls, impeccably arranged. We cut and iris out to reveal that Amanda has given Lavender's mane a wash and set. Part of the pleasure of this sequence is the superbly cinematic way it has been done—the pouring rain, the miserable tenement, the horse galomphing around the bedroom with Amanda aloft, and the ceiling collapsing on the family beneath. As the above photo shows, the scene had an air of surrealism before the word *surrealism* was invented. One wonders if Luis Buñuel ever saw this sequence before making *Un Chien Andalou.*

    The trouble with Lavender, allegedly an ex-polo pony, was that however starved it looked when first brought to the studio, it ate so well in Douglas Fairbanks's stable that its ribs had to be painted on its side when it came time to film.

    If Mary had any idea of redoing Chaplin's *A Dog's Life* with a horse, she abandoned it after the sequence in the tenement. She introduces an aristocratic lady with a country estate who does charitable work in the slums. The woman takes the horse, soon after this scene, and lets it loose in her fields.

    Mary had trouble with the ending. Horace, the man she loves (Albert Austin), agrees to pretend to be her fiancé, but when he sees how shabby she looks, he abandons her. This was

Amanda (Pickford) has brought her horse Lavender in from the rain—to her second-story flat.

Having saved Lavender from the glue factory, Amanda is mocked by the local street children.

admirably honest and realistic, but people were so downcast by it that exhibitors demanded a more heartwarming conclusion. Luckily, there was another boy in the story, the laundry driver Ben (Harold Goodwin). In the revised ending Ben appears, carrying two carnations.[201] He misinterprets the sight of Amanda with Horace and withdraws, clearly upset. It isn't terribly convincing, because we have never seen him give Amanda so much as an affectionate glance. But even that was not enough. The film finally ends with Mary and Lavender reunited on a country estate. Ben is with them. Lavender gallops around with Amanda until a wasp sting causes the horse to throw her into a stream. Final title: "There's gratitude for you."

The film did not make as much money as most Pickford films: $722,155.97. Yet it was one of the few that Pickford liked.[202] William K. Everson presented *Suds* at his Theodore Huff Memorial Film Society in 1965 and regretted that, as most of the Pickford films were locked in her vaults,[203] this atypical film was likely to be the only one modern audiences saw.

One of the most important events in Mary's life took place during the production of *Suds*, her semi-secret marriage to Douglas Fairbanks. Mary came to the studio (to play a lovesick slavey!) with adhesive tape covering her wedding ring. Everyone guessed at once what had happened and congratulated her. This wedding could so easily have caused a scandal. Mary was Catholic, and her divorce from Owen Moore was not accepted in some quarters. Fairbanks was also recently divorced. They agonized over the decision to marry for months, fearing that their union might destroy their careers. Finally they decided that they both had enough fame and money, and if the public dumped them, so be it. To the contrary, their wedding became an occasion for worldwide rejoicing as soon as it was announced. "This America's Sweetheart business must stop," joked Fairbanks. "She's my sweetheart. And if the world doesn't like it, they know the way to Beverly Hills."[204]

**Pickford and Fred Thomson
in *The Love Light*.**

THE LOVE LIGHT
RELEASED: JANUARY 9, 1921

The Love Light was a radical departure from Pickford's lighthearted comedies. Angela (Pickford) tends the lighthouse in an Italian fishing village. When war comes, her elder brother volunteers and is killed. Her younger brother, Mario, and her fiancé, Giovanni, depart for the front. She finds a sailor washed up on the rocks. He says his name is Joseph (Fred Thomson), that he is an American deserter. Will she hide him until he can return to the safety of his ship?

A woman concealing a man in her house was an extremely daring situation for a film of the time, and perhaps only Mary Pickford could have gotten away with it. In the first *Tess of the Storm Country*, she was shown innocently asleep with a man in the next bed, but this was far more risqué. A secret marriage is referred to in a title, but not shown—as though dropped in to placate the censors. At the height of their affair, Joseph persuades Angela to send a "love signal" to him at the village on the stroke of midnight. The "love light" serves to alert a U-boat; Joseph is a German spy. He convinces her that it is dangerous for him to stay. To supply provisions for his escape she steals chocolate from a neighbor. The theft is quickly discovered, and although Angela reaches home, a group of men have set out in pursuit, a dog following her scent.

The above photograph shows the moment when Angela's innocence is snuffed out. Leaning over the sleeping Joseph, she hears a murmur, "Gott . . . mit . . . uns." Her horrified reaction wakens him. "You—a German!"

"Angela, I am an enemy of your country, but not a traitor to you. You can't hate me for serving my own country. It is every man's duty."

Angela hides him from the mob, but when the villagers tell her that a ship was sunk the previous night and that Mario was among the dead, she hands Joseph over. After a brief struggle, he leaps over a cliff and dies on the very rocks on which he was found.

Angela gives birth to the child of the German spy—the situation must have caused near heart failure for some of Pickford's fans. The baby is stolen by Maria, a neighbor who has recently lost both her husband and her child. Maria manages to keep the child by telling the nuns at the convent that Angela is insane. When Angela goes to the convent, seeking the baby, her desperate expression and wildly waving hands merely seem to confirm that allegation.

As Angela gazes at her baby clothes at home, utterly distraught, her old fiancé Giovanni returns from the war—blind. Giovanni moves in with Angela, who becomes his eyes. Oddly, there is no reaction from the villagers. However, a title tells us, "An outcast from the village, Angela devoted her life to the mothering of Giovanni." When she encounters Maria with her baby, she assumes it is Maria's own child. Back in her kitchen, the memory hits her—Maria's child is dead! Maria, terrified that Angela will

Angela (Pickford) holds the baby who later causes her overwhelming agony.

Above and opposite:

The convent scenes are presented with a cool detached beauty, as in these remarkable photographs. The authentic and grandiose sets were created by Stephen Goosson, later famous for his work on *Lost Horizon* (1937).

want the baby back, accepts the offer of a boat trip to Genoa. A storm is rising, and all Angela can do is to operate her lighthouse. But its light is failing. In extremis, with the boat being pounded on the rocks, she sets her house on fire. Angela's home, as a title tells us, "becomes a beacon light to save her child."

By now the film has gone so far over the top that all credibility has vanished. She clambers over the rocks and through the boiling surf to rescue her baby—and to establish that Maria has died.

"After Angela's marriage to Giovanni, they sought the harbor of his home." And the film ends with a tableau of the couple playing with the baby, in the welcome company of Father Lorenzo.

This was hardly the sort of story people wanted to see from Mary Pickford. But Frances Marion, who directed, had returned from the war determined to avoid "filmic fluff." In Italy, she and Fred Thomson had been told of this incident: a German spy had infiltrated himself into an Italian village and married the girl whose father kept a lighthouse. When he took over this duty, she began to grow suspicious; Italian ships were wrecked off the coast, torpedoed by German submarines. She faced him with the truth, and he didn't deny it, but she was carrying his child. She kept quiet until another ship was wrecked—a ship carrying her two brothers. Frantic with grief, she turned him over to the police, and he was shot the day her baby was born. Had Marion filmed the story in realistic style, it might have been a moving tragedy. Admittedly, truth is sometimes stranger than fiction, but the picture is Melodrama with a capital M.

Mary Pickford identified the personnel in this photograph, taken in Monterey, California, in 1920, as follows: Top row: Aaron Johnson, assistant electrician; Ralph Angel, head carpenter; Mme. Bodamère, Mary Pickford's personal attendant; Bill Johnson, head electrician; Jack Wallace, property man; Ed Benshoff, assistant property man. Second row: Jack Jacob, assistant cameraman; George Rigas, Italian actor; Charles Rosher, chief cameraman; Alfred Werker, assistant director; Ray Binger, assistant cameraman; Henry Cronjager (in back), second cameraman; Eddie Phillips, actor, in front of Cronjager. The others are unidentified, or given a first name and a query. Seated: unidentified French actor; Frances Marion, director; Stuart Heisler, editor; Mary Pickford; Raymond Bloomer, actor.

Robert Cushman finds most of the film riveting, and a courageous experiment, considering what Pickford fans generally expected. Indeed, one critic remarked, "catastrophe and the theft of her child shatter her reason; for in one reel she plays a sort of peasant Ophelia. . . . [I]n many of the scenes there is a new quality about her, a wistful Botticelli quality never before displayed. She is working against all the Pickford traditions."[205]

The role of religion in *The Love Light* is both fascinating and curious. Apart from the secret marriage, the priest is characterized as being unusually liberal. Yet he remains merely a comforting presence, never intervening in the drama, and once is even used as comic relief when his blessing is so long it delays the hungry brothers from getting to the food. When Angela's baby is stolen, it is the convent that adjudicates ownership, not a magistrate.

Religious symbols proliferate; when Angela learns the truth about Joseph, she knocks over a religious statue, which shatters on the floor. Pickford was Catholic, and her religion became more important to her as she got older. But one senses that the film's writer-director must have been a convinced atheist. Or was it just a plot contrivance that showed the nuns to be so irredeemably cruel? Was it just convenience to show both sets of lovers living together with the apparent connivance of the priest? I checked with Frances Marion's biographer, Cari Beauchamp, and she confirmed this, even though her husband, Fred Thomson, had been an army chaplain. "Frances was adamant in her lack of religion, and grew more and more resentful of organized religion as she aged."[206]

There are two versions of *The Love Light* in existence. In one, a title says "To Angela a child was born and they named it Dolora—which means sorrow." In the other, "In the shelter of the convent a child was born to Angela, but the little mother's mind lay sleeping—stunned by successive shocks of sorrow." In the original cut of the film the religious order seized the baby, but scenes were reshot to show Maria stealing it.

All the evidence shows that Pickford had a hard time editing the film. She apparently employed no fewer than three title writers. The editor, Stuart Heisler, recalled many retakes to compensate for Fred Thomson's inexperience.[207] But despite rumors to the contrary, he is not the star of the film and never could have been. In any case, his character is killed just over halfway through. So the stories of Mary objecting to Frances Marion giving too much screen time to Thomson fail to stand up. (She is supposed to have reminded Frances repeatedly that they were making a Mary Pickford picture and not a Fred Thomson one.)

Photographically, the film is ravishing. Marion displayed the influence of Maurice Tourneur. She not only had Charles Rosher to guide her, but also Henry Cronjager, a pioneer who would be her cameraman again on the only other film she would direct, *Just Around the Corner* (1922).

Reviewers objected to the morbid story, but the picture turned a healthy profit, despite the general postwar slump into which it was released. *The Love Light* stands today as a worthy experiment—intensely felt, beautifully staged, but ultimately closer to grand opera than to reality.

THROUGH THE BACK DOOR

RELEASED: MAY 17, 1921

"Boring," said *Motion Picture Classic*.[208] "Wonderful," said *Picture Play*.[209] "Can it be that we are growing up faster than our films?" asked Frederick James Smith. "Is it possible that this juvenile food is too weak for us?"[210]

This was not a picture Pickford encouraged with a revival, although a very funny sequence was included in a compilation of her work that she released. In it she is faced with scrubbing a floor she has covered with muddy footprints. She straps brushes onto her feet, sloshes soapy water over the floor, and skates across it at high speed, as shown in the above photograph. This is not the only moment that could be described as Chaplinesque.

The story concerns a Belgian girl whose mother has remarried, and the new husband is jealous of the child. She is brought up by a peasant woman. Years pass, and the mother comes to collect the girl. The foster mother pretends she is dead. As the mother drives off, weeping, her car sweeps past Mary's character, sitting by the roadside, enveloping her in a cloud of dust. The scene anticipates the ending of Chaplin's *A Woman of Paris* (1923).

The Chaplin connection is hardly surprising. After Pickford and Fairbanks married in 1920, "the three of us became virtually inseparable," wrote Mary. "We had become virtually one family."[211] They watched movies—their own and everyone else's—analyzed their success or failure, and revealed their innermost thoughts. As James Card wrote, "It is not surprising their work bears both visible and intangible kinship."[212]

While the film was in production, no one was certain what to call it; the Pickford staff panicked when the advertising department jumped the gun and announced it all over the country as *Through the Back Door*. The plot suggested no reason for calling it that. It fell to the already overworked title writer, Gerald Duffy, to connect the main title to the plot. In the scene where the Belgian girl immigrates to America, he came up with the title, "Ellis Island—the back door to America." So Mary's character came "through the back door," and the result was so smooth it seemed as though the title had been written before the picture was named.[213]

Jack Pickford co-directed the film. "Jack was completely different from his sister," wrote Adolphe Menjou, who played a suave blackmailer in the film. "He had a great antipathy for hard work and had no idea whatever of the value of money. While he was making $2,500 a week, he was spending $3,500. He threw elaborate parties, gave expensive presents to people he liked, bought a new automobile every few months, and was continually falling in love."[214] Olive Thomas, Jack's wife, had died in Paris the previous year (hence the mourning band on his arm in the photograph on page 184), and Mary probably suggested this job to help him through a difficult time. After the bland beginning and the superfluity of titles, the picture becomes highly entertaining. Juvenile it may be—the early scenes feature Mary as a child, and include some very funny gags with animals—but once the story reaches America, it switches to a more serious note. The Belgian girl tries to make contact with her real mother, who wants nothing to do with her, and she gets involved in marital drama. The direction may be a little stiff at times—it lacks Neilan's easy flow—but it is well up to the standard of the time and results in a rewarding and handsome production.

Charlie Chaplin and Douglas Fairbanks visit Mary (in costume) during the making of *Through the Back Door*.

Mary Pickford poses with the script for *Through the Back Door* with Johnny Harron (who played Billy Boy in the film), the brother of the D. W. Griffith star, Robert Harron, who had died the previous year.

This was the first film to be co-directed by Alfred E. Green, Marshall Neilan's assistant, and Jack Pickford, seen here to the right of Charles Rosher's camera. Seated in the background is Mme. Bodamère, Mary's maid—she preferred to be called her attendant. Mary's character in this picture was named Jeanne Bodamère in her assistant's honor. The musicians seem to be taking a break.

LITTLE LORD FAUNTLEROY

RELEASED: SEPTEMBER 11, 1921

Around 1921, Hollywood features began to emerge from their infancy and aim at bigger things. The sets got bigger, the budgets higher, and the films longer. A lot longer. Whereas Mary had been turning out five-reelers a few years before, *Little Lord Fauntleroy* was ten reels and came equipped with its own score by Louis Gottschalk, who had written the music for Griffith's *Broken Blossoms*.

Based on the famous novel by Frances Hodgson Burnett, it is the story of a boy called Cedric, who lives in New York with his widowed mother. (Pickford plays both roles.) They are brought to England because his father was heir to the Earl of Dorincourt, and the old earl wants to prepare Cedric for the title of Lord Fauntleroy. The mother is banished from the castle because the earl unjustly accuses her of marrying for money. But Cedric so captures the earl's heart that he brings about a reconciliation.[215]

I had heard so much about how this film dragged that I expected to be bored and impatient. Far from it. I enjoyed its storytelling flair—being fascinated by Pickford's performance as a boy—and feel it would still play superbly on the big screen with a live orchestra. With its remarkably high standard of production, its influence—upon films as diverse as Hobart Henley's *A Lady of Quality* (1924) and Buster Keaton's *Our Hospitality* (1923)—cannot be denied. The art direction, by Stephen Goosson, convincingly creates two worlds: old New York and England. The former is full of dust, horse-drawn traffic, and clapboard houses; the latter is highly atmospheric, with oak beams and massive furniture. The characters never fail to come alive, especially the earl, whose tetchiness and bad temper launched an elderly English actor, Claude Gillingwater, on a new career.

Of course, the picture would drag if shown at the wrong speed. But cameramen in Hollywood had greatly increased their speed to keep pace with the practice of some exhibitors of "racing"—showing films too fast—and if the picture is shown close to the speed of sound, it looks excellent.

Doug Fairbanks's *The Three Musketeers* opened just before this film. Mary said that while playing the boy was the most difficult thing she had done, she got the walk from watching Fairbanks's swagger in that film. As David Robinson wrote, "She never for a moment looks like a real boy . . . and yet she still compels belief by her own integrity and conviction."[216]

Mary, in costume for *Fauntleroy*, clowns with Doug on his set for *The Three Musketeers*.

Nothing can top the moment in which Mary, playing mother and son, appears in both parts in a single shot—and kisses herself, casting a shadow on her own face, as seen in this frame enlargement. This fleeting moment of a few seconds took Mary and Rosher fifteen hours to achieve; its complexity probably went unnoticed by eighty percent of the audience.

Pickford is full of surprises in *Fauntleroy*, both as actress and producer. There is enormous fascination in watching the creative devices conceived by Pickford and cinematographer Charles Rosher—double exposures, double performers, and a depth of focus worthy of *Citizen Kane*. The intricate trick shots were acclaimed as the finest that had ever been made. The trade paper *Wid's Daily* said, "When Pickford kisses herself as 'Dearest' and hugs herself, and when both characters walk off together, one ahead of the other—well it's almost uncanny. Hats off to Rosher."[217]

According to second cameraman Lewis William O'Connell, the shadow cast on Pickford's face during the kiss shot was accomplished by having a double who fitted the exact shape of the matte—the masking device placed in front of the lens—present when Mary (as the boy) leaned forward for the kiss. There was actually a person there to cast the shadow.[218]

In these days of computer animation, it is all too easy to overlook such an achievement. In those days, there were no "process shots," combining two different actions from two separate negatives, as there are today. This all had to be done on one piece of film, exposed once for the first action, rewound inside the camera, the matte changed, and exposed a second time for the second action. First, Rosher had to build a camera stand weighing two thousand pounds.

Steel girders formed the framework; the base was lined with sand bags and a huge, hollow block of steel supported the pan and tilt head. The contraption would be moved around on casters, but when I'd lined the shot up, jacks secured it to the floor. Jacks held the pan head rigid, too, once it had been positioned. In front of the camera was the matte frame, and I moved the matte as Mary moved.

High atop the ladder, Mary Pickford, costumed as Little
Lord Fauntleroy, oversees and supervises her production.
Among those below are Lewis William O'Connell, second
cameraman; Charles Rosher, first cameraman; director
Alfred E. Green, at far right; and Mme. Bodamère, Mary's
personal attendant, in the foreground.

The whole setup was so solid that you could jump around the floor without shifting it a thousandth of an inch.[219]

None of the critics thought that Mary made a convincing boy. With hindsight, Mary thought the double role a mistake, "because no one in the audience could feel very keenly for me when I was playing my own mother and also my own son." She added, "I should have been content to be Dearest and engaged a real little boy for Lord Fauntleroy."[220]

Once again, Mary dispensed with her star director, and Alfred E. Green worked in collaboration with her brother Jack.[221] "It was understood from the start that Al Green was the senior director," said Mary, "and I never overruled him in the few instances when he and Johnny [Jack] disagreed. They were both on the set at all times. Johnny thought more in terms of gags and business while Al was better with the acting and camera angles."[222]

Charles Rosher was more dismissive of Mary's beloved brother: "Al Green did the directing. Jack would show up at the studio when he felt like it. He seldom took any active part other than suggesting a few gags."[223] But *Variety* said, "only Jack could have introduced the whimsical and always amusing touches of raw boyishness in the fighting, grimacing, scheming, lovable kid that Mary Pickford turns out to be."[224] *Motion Picture Classic*, however, concluded that although the directing credit was officially given to the two men, ". . . personally we hand it to Mary Pickford herself. We detect her discerning hand."[225] Several critics also commented on the influence of Fairbanks in her athletic leaps, tumbles, and handstands.

Mary plays both characters, with Joseph Dowling, as the earl's solicitor, in the center. This is not a frame enlargement but rather a double exposure created by combining two still-photograph negatives into one.

Opposite:
Mimicking Douglas Fairbanks, Pickford routs the cast and crew of *Little Lord Fauntleroy*. Her right boot is on brother Jack's face. Director Al Green lies next to him.

P.161

Little Lord Fauntleroy (Pickford) asserts his physical authority over the young impostor (Francis Marion—no relation to the screenwriter Frances Marion) who is trying to usurp his title.

Little Lord Fauntleroy is about to remove the root cause of a particularly painful toothache.

TESS OF THE STORM COUNTRY

RELEASED: NOVEMBER 12, 1922

This second version of *Tess of the Storm Country*, directed by John S. Robertson, gave Mary the opportunity to re-create her favorite role, while bringing the outmoded techniques of early cinema up to date. And nothing demonstrates the staggering advances made in the silent era more than a comparison of the 1914 and 1922 films. The first, raw and theatrical, moving forward in a series of jerks, has much to commend it, but it fails to make any emotional impact on an audience brought up on far more sophisticated stories. The second, beautifully mounted and exquisitely photographed, is, by any standard, a work of art. It is hard to believe there are only eight years between them.

"This new *Tess* is superbly moving," said *Photoplay*,[226] while acknowledging that it was an old-fashioned plot, full of obvious and clichéd characters. "But you never realize that until long after. There is too much in Miss Pickford's art to permit it; her performance is too full of human touches spanning the gap between mere acting and genius." This rave review appeared in the *Exhibitors Herald*:

We think that this new *Tess* should be scrutinized by the most competent dramatic critics of the day in order that authoritative opinions might be written into the history of the drama which we believe would place Miss Pickford with the few really great actresses, past or present. . . . Apparently with no effort she is able to register what she means to convey with an astounding swiftness and certainty. There is a conspicuous absence of reaching after effects, which results in her work carrying with it the highest degree of conviction. She proves very pointedly in *Tess* that she is the peerless player of the screen.[227]

The new version did not try to sedate the melodrama. The heavy, played by an actor later noted for his benevolent roles, Jean Hersholt, was possibly the most repellent individual yet put on the screen. Yet the characters are much more convincing; they have a life of their own, and this gives John Robertson's film an emotional force completely missing from the original.[228]

Over the Santa Monica Mountains, three hours from Hollywood in those days, is a reservoir called Lake Chatsworth, which doubled as Lake Cayuga in this story of rural squatters. Robert Florey, a young Frenchman who was publicity man for the Pickford-Fairbanks studio, correspondent for *Cinémagazine* in Paris, and later a director himself, left us a unique account of the filming:

The village is very strange, like thirty sheds built on top of each other. It seems as if the village has been here for centuries. Shaw Lovett, Robertson's assistant director,[229] must have had a tough time getting these prehistoric accessories up here. It was almost as if they'd turn to dust if you breathed on them.[230]

Charles Rosher faced a colossal lighting job, since many of the most dramatic scenes, such as the murder of a gamekeeper, took place at night. In the 1914 version of *Tess*, these were shot by day and tinted blue to resemble night. Although that convention was still practiced in 1922, Rosher preferred to do the job properly. An enormous amount of equipment had to be shipped over

In a shot that could be from a great German art film, Tess watches over Teola's newborn baby; Teola lies in the back of Tess's hut while an old squatter woman, who has served as midwife, puffs on her pipe.

Jean Hersholt as the villain is attacking Tess,
who is about to throw scalding water on him.

the mountains. The generator alone cost three times the budget of the 1914 film! There were also two giant aviation motors to provide the storm, and, since most Hollywood films had music on the set, Mary provided no less than a dozen musicians.

Florey recalled them playing rather doleful melodies, like "Little Grey Sweetheart of Mine," while everyone prepared for a shot.

Suddenly, everything lights up. Little Mary has made her appearance, golden hair flying in the wind, dressed in a horrible dress full of holes, with dirty hands, arms and legs, she arrives running. In one go, she leaps into her father's boat, she pulls his hair, throws his hat in the water, covers him with kisses, sits on his knee and tells him stories—and the whole scene is illuminated by the divine smile of Mary. The orchestra has abandoned its lugubrious lament for a light and devilish air. Everyone seems at ease. Mary is here.

At lunchtime, Mary speaks to her husband in Hollywood, thanks to a radio post which has been installed next to her cabin; she promises to meet Doug at the studio at seven. (His current picture is *Robin Hood.*) After lunch, the heat is unbearable. To save Mary standing out in the sun while the cameras are set up, a wax model is used, its face sculpted so that it closely resembles hers. When the day is over, Mary's secretaries arrive, she signs urgent letters, dictates replies to telegrams and goes to her hut to take off her makeup. When she is ready, she tells Chevalier, her French chauffeur, to drive quickly; she doesn't want to keep Douglas, the Earl of Huntington, waiting.[231]

Cinematographer Charles Rosher, director John S. Robertson, and Mary Pickford pose with Frank Ormston's model for the squatters' village, which has been erected behind them. Robert Florey is in the white shirt.

P.317.

Why did Mary Pickford refuse to preserve *Rosita*—which she insisted was one of her worst films—when it proved, once it was recovered from archives in Russia, to be surprisingly good?

It was a curious saga altogether. Pickford's films had reached a high standard by 1920. Indeed, there was no one to touch her for the combination of audience appeal and artistic excellence. Suddenly, German films had appeared. The best of them were even more spectacular than American films and often more courageous in their subject matter. These invariably had the name Ernst Lubitsch attached. Lubitsch had started his career in the theater with Max Reinhardt, and he acted for a while as a Jewish comic on the screen. Besides his skill at directing uproarious farce, he had an astonishing ability to stage epics. In some ways, he was even more versatile than D. W. Griffith.

Douglas Fairbanks, a connoisseur of such things, probably advised Mary to put Lubitsch under contract before someone else did. She was nervous about the reaction—anti-German feeling was still very strong. But she chose a politically harmless subject, *Faust*. When Lubitsch reached Los Angeles, he was confronted by the American Legion, protesting his very presence— and he one of the few Germans who had not fought in the war.

Lubitsch spoke of nothing but *Faust*; he was anxious to get to work. He must have been shattered to hear that *Faust* was off. Mary's mother, Charlotte, refused to allow Mary to play anyone who kills a baby, especially her own illegitimate one! He refused to direct the proposed alternative, *Dorothy Vernon of Haddon Hall*, and so everyone settled on what was initially called *The Street Singer*, an adaptation of the play *Don Cesar de Bazan*.

By an odd coincidence, Famous Players-Lasky was adapting *Don Cesar de Bazan* for its new star Pola Negri. Despite all the trouble he had, Lubitsch produced the more sophisticated picture, sly and sexually aware in a way Mary Pickford films never were.

Rosita is a Spanish street singer who loves an impoverished nobleman called Don Diego (George Walsh). She is arrested for singing a song lampooning the king. Diego tries to defend her—but the king has fallen for Rosita and orders his rival shot. Although the king tempts her with lavish gifts, Rosita remains true to Diego. The king obligingly arranges their marriage before the execution, but the queen saves Diego's life by substituting blank cartridges. Diego pretends to be dead and is brought to Rosita's villa, where he saves the king's life just as Rosita raises a knife to stab him.[232]

Pickford's antipathy for *Rosita* and for Lubitsch was not apparent in the beginning. The film was intended to launch a new, mature Mary Pickford, capable of seductiveness as well as playfulness. She wanted to surrender her burden of responsibility to a director. Edward Knoblock, who worked on some of Fairbanks's successes, would supervise and write the picture.

"I wish you could tell me who to get as a director," she had said to journalist Edwin Schallert.

I would like to have Ernst Lubitsch, because he seems to understand so thoroughly the meaning of historic reality and atmosphere. It would be so much better, too, for me to engage someone who does not know me too well, and who would consequently assume complete charge over me. Most directors that I have defer too much to my opinion. I wish they wouldn't.[233]

Rosita dines with the king (Holbrook Blinn) on one of the magnificent sets designed by Sven Gade and William Cameron Menzies.

Schallert was invited to watch the film being made, and he was struck by the relaxed and assured Pickford he saw. He gave no hint of any conflict. "I saw Mary shortly after she had begun her portrayal. She appeared more content than I had known her to be in years. She positively radiated assurance."[234]

When the picture was finished, *Picture Play* announced that Mary was so well pleased with what Lubitsch had done in *Rosita* that she had secured him for one production a year for the next three years.[235] She told Schallert that Lubitsch was one of the best directors she had ever worked with. "And we have a suspicion," he wrote, "that when she said this she meant the very best, but didn't want to make such a statement for publication lest she offended some of those who have helped her produce her pictures heretofore."[236]

Two weeks after *Rosita* was finished, Pickford wrote to her attorney, "I still think he is the greatest director in the world."[237] As late as 1928, she was quoted as saying, "*Rosita* wasn't so very bad, but I might have known I am not the Spanish type."[238]

And in public, Lubitsch never had anything but praise for Mary Pickford: "The most practical artist I have ever met. She can dictate policies, handle finances, bargain with supporting players, attend to booking problems, and still keep her mind on acting. It is no wonder that she held her place at the top longer than any personality in motion pictures."[239] And the film? "I have made better, more significant pictures than *Rosita*," he said, "but never one that I have loved more. Because with that I associate the finest thing that ever happened to me—the opportunity to come to America, to become a citizen. Besides that good fortune, all else pales."[240]

For publicity purposes, Lubitsch pretends to sign the contract that would lead to *Rosita*, under what looks like a highly suspicious gaze from Charlotte Pickford. (The contract had actually been signed long before.)

Pickford wanted the settings of *Rosita* to be as elaborate as those for Douglas Fairbanks's *Robin Hood* (1922). She hired the Danish designer Sven Gade[241] to work with William Cameron Menzies to create the sets. These stills show how brilliant they were. It is hard to believe it is a set at all, let alone one put up on the backlot of the Pickford-Fairbanks studio in Hollywood. The distant section of the city, seemingly on a hill, was built in miniature on top of a stage, just 300 yards from the camera.

The production was one of startling beauty, in which the heroes, besides Lubitsch, were Gade, Menzies, and Charles Rosher. While Rosher had been a pioneer of backlighting, he felt it was being overused. For *Rosita* he created a technique that he called *Perspectography*. It was a method of light separation that made the subject stand out from the background without the use of

Above, art director Sven Gade shows the model of the Seville set to Lubitsch and Pickford. Below, the end result.

backlighting. Alas, Mary would not allow a penny to be spent on preserving the original print or the negative, and all we have left is a print of poor quality from the Russian film archive, Gosfilmofond. The Russians reduced it by at least a reel, and while the film is still impressive, its impact is also reduced. (Russian titles don't help!)

Since it is such a fine film, one should try to understand why Mary Pickford did not like it. One possible reason: she is secondary to the decor, as is Fairbanks in *Robin Hood*. It is one of the few Pickford roles that any competent actress could have played. And her performance is molded by Lubitsch to the demands of the drama. She has one sequence as the old feisty Mary, when avoiding the king's attempts at seduction.[242] Other than that, she seems to be slavishly obeying Lubitsch's direction, and while this results in a portrayal of earthy vulgarity at the beginning, she goes over the top by the end. Lubitsch was a genius, and Mary recognized that. She probably failed to exercise her usual level of control, and she came to regret the result. And yet it is a film that anyone else would have been proud of.

Both *Variety* and *Photoplay* thought Mary's acting in *Rosita* was better than in any of her other pictures.

There is probably no actress today who could portray the gay, graceful, coquettish little street singer of Seville who "vamps" a king, as she does. The production is incomparably beautiful. It shows why Ernst Lubitsch holds his place among the leading directors of the world.[243]

"This comes mighty near to being a perfect photoplay," wrote Frederick James Smith in *Screenland*. "You will go many, many months before you see a drama told so dextrously. . . . and yet I must honestly admit her performance to be inadequate."[244] Smith thought she was nothing but Pollyanna with all the old Pickford tricks.

There were not many reviews like that, but their effect must have been traumatic. And further disapproval must have grown in Pickford's mind because she had allowed herself to be talked out of *Faust*. It was to have been the one film in her career made purely for art's sake, without any commercial considerations whatsoever. She expected to lose money on it, and she expected a great many people to be thoroughly disgusted.

I'm going to turn myself over to Lubitsch, who wouldn't dare go back to Germany if he took liberties with Goethe. There will be no curls. There will be no girlish stuff with domestic animals. There will be no hokum of any kind. It will not be a star picture. The unity of characters will not be violated. I want Faust and Mephisto to be equally prominent with Marguerite.

However good it was, *Rosita* came nowhere near the heights she hoped to achieve with *Faust*. Perhaps she took out her frustration on the film that her advisers (particularly her mother) persuaded her to make, in place of the one she so longed to make.

DOROTHY VERNON OF HADDON HALL

RELEASED: MARCH 15, 1924

When Mary brought Ernst Lubitsch over from Germany, he thought he was going to direct her in *Dorothy Vernon of Haddon Hall* after *Faust*. He had read the script in Germany, but when he reached Hollywood, he turned against it. "Der iss too many qveens and not enough qveens." Queen Elizabeth and Mary Queen of Scots could have been a story on their own, but there was not enough in the script to make that possible. He objected to Elizabeth and Mary being more interesting than Dorothy herself.

So the picture was set aside until Marshall Neilan was available. He had no such objections. Knowing he might do his disappearing act, Mary ensured that shooting began with the heart of the drama. And disappear is just what he did. An elaborate procession filmed in San Francisco's Golden Gate Park with scores of extras in Elizabethan costumes was ready for shooting, but Neilan failed to arrive. He had evidently gone on a bender with his pals Jack Pickford and Norman Kerry. Mary Pickford had to direct the scene herself.

In retrospect, Mary felt she had made a mistake in trying to compete with a flurry of other costume pictures "and most of them done better than mine."[245] She was being unnecessarily harsh on herself, for people loved the film at the time.

When she was asked why she chose *Dorothy Vernon*, she replied, "Because it had big characters in it."

I did not consider the story because it had a big part in it for me, and that is the truth, but because in it were the conflicting emotions of Queen Elizabeth and Mary Queen of Scots. A story concerning those two women is bound to be interesting. There was not so much pathos as there was, for instance, in *Stella Maris*, for although Dorothy's heart may beat as poignantly as did Rebecca's or Unity's no audience can see a heart beat under lace as clearly as under calico.[246]

Picture Play hailed it as

the best of all the costume pictures. . . . When the first closeup of Mary Pickford appeared on the screen, the audience at the Criterion Theater in New York let out a noise something like a thousand tires going off at once. . . . the beauty of the picture and the beauty of Mary—the two are bound up together—are the chief things that will make you remember *Dorothy Vernon* . . . you have never seen such exquisite posing in your life.[247]

An extra on *Dorothy Vernon of Haddon Hall*, journalist Margaret Reid, wrote an eyewitness account of making the film. She described the tensely dramatic scene in which Dorothy Vernon betrays her lover and Mary Stuart to Queen Elizabeth:

There was fire and rage in this, and at the end Mary Pickford broke into tears—real tears—and some of the spectators did, too.

There is a long pause before the next shot, while Mary sits limply in a corner with sobs still shaking her poor little shoulders. Everyone wanders tactfully away and Mickey Neilan sits down at a piano and plays melting, soothing little melodies—some his own, some not. He plays like a young Pan, putting all his Irish heart into the keys, and sometimes sings softly in a fine, mellow voice. And then, at some unknown signal, he is up with a shout, chasing a howling prop boy up the gorgeous silver *Thief of Bagdad* stairs that stand near our set. There is a terrible commotion and shouting and suddenly Mickey comes down an unexpected ladder, barking and whooping like a sea lion—and the place goes crazy. Douglas Fairbanks and Charlie Chaplin, coming in then, join the fight at once with all their well-known zest, and the result looks more like a schoolboy's free-for-all than a motion picture company during working hours.

You see, when these people work, they work like Trojans, and naturally I suppose they must play with the same energy. Then, too, many of them, like Charlie Chaplin, had no opportunity in childhood to indulge their natural instinct for play and are trying to make up for lost time now. It is, indeed, an inspiring sight—three of the most powerful men in the business playing tag up and down ladders and shrieking like wild things. But work must go on some time, so all at once Mickey decides to continue the picture.[248]

Mary as Dorothy with her father, played by
Anders Randolph. "I will break that spirit of
yours," he says, "if I have to kill you." Her lover,
played by Allan Forrest, is concealed beneath
Mary on the chair.

A remarkable incident occurred on location in San Francisco's Golden Gate Park. Mary was riding a horse called Pearl alongside the camera car. Worried that Pearl might slip on the asphalt road, the crew had fitted her with rubber shoes. As Mary wrote,

I was riding along at increasing speed, when I suddenly heard them shrieking at me in one voice. Pearl, it seems, had cast off one of the rubber shoes from a hind hoof. Panic-stricken, she began to race like mad trying to outdistance the car. To add to her panic, I was, of course, riding side-saddle, to which I was totally unaccustomed, and twenty-odd pounds of multiple skirt were flapping wildly in the wind over her flank. The risk of a sudden fall was very great indeed, and I could understand the wild shouting and gesticulating of the men in the car. I tried to remain calm, because I knew better than they did what would happen if I lost my head. I shouted back to them to reduce their speed gradually.

Directly ahead of me was an intersecting highway, with automobiles racing in both directions. Pearl was . . . blindly plunging toward that highway.

Mary spoke into Pearl's ear, patting and smoothing her neck while gently pulling the reins. "Just as we reached the intersection, I gave the reins a quick jerk with both my hands, and Pearl reared, half-stumbled and landed in a culvert on all fours. I am proud to say I did not lose my seat."[249]

Mary costumed as Dorothy Vernon assists Douglas Fairbanks with his makeup on his *Thief of Bagdad* set.

Opposite:
Pickford sits at her dressing table on location in San Francisco's Golden Gate Park. This was the day that director Marshall Neilan failed to show up.

P.735.

The ride is as elaborate as Griffith's ride of Paul Revere in *America*, which was released a few months after *Dorothy Vernon*, but it is even more exciting because of the plot. Dorothy, imagining her lover has been deceiving her, betrays his closest-guarded secret: the presence of Mary Queen of Scots at nearby Rutland Castle. Her horse gallops only a length or two ahead of Queen Elizabeth's army.

Dorothy Vernon was a combination of high art and low slapstick, of history and hokum. The final result is an exceedingly impressive and entertaining picture, the closest to a Douglas Fairbanks production of any that Pickford made. The actor cast as the hero, Allan Forrest, even looks like Doug, with a similar moustache, although his limited athletic ability is evident when the film editor cuts away as soon as he tries to climb up or down anything. Forrest was the husband of Lottie Pickford, who has a fairly prominent role as Jennie, Dorothy's faithful maid. (Actually, Douglas Fairbanks did appear in the picture. For a shot in which Forrest's bare back is featured, Fairbanks stood in, since he had a more impressive physique.)

One can see why Pickford originally wanted Ernst Lubitsch to direct *Dorothy Vernon*. The very style of such historical romps has its origins in Lubitsch's "humanizing of history" with films like *Madame Dubarry* (a.k.a. *Passion*, 1919) or *Anna Boleyn* (a.k.a. *Deception*, 1920). *Dorothy Vernon* is the antithesis of the historical epics produced by William Randolph Hearst, where dignity is all and the people of history are not supposed to crack jokes or fall on their rears. Mind you, Neilan indulges in a bit too much of that, and such *lèse majesté* as the sight of the immortal Queen Elizabeth tucked up in bed, shorn of all her finery, still startles English sensibilities, as does the sight of Mary Queen of Scots being kissed by Sir John Manners.

Anders Randolph (playing Dorothy's father, Sir George Vernon) looks very much like Emil Jannings as Henry VIII. He is exceedingly bad tempered, but Pickford outplays him. When she flies into a storm, the heavens themselves do tremble. Only when she has to emote in scenes of high drama does Neilan encourage her to overact. Costume drama was traditionally played in the grand manner (see *Ben-Hur* [1926] and *Scaramouche* [1923]), but here only Clare Eames, as Queen Elizabeth, is allowed to act in a purely theatrical style. Pickford is splendid with comedy and fury, and quite touching in the love scenes. A live orchestra and a big screen would no doubt restore to her big moments the right sense of proportion.

In a tense scene, Mary as Dorothy Vernon protects Queen Elizabeth (Clare Eames) from would-be assassins. The spontaneous action in this photo was caught on a 5x7 negative, whose speed was faster than the 8x10 plate and therefore permitted more movement during exposure.

Allan Forrest and Pickford indulge in a laugh between
takes on location for *Dorothy Vernon of Haddon Hall.*
On the left, a grip is holding up a huge scrim. Placed
behind the actors, it had the effect of casting the
background into soft focus.

The costume designer for *Dorothy Vernon of Haddon Hall*, Mitchell Leisen
(later a prominent Hollywood director), confers with Mary on the lawn of the
Pickford-Fairbanks studio, as director Marshall Neilan (directly behind Mary)
and other production associates look on. A model of one of the *Dorothy Vernon*
sets sits on the table.

LITTLE ANNIE ROONEY

RELEASED: OCTOBER 18, 1925

"Everyone seemed to resent so much the two grown up parts of Rosita and Dorothy that I felt I had to return to a little girl role," wrote Mary.[250] The box office and the fan letters had spoken. *Photoplay* claimed she had received 20,000 letters in answer to her appeal for her next story; her public wanted her as a child again. She felt her two recent adventures into adulthood had been costly and embarrassing. No doubt it was a relief to get as far away from them as possible, and to produce a slam-bang comedy of the Marshall Neilan sort.

She and Neilan were going to make a story of his called *Patsy*, but they had an argument about it.[251] Neilan made it anyway, for M-G-M, as *Mike*, discovering Sally O'Neil for the lead. Mary decided to do *The Rooney Family*, later called *Little Annie Rooney*. She thought of the idea while walking through empty sets of the lonely studio at night and wrote the story in two weeks because she was so pressed for time. Whimsically, Mary gave story credit to Katherine Hennessey, her Irish grandmother.[252]

The daughter of a policeman, Annie Rooney spends her time fighting the neighborhood kids and caring for her father and brother, Tim. After her father is shot, Annie and Tim set out for revenge. When they mistakenly believe that the culprit is Joe Kelly (William Haines), the man Annie loves, Tim takes his father's gun and shoots Joe. Meanwhile, Annie captures the real killer. When she finds Joe in the hospital she gives her own blood for a transfusion that saves his life.[253]

Pickford chose as director a former prop boy from Biograph, William Beaudine. Like Sidney Franklin, Beaudine had become a skillful director of kid pictures; Neilan had directed *Penrod* in 1922, and Beaudine had directed the charming sequel, *Penrod and Sam*, in 1923. He seemed a sensible choice. The result was superb.

Wrote Pickford biographer Eileen Whitfield, "One watches in amazement as Pickford, at thirty-three, fresh from the seductions of *Rosita* and the stiff declamations of *Dorothy Vernon*, slips into the body of a twelve-year-old tomboy, chugging her little legs, puffing up her flat chest, throwing punches."[254]

Both comedy and tearjerker, it is one of Pickford's most successful films. The more naive jokes are reminiscent of Hal Roach's "Our Gang" series, but there are some exceptional moments. The fight among the kids, which at first seems so funny, proves to be the training ground for the deadly serious fighting among the neighborhood's young men.

The production is of a very high order; the art direction by John D. Schulze[255] is impressive; and when you think that it was all shot on the Pickford-Fairbanks backlot, flat California land converted into cobbled streets and rotting tenements, with a neighboring gasworks in the background, it is all the more remarkable.[256] The use of ethnic stereotypes is fascinating, because while the kids are at each others' throats, the parents are united by anxiety, and all troop for advice to Annie's father as though he were the neighborhood doctor. They are free of the usual embarrassing gestures: all are treated as natural neighbors. Annie's most helpful pal is Jewish. One critic thought the film ought to be called *Abie's Irish Annie*. Except for a Greek, the gangsters are as Irish as the cops.

Pickford, at age thirty-three, maintains her youthful demeanor as Little Annie Rooney.

Pickford's heartwarming grin in the photograph on the opposite page belies the heartbreaking nature of this scene. Little Annie Rooney, the tomboy of the tenements, is preparing a birthday party for her policeman father. In a brilliantly directed sequence, a gangsters' dance gets out of hand, the lights are doused, a pistol fires, and Annie's father is accidentally shot dead. We cut to Annie; she has put a notice on the door: "Dear Pops, please knock before you come in." A fellow policeman has the unhappy duty of breaking the news, and of course he has to knock. We cut to Annie lighting this eccentric group of candles. She then hides underneath the table. The policeman enters. From her vantage point, all is normal; she sees what appear to be her father's uniform trousers and giggles. The policeman, seeing no one, stands stock-still. This strikes Annie as odd. She waits for the reaction and emerges only when there is none. We then tilt slowly upward to reveal the strange face beneath the familiar peaked cap. The man looks wretched. Annie, guessing something is wrong, asks if it is her brother, Tim, or her father. "It's your Dad. He's not coming home."

If the audience isn't in tears by this time, they must be uniquely hard-boiled. Annie weeps wholeheartedly,[257] puts out all the candles but one, and uses that to pray by. If any two sequences were needed to prove the power of the silent film, the gangsters' dance and the cop's visit should do it. All the artistry, technical skill, and emotional impact of a medium only thirty years old shine triumphantly through.

During the making of *Little Annie Rooney*, the police learned of a plot to kidnap Mary and hold her for ransom. A stool pigeon had revealed that other prominent people were on the kidnappers' list, including Jackie Coogan and Pola Negri. The police knew who the crooks were but could take no action until they did. Mary was ordered to behave

The neighbors seek the advice of Officer Rooney, at left, who is played by Walter James, the unforgettable father in Harold Lloyd's *The Kid Brother* (1927).

Mary lights the candles for the birthday party

that never happens.

as if nothing was wrong and to keep to her normal schedule. A detective, assigned to protect her, was introduced to a puzzled cast as an actor.

Every day for two weeks, the kidnappers parked a few blocks from the studio. A Shriners' convention gave them a brain storm: they adopted Shriners' hats so that if they grabbed Mary, onlookers would assume it was all part of the fun, even if she screamed.

One night Douglas Fairbanks picked up Mary in his Rolls-Royce, and a convertible gave chase. Fairbanks had a sawed-off shotgun beside his seat, and he told Mary, "If the shooting starts, drop to the floor of the car!"

Fairbanks drove at a frightening speed, nearly wrecked a Ford in his path, and screeched to a halt in front of the Beverly Hills Hotel. He leaped in front of the kidnappers and leveled his shotgun. A screech came from the convertible. "Stop, Douglas, we're the police! The kidnappers were in the Ford you almost turned over!"

When the crooks appeared in court, their attorney tried for the sympathy vote, comparing Fairbanks's Rolls-Royce with the humble vehicle used by the kidnappers. Pickford rounded on him with fury, and what a scene it would have made: "To the annoyance of the judge I proceeded to give him a good tongue-lashing, stating that my husband had bought the Rolls-Royce with hard-earned money, while they had stolen their 'humble vehicle.'"[258]

She was dismayed by the light sentence the kidnappers received and installed watchmen day and night, together with a squad of well-trained watchdogs, at Pickfair. And the following year, she incorporated a kidnapping theme into *Sparrows*.

In the foreground is the baby spotlight (not on for this picture), introduced by Mary in 1917, which was used to enhance her youthful look by flattening wrinkles. Director William Beaudine sits in the director's chair wearing a straw hat, a fashion borrowed from his former employer, D. W. Griffith. In his hand is a tiny megaphone. Behind him, Charles Rosher cranks the first camera to come from the Mitchell factory, and behind him is second cameraman Hal Mohr, soon to be a great cinematographer in his own right. And standing by the door, a tenor provides mood music. The instrumentalists are, presumably, off camera.

Mary and the children in the cast of *Little Annie Rooney* pose with Helen Keller, who visited the set at the Pickford-Fairbanks studio. One reviewer thought the gang looked like a "junior League of Nations."

Mary Pickford poses with her production team on the set of *Little Annie Rooney*. In the front row (left to right) are Tom McNamara, title writer; William Beaudine, director; Mary; E. de Beaumont Newman, Mary's production manager; a gentleman called "Frenchie" (whose function is unknown); and an unidentified man. In the back row (left to right) are Harry Oliver, art director; Hal Mohr, second cameraman; William Johnson, head electrician; and Charles Rosher, first cameraman.

Fleeing through the swamp, Pickford and the children are suspended on a crumbling branch above the alligators. The top and bottom portions of this double-exposed still were from two separate negatives that were subsequently pieced together. The splice is undetectable.

RELEASED: SEPTEMBER 19, 1926

Douglas Fairbanks and Mary Pickford's visit to Berlin in 1925 had an impact on the way they made pictures. In Pickford's case, *Sparrows* was surprisingly Teutonic in its treatment, partly because the German UFA studios had hired its cinematographer, Charles Rosher, as photographic consultant on F. W. Murnau's *Faust*; he and Karl Struss ended up photographing Murnau's first American picture, *Sunrise* (1927).[259] The strongest influence, however, was Charles Dickens. This was a story of mistreated orphans. Its first title was *The Baby Farm*, later changed to *Scraps*, then finally *Sparrows* just before release. Scott Eyman describes it as Dickens laced with Edgar Allan Poe.

Mary plays a teenager who takes charge of a group of orphans on a "baby farm" in the Deep South. It is run by the evil Mr. Grimes, played by Gustav von Seyffertitz, who limps through the swampland like Nosferatu. This seemed a curiously foreign concoction to American audiences, and many people, expecting the usual Pickford sunshine, were upset by it.

"There isn't a ray of brightness," said *Variety*, ignoring all the comedy. "For once a Pollyanna is submerged, smothered and muffled in sinister gloom. There are reeks of agonies and the cumulative effect is oppressive."[260] Grimm's fairy tales may have exploited just such elements, but the movies were not supposed to be disturbing. Members of the public registered complaints, alleging that the children in the cast must have undergone terrible privations making the film, which was a left-handed compliment if ever there was one.[261]

Pickford told me that she had taken a risk for the film—by planning to cross a narrow board (and a low-hanging branch) over an alligator-infested swamp with a baby on her shoulders. She said to director William Beaudine that she would have to rehearse it with a weight. Before she finished rehearsals, Fairbanks heard about the plan and put a stop to it. While stars often like to give the impression that they did their own stunts—even when insurance companies would not have permitted it—there might have been some risk at some point. Both Rosher and Karl Struss, the chief cameramen, spoke of it, as did prop man Irving Sindler. I spoke to William Beaudine in 1969, and he said, "I wouldn't want to contradict Mary, but I doubt if we'd have had loose alligators in there. I don't remember, but if Mary says there were alligators there, there were alligators there."[262] In 1972, Robert Cushman interviewed cameraman Hal Mohr, who shot the intricate double exposure we see in the final film. He said the alligators were photographed at one time and Mary and the kids at another and concluded that they "never got any closer than fifty or sixty feet, I can promise you that."[263] Mohr counted each turn of the crank, and the script girl kept a record of when the alligators made their leaps (at meat held out of the picture) so that the actors could recoil at the right moment. Beaudine's biographer, Wendy Marshall, interviewed Camilla Johnson Jones, one of the children, who said that at no point were they ever in danger, and that in fact Pickford had taken the greatest care of them. So the story is just that—a story.

Harry Oliver constructed the amazing sets for *Sparrows* on the backlot of the Pickford-Fairbanks studio. The hanging moss and the alligator-infested pools through which the orphans make their escape from the hated Mr. Grimes were aged in the same way as the forest of Fritz Lang's German film *Siegfried* (1924).

"Harry Oliver was one of the greatest art directors who ever lived," said Hal Mohr, third cameraman (he is the man peering from behind camera at right in the above photograph).

Harry would pick up a stick or some object with character and design the whole set around it. And he'd burn the wood. Every piece of the *Sparrows* set was scorched to age it. The quicksand was sawdust and cork, ground up, with water. And it had a bottom to it so that you couldn't actually go under. Spec O'Donnell's feet [as he sank in the quicksand] were resting on something solid; he couldn't go further down than his chin.[264]

The other cinematographers, Karl Struss and Charles Rosher, flank William Beaudine, standing in a straw hat. Beaudine was paid $2,000 a week by Pickford—he had been getting $600 at Warner Bros.—but he still felt like the Biograph prop boy he once had been.

I couldn't get it out of my head that she was the big star and I was just a punk. I was hesitant about saying, "Let's do it again," and finally she says to me, "Bill, what's the matter?"

I said, "I don't know, Mary, I just can't seem to get it. I'm hamstrung here."

She said, "Now, look. I am the star, I am the producer, and I am the owner of this picture. You don't want me to be the director, too, do you? If I didn't think you could do this picture, I wouldn't have hired you. Now come on, let's get to work."

So from then on, everything was great.[265]

Ernst Lubitsch[266] sent Mary Pickford a telegram describing *Sparrows* as one of the eight wonders of the world. Mary said she ought to die at once—at

Opposite:

***Sparrows* was a physically arduous production for everyone involved. In order to get exciting camera angles, the cameras, lights, and crew had to be positioned on scaffolding above the swamp set.**

last she had made a film that her most critical friends approved of. "Even Charlie."[267]

"Baby farms" were a well-known racket in certain states, and kidnapping held a lot of fear for wealthy parents—especially those in Hollywood. Exaggerated as *Sparrows* may seem, knowing that the background has its basis in reality makes a lot of difference. One of the most touching moments in the picture shows a farmer buying one of the children (for less than a hog) and taking him off as slave labor. As he leaves the baby farm, the boy looks to the barn where the other children are concealed. Tiny hands emerge from every gap in the rotten woodwork to wave farewell.

William Beaudine recalled enjoying working for Pickford, until the strain got too intense, toward the end of *Sparrows*:

Marshall Neilan said nobody can do two pictures in a row with Mary Pickford without going screwy. And I laughed at him, but towards the end of *Sparrows* I did get a little bit edgy. I don't know, we just didn't hit it off or whatever, and in fact I came home. I got to where one side of my face was paralyzed. I couldn't drink. It was nerves, that's what it was. It was a friction or something, and I was not getting anywhere. I finally figured it out, and I told Mary I'd like to go back to Warner's and let Tom McNamara finish the picture. He was my gag man. There was very little left to do, about two or three days, which was just pick-up stuff. I had a very good Christian Science practitioner—she sat in a chair, and I lay on the couch, and when I woke up it was gone.[268]

It is hardly surprising that creative people should experience such high tension when at work on so demanding a project. But what is even more surprising is that most of her coworkers remembered Mary Pickford and the atmosphere at her studio with nostalgia and affection.

Mary has an ice-cream break on the set of *Sparrows* with Gustav von Seyffertitz, who plays the monstrous villain Grimes. In the film Mary threatens to run him through with a pitchfork, after which he drives her and the children into the swamp, where he assumes they will all meet their demise among the quicksand and the alligators.

Opposite:

At the end of the day: Fairbanks, in costume for his Technicolor picture *The Black Pirate*, and Pickford, in her rags for *Sparrows*. A Technicolor test of Mary, shot around the same time, has recently been found at George Eastman House.

MY BEST GIRL

RELEASED: OCTOBER 31, 1927

Mary Pickford's last silent film was a return to first essentials—a simple, straightforward, and charming comedy. Pickford's character may seem sane enough—she is a shopgirl in a department store, in love with the owner's son (Charles "Buddy" Rogers). But her family is a nightmare. Mother (Sunshine Hart) ignores the housework and counts it a good day if she's managed to attend a four-handkerchief funeral. The sister (Carmelita Geraghty) has a vile temper. When Mary brings Buddy home, the crockery starts flying; she explains the chaos as rehearsal for a dramatic club. "What a lovely costume," she says, as a cop bursts in, in pursuit of the sister's shady boyfriend. "You look just like a policeman!"

Pickford kept as shrewd an eye on her competitors as they kept on her, particularly now that her supremacy had, inevitably, passed to others. The top box-office star of 1926 was Colleen Moore, a flapper comedienne, who had built her fame on Cinderella stories. (One of her 1926 titles was *Ella Cinders*.) Her popularity was about to be exceeded by that of Clara Bow. *My Best Girl* would have made an ideal vehicle for Moore or Bow, and it seems strange to see the buoyant bangs replaced by the golden curls, even if they are worn up. But Pickford was nothing if not versatile, and she plays the headstrong clerk with convincing skill. She studied for the part by working as a shopgirl in disguise.[269] Nobody recognized her, but several customers told her she looked like Mary Pickford.

Director Sam Taylor (shown in the still on the opposite page) was a splendid choice. He was a studious-looking young man, a graduate of Fordham University, and a former cutter and gag man who would display extraordinary talent in silent films before pulling out of the directing business, mysteriously, in 1935, to go into publicity. He came to prominence as co-director for Harold Lloyd. And he undoubtedly got on well with Jack Pickford. Before joining United Artists, he had directed *Exit Smiling* (1926), at M-G-M, with Beatrice Lillie and Jack.

My Best Girl was written by Kathleen Norris, a celebrated novelist.[270] The scenario was written by Hope Loring,[271] who had co-authored *Wings*; that film had starred Charles "Buddy" Rogers.

Rogers heard that Pickford was casting and went for an interview on a hopeful whim. A dozen others had assembled by the time he arrived, and his heart sank. Rogers remembered that the first time he saw Mary face-to-face was when she answered his knock at her dressing-room door with, "Won't you please come in?" Her golden curls hung well below her waist. He was so dazzled by this apparition that he could not recall what he said or how he got the part—but get it he did. And even more than *Wings*, it made him a star. He became known as America's Boyfriend.

Rogers played this boyfriend with immense charm, and he remained a close friend. In 1937, he married Mary in real life. Charles Rosher said he first noticed something between them during this sequence inside a packing crate. When the scene was over, he could not get them out. Coincidentally, it is the first real love scene in the picture; they seek privacy in the crate in the storeroom, and an old foreman, who spots them in there, pulls up a stool, considerately waiting until they emerge.

Pickford worked in disguise as a store clerk to prepare for her role in *My Best Girl*.

Opposite:
A gag still of Sam Taylor with Charles "Buddy" Rogers and Pickford.

The original working title of *My Best Girl* was *Paradise Alley*. Reviewers welcomed it as a refreshing return to the kind of story Mary Pickford did best. But there was no possibility of erasing the technical progress made since the war. Cinematographer Charles Rosher had just come from photographing *Sunrise*, and he employed the same care on this one. From the opening track back from a cash register—as five and ten cents are rung up—into a complex montage, all done in the camera, of department-store merchandise—cutlery, candles, hammers—one is aware of being in the hands of master filmmakers. The fluid technique and the immaculate lighting are a joy to behold (particularly if you are lucky enough to see an original tinted print projected on a screen). But one wishes there had been a trifle less elegance and a trifle more spontaneity, in the old Mickey Neilan tradition.

The company found that the exteriors could be filmed in downtown Los Angeles during the day, but night scenes were impossible. So Pickford adopted the solution used by F. W. Murnau and built a huge set of the business district on the Pickford-Fairbanks backlot. It took a month to build and occupied the space of two city blocks. Almost a mile of temporary track had to be laid to admit streetcars to the studio. An elaborate sprinkler system was installed for a scene that takes place in the rain. Truckloads of merchandise had to be brought in to dress the counters of the store set.

The film was used by heads of state to raise funds for charity: in Rome at a benefit sponsored by Queen Elena; in Spain at a command performance for King Alfonso and Queen Victoria; in Prague before President Masaryk; and in Brussels at a charity benefit under the patronage of Queen Elizabeth.[272]

For this film, critic Norbert Lusk of *Picture Play* paid Mary the following tribute:

Mary Pickford is one of the great intelligences of the screen, more akin to genius than those to whom the word is more often applied. Say that she repeats herself and is an institution rather than a many-sided artist, but do not forget that she is a supreme actress. Her portrayals of childhood and youth are unequalled, of course, but more than that she touches depths of feelings in her roles, and conveys the most delicate shading of mood, with a sureness that is inspiring to watch. All of which—and a great deal more—can be seen in her new picture, *My Best Girl*.[273]

Above:

It is hard to believe that this group, which might be working in a bank, was responsible for such a delightful creation as *My Best Girl*. From left, they are writer Allen McNeil, writer John Grey, cinematographer Charles Rosher, Mary Pickford, director Sam Taylor, and assistant director H. Bruce "Lucky" Humberstone. It is no coincidence that McNeil, Grey, and Taylor were associated with Harold Lloyd. A close friend of Mary and Doug, Lloyd would undoubtedly have recommended them, and made sure he got them back when shooting was finished. The picture was taken in Mary's bungalow on the Pickford-Fairbanks lot.

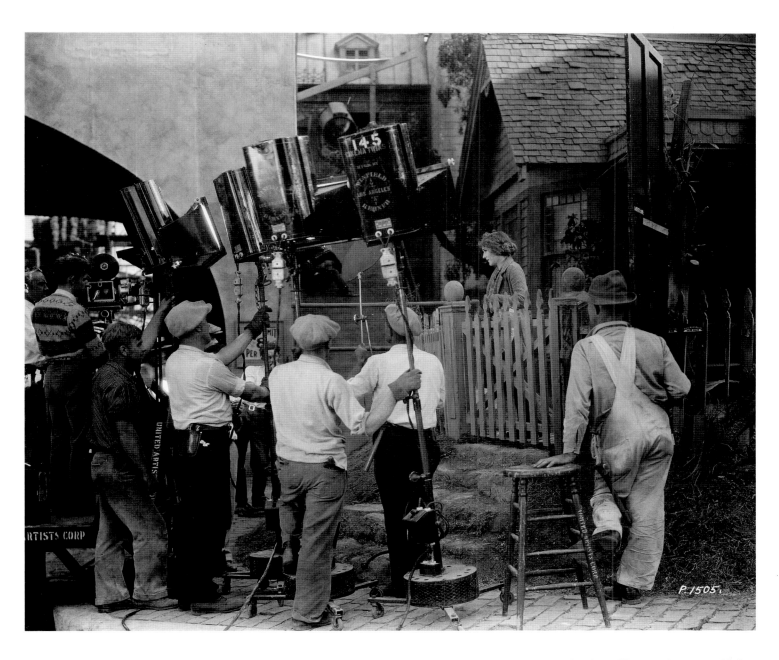

In this production still, a massive array of lights and reflectors illuminates Mary. She is surrounded by her crew. Sam Taylor and Charles Rosher, with a Mitchell camera, are at the far left.

Opposite:

Mary (out of costume) sits on the truck used in *My Best Girl* with the cash register that opens the film. On the right is D. W. Griffith, back with the United Artists he had helped to found, whose president, Joseph M. Schenck, can be seen lighting a cigar. The young man in the middle is visitor Irving G. Thalberg, vice president in charge of production at M-G-M.

In her first scene in *My Best Girl*, Mary demonstrates the rigors of being a stock girl at Grant's Department Store.

P. 1527.

With a coat covering her *My Best Girl* costume, Pickford stands
with a battery of Mitchell cameras. She bought the first Mitchell
for her cameraman, Charles Rosher. Third from left is a Bell
and Howell 2709.

COQUETTE

RELEASED: APRIL 12, 1929

Here are the men (and one woman, script girl Cora Palmatier) who got Mary through her first talkie. Director Sam Taylor is seated next to Mary. The man in the fedora is the assistant director, H. Bruce "Lucky" Humberstone. Cinematographer Karl Struss stands behind him, in glasses. You may notice one important face missing. Where is Charles Rosher? According to Mary, she was deep into a highly emotional scene, working herself up to a hysterical outburst, when Rosher stopped the camera and complained of a stray shadow on her face. Mary wrote that she lost her temper. She found it impossible to get back into the mood and decided she and Rosher had to part.

According to Rosher, he was brought back from Canada, where he was filming an Ernst Lubitsch picture, and presented with a fait accompli. Sam Taylor had worked out a system of shooting with multiple cameras in collaboration with the sound engineers. Even the lighting had to be controlled by these godlike men. Rosher said he decided to leave then and there and actually photographed nothing. "I expressed myself freely, and my career with Mary Pickford came to an end, fortunately without any unpleasantness," said Rosher.[274] But Karl Struss told Robert Cushman that Rosher did start the film and was indeed fired by Mary Pickford.

Opposite:
Mary was careful not to cut her curls until her mother had died. Charlotte was so enamored of Mary's image, for which she had fought so long, that Mary had no alternative but to hang on to it. Photograph by Edwin Bower Hesser.

HP.347

C-72.A.

She did not care how she looked for the film; she would look thoroughly unglamorous, when necessary, to be true to the part. "I was out for the Oscar," she said. "I didn't want to look like a candy wrapper valentine." She said she lacked the courage to face Rosher and left him a letter.

His successor, Struss, had worked on *Sparrows*; more importantly, he had collaborated with Rosher on *Sunrise*, which would bring them both Academy Awards (not yet called Oscars). He did his best to cope with the superhuman demands placed on him by the use of multiple cameras, which made beautiful lighting no more likely than in live television, two decades later.

The picture looks as theatrical today in its own way as the 1914 *Tess*, with which it shares some slight coincidences of plot. The girl is rich this time, and the boy lives in a shack, but once again it is the proud father who ruins their lives. In 1935, Pickford toured *Coquette* as a stage play, and in the scene where she is told of her lover's death, she wept so hysterically that on one occasion, the curtain had to be lowered. While making the film, she cried steadily for twenty-four hours, and production had to be shut down to enable her to recover from what was evidently some kind of nervous breakdown. Mary had lost her beloved mother in 1928, not long before shooting this film. Despite the image conveyed by her photographs and her formidable business acumen, Charlotte was by all accounts witty and delightful. Adela Rogers St. Johns described her as "the most charming woman I have ever known."[275] Pickford would lose her brother Jack in 1933 and her sister Lottie in 1936.

When it could no longer hurt her mother, Pickford cut her hair in June 1928. It was almost as though she had died. "Literally millions of her fans mourned the loss of those golden curls as sincerely as though they were their own," wrote a correspondent to *Picture Play*.[276] She pointed out that it gave her the freedom to play the kind of serious parts she had longed for, yet she had played many dramatic parts with her hair piled on top of her head.

Mary had been America's Sweetheart for fifteen years.[277] Now she had to find the courage to turn her back on parts that had won her that title and face a new generation of stars—Greta Garbo, Clara Bow, Corinne Griffith. Mary had been acting longer than these women had been alive, but they presented strong competition. They merely had to sidle on to the screen to make males go weak at the knees. It would have been hard enough to compete in the familiar territory of silent films, but sound had arrived. Mary had to conquer the new technology as well.

At the urging of Lillian Gish,[278] she chose a Broadway play called *Coquette*, about Norma Besant, a wealthy Southern girl—played by Helen Hayes on the stage—who behaves like an irresponsible flirt. After she spends the night with a boy (Johnny Mack Brown) from a socially inferior family, her father (John Sainpolis), considering him worthless, shoots him. In the play, this leads to her suicide, but for the film, the ending was changed. We discover that her honor is unsullied, and the father shoots himself instead.

Pickford recalled a man who had written to Fairbanks, telling how, on the verge of suicide, he had wandered into a theater where he saw *The Three Musketeers*: "He wrote Douglas that he came away from that theater alive and laughing at his own humorless despair of an hour or so before," said Pickford.

He enclosed the bullet he had intended to send into his brain. It is because the screen has such a tremendous power of suggestion that I refused, in *Coquette*, to

Pickford basks in the undivided attention of nearly all the local young men, relishing her position as "belle of the ball" at a party.

commit suicide, although the heroine did commit suicide in the stage version. Some of the critics roasted me for that, but I knew that every girl and woman in the audience all over the world would be vicariously living that role. Most of them had, or some day would have, some serious problem to face, and I refused to set an example or suggestion of suicide as a way out.[279]

The play *Coquette* was purchased in August 1928. The first talkie undertaken by a major silent star, the film went into production when sound was still at a very primitive stage. The production was a nightmare. One of the sound recordists was Ed Bernds. He wrote.

In the silent era, Mary had been in control; she was film-wise, camera-wise and story-wise. Now she no longer had that control. Scenes were shot with agonizing slowness; we, in sound, took too much time setting our microphones. A grip would go high up to the stage catwalk and drop a rope to us. We would tie a microphone to it; it would then be raised to clear the top frame-line of the widest-angle camera, and ropes from the light platforms would be used to pull the mike into position. It was laborious and time-wasting, and if the staging of a scene or the camera set up was changed, our mikes had to be repositioned in the same cumbersome way.[280]

The multi-camera system increased the problems for the cameraman. The camera booths took up space that should have been used for frontlighting. There was the maddening problem of "kicks"—reflections on the glass fronts of the booths. The use of so many cameras hurt the sound, too. The top of the picture, below which the mikes could not stray, was determined by the camera with the widest lens. But other cameras were taking closeups, and the microphones were often too far from the player to provide good closeup quality. This was distressing in Pickford's case, as she did not have a strong voice. It also meant that everyone in the cast had to speak too loudly.

The picture was booed in Britain, apparently because audiences fresh to American accents simply could not cope with a Southern drawl.[281] But on the whole, the critics were kind to Mary. *Photoplay* reported that she "turns in a remarkable performance. Her voice records nicely and she reveals surprising emotional force."[282] And *Motion Picture Magazine* felt that Mary had passed her talkie test "with high honors."[283] And she won the Academy Award for Best Actress—the first given to an actress in a talkie. It was undoubtedly a retrospective award for her dazzling career, but warm consolation nonetheless.

When *Coquette* was released, three thousand theaters were unable to show it because they had not been wired for sound. Yet it made $300,000 more than any other picture Pickford produced,[284] an astounding record considering those circumstances.

Mary poses with Johnny Mack Brown and director Sam Taylor. Poised over their heads is a microphone the size of a World War I bomb. Photograph by K. O. Rahmn.

P.1608.

THE TAMING OF THE SHREW

RELEASED: OCTOBER 26, 1929

"By William Shakespeare. With additional dialogue by Sam Taylor." The joke swept Hollywood, and it is disappointing to find that original prints bore the credit "Adapted and directed by Sam Taylor." However, it seems that the credits were remade; reviews of the opening night recorded the "additional dialogue" credit, presumably sending Taylor rushing back to the title department.[285] In later years, Mary insisted there was never any such credit.

This was the first Shakespearean talkie and was technically far superior to most other sound films of 1929. And yet *The Taming of the Shrew* was a sad occasion: the only time Fairbanks and Pickford ever co-starred in a film and the beginning of the disintegration of the world's most celebrated marriage. Scenes in the film were a mirror of reality.

Mary studied the part with Constance Collier, a celebrated English actress of an earlier generation,[286] then working as an elocution teacher. Journalist Dorothy Manners[287] spoke to Fairbanks just as *The Taming of the Shrew* was going into production. He was far from happy in his role of co-producer of a talkie. His restlessness cast a damper over his spirit that was foreign to his method of working. He spoke of making pictures as an "obligation" to his associates—Mary, Schenck, Chaplin. Doug was fed up. The reception of the film did not revive his spirits. Both he and Mary realized it had been a mistake. According to Mary,

It was very hard for us to find a play that would give us equally important parts. Douglas' leading women have always been just figureheads to be saved in the end. My leading men, with one or two exceptions, have been just the same. Petruchio is very much Douglas' type; he's a very positive character. Katherine is very positive, too. I couldn't play a negative part. Strangely enough, one of my first successes was in a part of that kind. *Wilful Peggy* [1910] it was called. She was very nasty and mean. And *Tess of the Storm Country*, another milestone in my career, was a very positive and rather disagreeable character. Not quite as much of a shrew as Katherine, of course, but the same sort of person.[288]

However, Mary was not pleased with her role. She felt it was subordinate to Doug's and that it was too great a departure from her usual vehicles. But very impressive she seems today, her performance hardly dated at all, while other pupils of Constance Collier are destroyed by their "pear-shaped tones." Her best moments, however, are the silent ones, as in the wedding scene on page 236.

Variety greeted *The Taming of the Shrew* with tremendous enthusiasm: "A money picture, easily, for it's worth 75¢ for anyone to see Mary Pickford and Douglas Fairbanks do this kind of stuff in a vastly extravagant burlesque of Bill Shakespeare's best laugh. The two stars often turn that into a howl. So many ballyhoo and exploitation angles, there's not one town where it should fall down."[289] The *New York Times* named it as one of the "Ten Best of the Year,"[290] after which, like most of the early talkies, it disappeared from distribution.

When she showed it in Paris in 1965, Mary Pickford was given a standing ovation, and she decided to reissue it. Matty Kemp, a former actor who then held the post of the director of the Mary Pickford Company, brought the film out in what he called a "modified" version in 1966. He cut about seven minutes and once more replaced the credit titles. He had new music recorded and laid new sound effects.

Mary Pickford as Katherine. Photograph by Charles E. Lynch.

This is now all that is available, and one can only hope that the Mary Pickford Foundation will restore the original.

Fairbanks was never regarded as a gifted actor. He survived on the strength of his personality—his sheer charisma—but in this he emerges as a marvelous talking-picture player. His expansive gestures are splendid; his grin, his laugh, and his worried look may be the full extent of his repertoire, but his delivery is excellent, his timing impeccable, and his personality tremendously attractive. Mary is ideally suited to the role of Katherine, playing it not as a lusty wench (the Elizabeth Taylor way) but as a spitfire. She is both funny and, at the end of the bedroom scene, touching. And her closeups, lit by Karl Struss, are ravishing.

Sam Taylor's comedy training produces many unexpected laughs, and thanks to his sense of cinematography, Karl Struss produced some impressive camera movements. The opening was described at the time as the longest traveling shot ever. (But what would audiences have made of the silent version, released for theaters that were not yet wired?)[291]

Shakespeare has never been a box-office draw in the cinema, and although *The Taming of the Shrew* brought in a respectable $1 million, neither Mary nor Doug was happy with it. "I have no qualms about admitting that Katherine was one of my worst performances," said Mary.[292] Matty Kemp, who was seated next to Mary at the Cinémathèque Française when it brought the standing ovation, recalled her grabbing his arm and saying, "I cannot *believe* this is happening."

Katherine (Pickford) glowers at Petruchio (Fairbanks), her husband-to-be, who arrived at her wedding with a boot on his head and is crunching an apple.

In this scene, Petruchio tempts the exhausted, famished, and bedraggled Katherine with a fine feast, only to dash the whole tableful to the floor moments later, claiming the meat to be burned, before she can swallow a single mouthful. Photograph by K. O. Rahmn.

FOREVER YOURS

1930, Uncompleted first version of
SECRETS

Mary Pickford personified the silent era, so it was poetic justice that she should suffer so much when sound came in. Norma Talmadge had made a popular stage play into a silent film called *Secrets*, directed by Frank Borzage, in 1924. Mary decided to remake it as a talkie, under the title *Forever Yours*. She must have been aware that Marshall Neilan was now virtually unemployable, thanks to his drinking; but he had made several talkies. She brought him back as director.

The story covered three generations, requiring Mary to age across seventy years. Originally, it centered around the old lady sitting by her sick husband, recalling the dramatic events of her life. It was a hymn to family values—just what Mary needed after the loss of her mother, and the much-publicized wanderings of Douglas Fairbanks. For it showed a woman's lifelong devotion to one man, no matter what hardships, humiliations, and infidelities he subjects her to.

Talmadge's co-star had been one of Mary's early leading men, the reliable and rugged Eugene O'Brien. Mary chose Kenneth MacKenna, who, although thirty-one, photographed too young. But that was not the main problem.

Interviewed in 1933, Mary said she had felt from the beginning that something was wrong with the film but could not put her finger on it. Perhaps it just needed editing. She gradually realized that "the mood and spirit" were missing. She felt that the camera wasn't flexible enough—it was as though they were shooting the stage play. "Though it broke my heart, and, I'm afraid, the hearts of some of the others, I called them all one night and told them we were finished."[293] She abandoned the production and took a $300,000 loss.[294] She was convinced that she would never make another picture.

According to Paul O'Brien, who had taken over from his father as attorney to the Fairbankses, Mary had begun to drink more than usual, and it affected her ability to make decisions. Or rather, decisions were made, then countermanded, and the old atmosphere of confidence evaporated.

Neilan was as unreliable as ever. And he had long lost that magic touch he had brought to Mary's films between 1917 and 1919. Spirit and mood may well have been missing, but Mary undoubtedly recognized the work for what it was: unreleasable.

Pickford and co-star Kenneth MacKenna.

KIKI

RELEASED: MARCH 14, 1931

Mary was persuaded to make this frothy light comedy by Joseph M. Schenck, president of United Artists, who took over as producer and chose for her a story he had already produced with Norma Talmadge (then his wife) in 1926.[295]

Directed by Clarence Brown, *Kiki* was a French farce that had been adapted for the stage by David Belasco. It was the story of a frenzied French chorus girl, and while this characterization had been a relatively simple matter in the silent version, Pickford now had to adopt a convincing French accent. She studied with Fifi D'Orsay[296] and the wife of Maurice Chevalier.[297] She had long been fascinated by the French language and was able to throw in words and phrases she had picked up over the years, often from her maid, Mme. Bodamère.

The leading man was a surprise: comedian Reginald Denny, whose pukka English accent obliged him to abandon the all-American roles he had played in Universal silent comedies.[298] He played Victor, the theater producer at whom Mary hurls herself. It was surprisingly risqué French farce. Victor is depressed, now that his wife has divorced him, and he knows he cannot live without a woman. Kiki is in his office as he prepares to leave; switching the lights out, he trains the last one on Kiki.

Kiki (Pickford) tickles Victor (Reginald Denny), who is trying to talk to his ex-wife, in the hope of ruining his chances of a reconciliation.

M.P-5400-A.62

M.P.-5400-Pub.A.8

Pickford poses on the set of *Kiki*
with still photographer John Miehle.

"Why you look at me like that, with your lighthouse?"

"I hadn't noticed you before. Not bad. I'll take you along with me."

"Where?"

"Home. My apartment."

"Excuse me. Do you mean you want me to be your girlfriend?"

"You're very bright."

"At least you might ask me if I am willing."

"Are you?"

"No, no, no, no, NO!" Rapid dissolve, and Kiki is sitting on the sofa at his apartment.

The Hays Office let the situation through because Victor's ex-wife is also having an affair. This was the era before the Production Code and the Legion of Decency removed such charming suggestiveness from the screen. In a way, it is upsetting to see Pickford as a sex object. The odd thing about it is that she pulls it off—she *is* sexy, and her competition is the ravishing Margaret Livingston.[299] But after twenty years of seeing Mary as a child or young woman in usually asexual roles, one can understand why audiences did not embrace this one.

The film displayed an opening that was a fine mixture of silent and sound techniques, in the style of René Clair's *Sous les Toits de Paris* (1930), which no doubt inspired it. It was shot with a camera mounted on a perambulator-elevator, suspended from a rail in the studio roof—a prehistoric version of the Steadicam—which required six men to operate it. We fade in on a pair of feet, crossed on a table. We hear the sound of the dance director and the dance band. The shoes keep time. Pan along the legs and track slowly back to reveal that they belong to an old stagehand,

Above:

Pickford confers with director Sam Taylor on the set of *Kiki*, as Margaret Livingston has her make-up adjusted at left. William Cameron Menzies's highly stylized set looms in the background.

Opposite:

Kiki, the troublemaking chorus girl, is banished to the prop room.

sharpening a pencil in time to the music. Track past other stagehands pasting up posters, hammering, or sawing in sync to the music. A huge prop elephant dances on stage. Crane up to reveal the chorus line. Pan over to office door and mix. Victor, the producer (Denny), is pacing up and down. Intercut with Paulette Vail (Margaret Livingston), his temperamental star (and ex-wife), doing the same. Scream. Denny exits and looks down to where the chorus girls are running and shrieking. Kiki has been causing trouble; she is thrown into the prop room where, in furious French, she addresses a bust of Napoleon.

It was not a film Pickford approved of. "A misadventure," she called it.

We should, all of us, listen to that still, small voice within us more than we do. It tells us the truth. I did NOT listen to it when I made *Kiki*. I never liked that story. I saw nothing in it. I never liked the character. I even went so far as to tear the script in pieces one night. But I allowed myself to be advised and overruled. I allowed that still, small voice within me to be drowned out.[300]

She would be surprised at the reaction today. "While much maligned at the time," wrote Scott Eyman, "*Kiki* seems to modern eyes an enjoyable romp in roughhouse courtship à la *Taming of the Shrew*. . . . It's a pre-Production Code romp, thoroughly artificial in the best sense, with Mary flouncing around as a self-absorbed, self-dramatizing floozy, albeit a good-hearted one."[301]

Kiki cost $810,568 and returned a mere $426,513 domestically.[302] It was the first Pickford film ever to lose money. But there were mitigating circumstances: the Depression had cut audience attendance from 110 million in 1930 to 60 million by 1931.[303] Even so, one of the reasons Mary Pickford resuscitated and finally completed *Secrets* was that she simply could not let people remember her as Kiki.

ALICE IN WONDERLAND

1933, unproduced

Silent comedy had been eclipsed not so much by the arrival of sound—the two-reelers continued for many years in a more labored form—but by the coming of the cartoon. Cartoons could reach a level of humor denied the live-action pictures, even though they occasionally employed animation for special effects.

Mary admired Walt Disney profoundly and encouraged United Artists to sign him in 1932. And when, in 1933, an acquaintance suggested she star as Alice with Disney providing Wonderland, it seemed an irresistible idea. Mary saw it as a way of returning to the front rank, starring in a film that would combine the simplicity of silent comedy with the sophisticated appeal of the animated cartoon.

Disney reacted coolly to the idea. His career had started with a series of Alice comedies, combining live action with cartoon. But Disney's Alice had been a real child. Mary had turned forty in 1932. Disney was also deterred by the problems of achieving technical perfection and by the prospect of filming in Technicolor. Mary guaranteed him the kind of profit he was getting from his most successful shorts, multiplied to feature length. She even proposed paying this guarantee during the making of the film—an unheard-of thing—and offered to finance the picture herself.[304]

One can imagine Disney's feelings. "As I tried to explain to you at our last meeting," he wrote, "The apparent lack of interest on my part was due to my reluctance to work myself up into an enthusiasm which would lead to great disappointment should the deal fall through."

He sensed a lack of momentum from Mary's side. She was good at pep talks, not so keen on following through. Now Disney delivered a pep talk of his own:

Nothing has been done from your end which would indicate you seriously intended going ahead. . . . I would suggest you immediately delegate someone from your organization to get together with our business representatives and work out a mutual business arrangement. . . . In closing, I would like to say that I sincerely believe a Pickford-Disney production of *Alice* would be a sensation.[305]

But Paramount was planning to make the subject. They broke the news to Disney—who was no doubt relieved, although some footage had been shot—in May 1933. The Paramount version, all live-action, starred Charlotte Henry (who was twenty). It was a flop. Disney left United Artists two years later. He eventually made a fully animated version of *Alice* in 1951.

Mary, wearing her Alice costume at a party, socializes with Joan Crawford and Gary Cooper.

Opposite:
This publicity still was taken at Pickford's studio. The toy Mickey Mouse had been presented to her by Disney three years before. She also filmed a three-strip Technicolor test on this same set. (The Academy Library has the few surviving original film frames.) She still looks youthful enough to play a child.

SECRETS

RELEASED: MARCH 15, 1933

After the failure of *Kiki*, Mary returned to her obsession with *Secrets*, this time called initially *Yes, John*. She recast every part but her own. To ensure a fourteen-karat picture, she hired the director of the Talmadge original, Frank Borzage, and her old scenarist Frances Marion, who had written the original, and she tried to get Gary Cooper as the lead.[306] However, Paramount refused to loan him, and she chose instead Leslie Howard, the British actor who had played opposite Norma Shearer in the remake of *Smilin' Through* (1932). (That success gave Mary the heart to tackle *Secrets* again.[307])

The picture has that quality common to much of Borzage's work, in which you feel that everything is overdone and the sentiment is slightly cloying, until you find yourself wiping away the tears. It contains a stunning sequence in which Mary's baby dies during a siege on her cabin by cattle rustlers. When she realizes what has happened, she sits, stunned, taking no notice at all of the flying bullets. There is also some touching dialogue; as Mary decides to elope with John, he says, "It will be a rough road, Mary. The west is a wild country. You've never known anything but ease and comfort. If you come with me, you'll know hardship, poverty—maybe hunger. Mary, you understand?"

"Yes, John, it all sounds so beautiful."

Secrets in production: the dolly, its tires covered with camera tape to deaden the squeak of rubber on polished floor, was built especially to film traveling shots. A light—for backlighting—is suspended from above. The camera is in a soundproof "blimp" behind lamp no. 6. Mary is dancing with Herbert Evans, playing Lord Hurley. Director Frank Borzage is standing on the dolly; Ray June, chief cinematographer, is seated peering through the blue-glass. Charles Cline, head grip, is leaning from the dolly. W. J. McClellan, gaffer (chief electrician), leans forward behind the grip at the right front wheel. The sound man suspends a microphone attached to a bamboo pole above the actors.

This is very much a film of the early 1930s. The Western sets are built in the studio, and despite the great Richard Day being responsible for them, they look artificial. Ray June's lighting is impressive, but it isn't up to Rosher standards. Although some scenes are shot on location, back projection and traveling mattes remove some of the freshness that had been such a feature of the silent film. The rather insubstantial feel of the film—which, for the first time in Mary's career, looks underfinanced—is alleviated by elaborate montages by John Hoffman,[308] using occasional stock footage borrowed from *The Covered Wagon* (1923) and *The Winning of Barbara Worth* (1926). Nevertheless, Mary Pickford produces a brilliant performance, and it is terribly sad that she did not continue to act, aging in her parts just as she ages in *Secrets*.

There is an uncanny, if not eerie, aspect to Pickford's scenes as the elderly Mary Carlton: when she speaks as an old woman in the film, she sounds almost exactly as she did in real life thirty years later when actually in her seventies.

Pickford's career in talking pictures seemed cursed. The film opened in twenty-five key cities the very day that President Roosevelt declared a bank holiday. The public had largely lost interest in Pickford, as it had with many other great silent stars, and wanted new faces and personalities that seemed to be more in step with the new styles and attitudes of the 1930s. The film was a financial disaster.

Fortunately *Secrets* turned out better than anyone had expected. "The 1933 *Secrets* is a very good film," wrote Scott Eyman. "If anything it's too short—for which no apologies need be made. Certainly it's Pickford's best late performance."[309]

32-430-P

Secrets would be Mary's last picture. When she referred to her retirement, she did not entirely mean it—as her attempt to make *Alice in Wonderland* would prove. And during the filming of *Secrets*, she spoke of remaking *Tess of the Storm Country* as a talkie, according to costume designer Milo Anderson.[310] Perhaps she hoped for a mass protest of her retirement from her fans. But Mary's career had been too full. She had not left her public wanting; hardly ever had she compromised. Mary Pickford was one of the happiest memories for anyone lucky enough to be born into the age of the silent cinema.

Right:

Mary Pickford, at age forty, shows how young she can still look in a scene with Sir C. Aubrey Smith. Photograph by K. O. Rahmn.

Below:

It was an amusing conceit for Mary and Leslie Howard to appear as an old married couple and to have their children in this final scene played by silent-film players—Theodore von Eltz, Ethel Clayton, Huntley Gordon, and Bessie Barriscale. None had acted with Mary before. This is the only still from *Secrets* known to exist showing Pickford in the makeup of old age.

The press continued to find Mary of enormous interest—
although she does not give the impression that the interest
was mutual. A great star at the twilight of her career, Pickford seems to communicate here that twenty years of public
adulation had become burdensome. With her popularity
subsiding and many personal issues that needed her full
attention, perhaps she knew that it was time to say goodbye.

NOTES

"INTRODUCTION"

1. Kevin Brownlow, *The Parade's Gone By*, p. 128.
2. Julian Johnson, "Mary Pickford: Herself and Her Career," part I, *Photoplay*, Nov. 1915, p. 53.
3. C. A. Lejeune, *Cinema*, pp. 57, 59–60.
4. Iris Barry, *Let's Go to the Movies*, pp. 58, 103–5.
5. Ibid., pp.199–200.
6. Idah McClone Gibson, interview with Mary Pickford, *Toledo News Bee*, Mar. 25, 1915.
7. Adolph Zukor, *The Public Is Never Wrong*, pp. 170–71.
8. Herbert Howe, "Mary Pickford's Favorite Stars and Films," *Photoplay*, Jan. 1924, p. 106.
9. Mary Pickford, "How Audiences Find Expression...," *Christian Science Monitor*, Mar. 13, 1928, p. 12.
10. Adela Rogers St. Johns, "Why Does the World Love Mary?" *Photoplay*, Dec. 1921, p. 110.
11. Kevin Brownlow, *The Parade's Gone By*, p. 134.
12. Herbert Howe, "Mary Pickford's Favorite Stars and Films," *Photoplay*, Jan. 1924, p. 28.
13. Mary Pickford, "Mary Pickford Has a Word to Say," *Harper's Bazaar*, Apr. 1917, p. 130.
14. Leslie Wood, *The Romance of the Movies*, p. 143.
15. George Cukor to author, Los Angeles, c. 1980.
16. From an untranscribed audiotaped interview with Mary Pickford, conducted by George Pratt for the George Eastman House of Photography, 1958.
17. Alice Coon Brown, "Mary Pickford and Others," *Cincinnati Journal*, June 27, 1915.
18. Herbert Howe, "Mary Pickford's Greatest Love," *Filmplay Journal*, Sept. 1921, p. 34.
19. Herb Sterne, "The Autobiography of a Film Fan," part V, *Script*, June 25, 1938, unpaginated.
20. Mary Pickford, "Future Service of Film Plays...," *Christian Science Monitor*, Apr. 10, 1928, p. 8.
21. Mary Pickford, "The Portrayal of Child Roles," *Vanity Fair*, Dec. 1917.
22. Mary B. Mullett, "Mary Pickford Describes Her Most Thrilling Experience," *American Magazine*, May 1923, p. 34.
23. Mary Pickford, "The Greatest Business in the World," *Collier's*, June 10, 1922, pp. 22–23.
24. Clare Boothe Brokaw, "Mary Pickford: The End of an Era," *Vanity Fair*, Aug. 1932, p. 51.
25. Mary Pickford, interview with George Pratt, 1958.
26. Mary Pickford, "Going Back to the Stage," *Pictorial Review*, Mar. 1931, pp. 16–17.
27. Mary Pickford, "The Greatest Business in the World," *Collier's*, June 10, 1922.
28. Benjamin Hampton, *A History of the Movies*, pp. 190–91.
29. Daniel Frohman, *Daniel Frohman Presents: An Autobiography*, p. 276.
30. Frederick James Smith, "Mary Had a Little Tear," *Motion Picture Classic*, Sept. 1917, p. 35.
31. Samuel Goldwyn, *Behind the Screen*, p. 42.
32. Charles Chaplin, *My Autobiography*, p. 223.
33. Videotaped interview with Roxanne Rogers Monroe, conducted by Nicholas Eliopoulos, Las Vegas, Mar. 14, 1996.
34. Edward G. Stotsenberg to author, Beverly Hills, 1993.
35. Interview with Mary Pickford, conducted for the Columbia University Oral History Research Office, c. 1957, transcript pp. 61–62, 70.
36. Herbert Howe, "Mary Pickford's Favorite Stars and Films," *Photoplay*, Jan. 1924, p. 106.
37. Kevin Brownlow, *The Parade's Gone By*, p. 359.
38. Hal Mohr to author, interview, Los Angeles, Feb. 13, 1972.
39. Mary Pickford, interview with George Pratt, 1958.
40. Samuel Goldwyn, *Behind the Screen*, pp. 31–32.
41. Mary Pickford, interview with George Pratt, 1958.
42. Cecil B. DeMille, foreword to Mary Pickford, *Sunshine and Shadow*, p. 9.

"THE SEARCH FOR MARY PICKFORD"

1. Mary Pickford's only two-reeler at Biograph was *A Pueblo Legend* (1912).
2. Although he most decidedly did not invent them.
3. Doris Stone was also English, and she appeared in a number of American silent films. She was not Rosher's first wife, however. He never told me about Odette, but I know that they had a daughter, who became actress Joan Marsh. A son, Charles Jr., became a cinematographer.
4. From City of Toronto birth records. The date is usually given as 1893.
5. Ruth Biery, "As Mary Faces Forty," *Photoplay*, May 1931, p. 67. Pickford states here, "I would rather be a beautiful illusion in the minds of people than a horrible example on celluloid."
6. Matty Kemp worked briefly at Mack Sennett studios near the end of the silent era and also appeared in a few films during the 1930s.
7. *The New York Hat* (1912).

"MARY PICKFORD ON FILM"

1. A competition was held to decide what to call motion pictures, and it was won by the term *photoplay*.
2. And for a while the sole director.
3. Formerly the Martin Van Buren mansion.
4. Mary Pickford, *Sunshine and Shadow*, p. 106.
5. Ibid., p. 109.
6. Mary Pickford and Florence Lawrence played together at Biograph in films like *The Country Doctor* (1909) and *Sweet and Twenty* (1909).
7. Campbell MacCullough, "What Makes Them Stars?" *Photoplay*, Oct. 1928, p. 108.
8. "Miss Mary Pickford," *Moving Picture World*, Dec. 24, 1910, p. 1462.
9. According to Irvin Willat, when IMP signed Mary Pickford, she made them take Owen Moore.
10. Mary Pickford, *Sunshine and Shadow*, pp. 137–39. Mary Pickford continued to work for IMP until the end of summer 1911.
11. Irvin Willat to author, interview, 1967, p. 3.
12. Review of *In the Bishop's Carriage, New York Dramatic Mirror*, Sept. 17, 1913, p. 28.
13. Review of *In the Bishop's Carriage, Bioscope*, Nov. 13, 1913, pp. 663, 667.
14. *The American Film Institute Catalog, 1911–1920*, p. 448.
15. H. Lyman Broening to Marc Wanamaker, interview, transcript pp. 4–5.
16. Ibid.
17. *A Good Little Devil* was the first Pickford Famous Players film to be produced, but it was not released until a year later, in 1914, the fourth of her feature pictures.
18. *The American Film Institute Catalog, 1911–1920*, p. 121.
19. Al Ray, "Pictures That Made the Stars," *Picture Play*, Mar. 1, 1916, p. 15.
20. Review of *Caprice, Bioscope*, Mar. 12, 1914, pp. 1178, 1181.
21. Ibid., p. 1181.
22. Review of *Hearts Adrift, Variety*, Feb. 20, 1914, p. 23.
23. *Bird of Paradise* was eventually directed as a talkie by King Vidor in 1932.
24. Mary Pickford, *Sunshine and Shadow*, p. 100.
25. Ibid., p. 164.
26. Scott Eyman, *Mary Pickford, America's Sweetheart*, p. 71.
27. Mary Pickford, "My Own Story," *Ladies' Home Journal*, Aug. 1923, p. 122.
28. Review of *A Good Little Devil, Bioscope*, Nov. 27, 1914, p. 909.
29. Review of *A Good Little Devil, Variety*, Mar. 13, 1914, p. 23.
30. Adolph Zukor to author, interview, 1964, transcript p. 9.
31. Soon to become the headquarters of the Rolin Film Co., home to Hal Roach and Harold Lloyd.
32. It was actually Edwin S. Porter who persuaded her to do another "grimy-ragged" heroine.
33. Mary Pickford to author, interview, 1965.
34. "Photoplay Classics: Reasons Why Certain Screen Immortals Live While Others Quickly Die," *Motion Picture Magazine*, Apr. 1916, p. 142.
35. Sime Silverman, review of *The Eagle's Mate, Variety*, July 10, 1914, p. 20.
36. Review of *Such a Little Queen, Motion Picture News*, Sept. 26, 1914, p. 32.
37. Julian Johnson, "Mary Pickford: Herself and Her Career," *Photoplay*, Feb. 1916, p. 51.
38. H. S. Fuld, review of *Behind the Scenes, Motion Picture News*, Nov. 7, 1914, p. 45.
39. Review of *Cinderella, Variety*, Jan. 1, 1915, p. 29.
40. Famous Players pressbook.
41. Ibid.; *The American Film Institute Catalog, 1911–1920*, p. 624.
42. Review of *Fanchon the Cricket, Variety*, May 14, 1915, p. 19.
43. Stephen W. Bush, review of *Fanchon the Cricket, Moving Picture World*, May 22, 1915, p. 1276.
44. *The American Film Institute Catalog, 1911–1920*, p. 265.
45. Robert Cushman heard that Adele didn't remember it, either.
46. Famous Players pressbook.
47. Review of *The Dawn of a Tomorrow, Variety*, June 11, 1915, p. 18.
48. Review of *The Dawn of a Tomorrow, New York Dramatic Mirror*, June 16, 1915, p. 28.
49. This was David Powell's first film. He went on to act with Pickford in *Less Than the Dust* (1916) and in later silents such as *The Green Goddess* with George Arliss.
50. Famous Players pressbook; *The American Film Institute Catalog, 1911–1920*, p. 197.
51. Julian Johnson, "Mary Pickford: Herself and Her Career," *Photoplay*, Feb. 1916, p. 51.
52. *The American Film Institute Catalog, 1911–1920*, p. 531; review of *Little Pal, Variety*, July 9, 1915, p. 17; Famous Players pressbook.
53. Review of *Little Pal, Variety*, July 9, 1915, p. 17.
54. Robert Cushman, notes, 1970.
55. Lynde Denig, review of *Little Pal, Moving Picture World*, July 17, 1915, p. 505.
56. Review of *Little Pal, New York Dramatic Mirror*, July 14, 1915, p. 28.
57. J. Farrell MacDonald, who was also a director at this period, was featured by Ford in such films as *The Iron Horse* (1924) and *Riley the Cop* (1928).
58. *The American Film Institute Catalog, 1911–1920*, p. 753; review of *Rags, Variety*, Aug. 6, 1915, p. 17.
59. James Card, *Image: On the Art and Evolution of the Film*, ed. Marshall Deutelbaum, pp. 125–26.
60. William K. Everson, Cinefest 1994 program, Syracuse, N.Y.
61. Review of *Rags, Variety*, Aug. 6, 1915, p. 17.
62. Booton Herndon, *Mary Pickford and Douglas Fairbanks*, p. 126.
63. Against fifty percent of the profits of the combined affiliates.
64. Mary Pickford, *Sunshine and Shadow*, p. 171.
65. Sime Silverman, review of *Esmeralda, Variety*, Sept. 17, 1915, p. 25.
66. Julian Johnson, review of *Esmeralda, Photoplay*, Nov. 1915, p. 83.
67. Originally a short story; *The American Film Institute Catalog, 1911–1920*, p. 244.
68. *The American Film Institute Catalog, 1911–1920*, p. 244; Famous Players pressbook.
69. The other was *Little Annie Rooney* (1925), which she wrote under the name of her grandmother.
70. Wid Gunning, review of *A Girl of Yesterday, Wid's Film and Film Folk*, Oct. 14, 1915, unpaginated.
71. This was a favorite theme of Mary Pickford's; see *Stella Maris* (1918).
72. The yacht was the property of the California multimillionaire John D. Spreckels.
73. Frances Marion, *Off With Their Heads*, p. 44.
74. Peter Bogdanovich, *The Last Pioneer*, Allan Dwan interview, p. 35.
75. Adolph Zukor, *The Public Is Never Wrong*, pp. 141–44.
76. Review of *Madame Butterfly, Variety*, Nov. 12, 1915, p. 22.
77. Synopsis of *Madame Butterfly, Moving Picture World*, Nov. 13, 1915, p. 1382.
78. Frances Marion, *Off With Their Heads*, p. 76.
79. Eileen Whitfield, *Pickford: The Woman Who Made Hollywood*, p. 139.
80. Randolph Bartlett, "Mary, the Well Beloved," *Photoplay*, Apr. 1920, pp. 28–29.

81. Mary Pickford, "My Own Story," *Ladies' Home Journal*, Aug. 1923, p. 16.

82. The estate of Mr. and Mrs. James A. Blair at Peapack, New Jersey.

83. Booton Herndon, *Mary Pickford and Douglas Fairbanks*, p. 132.

84. Review of *Poor Little Peppina*, *Variety*, Feb. 25, 1916, p. 22.

85. "'Peppina' Causes Riot at Theatre," *Moving Picture World*, Mar. 11, 1916, p. 1629.

86. Jack Spears, "Mary Pickford's Directors," *Films in Review*, Feb. 1962, p. 78.

87. Williams is not credited, but he was Pickford's cameraman at the time.

88. Sidney Lens, *The Labor Wars*. These are 1912 figures.

89. Peter Milne, review of *The Foundling*, *Motion Picture News*, Jan. 15, 1916, p. 258.

90. Edward Wagenknecht, *The Movies in the Age of Innocence*, p. 149.

91. Review of *The Eternal Grind*, *New York Dramatic Mirror*, Apr. 22, 1916, p. 45.

92. Review of *The Eternal Grind*, *Variety*, Apr. 14, 1916, p. 24.

93. Review of *The Eternal Grind*, *Everybody's Magazine*, June 1916, p. 681.

94. Review of *Hulda from Holland*, *Variety*, Aug. 4, 1916, p. 29.

95. *The American Film Institute Catalog, 1911–1920*, p. 432.

96. Famous Players pressbook; *The American Film Institute Catalog, 1911–1920*, p. 432.

97. Don Ryan, "Our American Critic Complex: An Application of Psychoanalysis to the Prevailing Style in Motion Picture Actresses," *Picture Play*, Nov. 1924, p. 96.

98. *Moving Picture World*, May 13, 1916, p. 143; James Wilde fax to author, May 15, 1997.

99. Mary Pickford, *Sunshine and Shadow*, p. 173.

100. In the cast was Cesare Gravina, to whom he entrusted a major role in *Greed* (1924).

101. *The American Film Institute Catalog, 1911–1920*, p. 510.

102. Emerson had directed Douglas Fairbanks at Fine Arts and would marry Anita Loos in 1919.

103. Booton Herndon, *Mary Pickford and Douglas Fairbanks*, p. 150.

104. Review of *The Pride of the Clan*, *Exhibitor's Trade Review*, Jan. 13, 1917, p. 422.

105. Richard Koszarski, "Lost Films from the National Film Collection," *Film Quarterly*, Winter 1969–1970, p. 34.

106. Bitzer was D. W. Griffith's cameraman. The second cameraman on this and the other Tourneur-Pickford was Lucien Andriot, a Frenchman who was also remarkably gifted.

107. Mary Pickford, *Sunshine and Shadow*, p. 174.

108. Lucien Andriot to author, interview, "Hollywood" television series, 1976; transcript p. 10.

109. "Mary Pickford in Dangerous Accident," *Moving Picture World*, Dec. 2, 1916, p. 1332.

110. Frances Marion, *Off With Their Heads*, p. 44.

111. Eileen Whitfield, *Pickford: The Woman Who Made Hollywood*, p. 155.

112. Ben Carré, unpublished memoirs, p. 207.

113. Review of *The Poor Little Rich Girl*, *Exhibitor's Trade Review*, Mar. 10, 1917, p. 976.

114. Ben Carré, unpublished memoirs.

115. Mary Pickford, *Sunshine and Shadow*, p. 180.

116. Ibid., p. 111.

117. Bert D. Essex, review of *The Poor Little Rich Girl*, *Photoplay Journal*, Apr. 1917, p. 33.

118. Robert Birchard, DeMille research notes, Pordenone (Italy) Silent Film Festival, 1991.

119. Edward Wagenknecht, *The Movies in the Age of Innocence*, p. 141.

120. Robert Birchard, DeMille Research Notes, Pordenone (Italy) Silent Film Festival, 1991. They could not know then that *The Poor Little Rich Girl* (in the can but not yet released) would prove a smash hit.

121. Vachel Lindsay, "Queen of My People," *The New Republic*, July 17, 1917, pp. 280–81; Edward Wagenknecht, *The Movies in the Age of Innocence*, p. 141.

122. Mary Pickford, *Sunshine and Shadow*, p. 182.

123. Ibid., p. 183.

124. Vachel Lindsay, "Queen of My People," review of *A Romance of the Redwoods*, *The New Republic*, July 17, 1917, pp. 280–81.

125. Neil Caward, review of *A Romance of the Redwoods*, *Picture Play*, July 1917, p. 122.

126. Charles Higham, *Cecil B. DeMille*, telegram dated Feb. 19, 1917, p. 66.

127. Cecil B. DeMille, *Autobiography*, p. 165.

128. Charles Frohman, brother of Daniel Frohman, the managing director of Famous Players, died on the *Lusitania*.

129. These scenes were probably filched from the novel, *The Four Horsemen of the Apocalypse*, which appeared in 1916. The novel and the film have much in common.

130. Inspired by *The Birth of a Nation*.

131. This may have caused the film not to be shown in France. It was not presented there until 1926, when it was dismissed as "puerile." (*Cinémagazine*, Sept. 24, 1926, p. 551.)

132. Frances Marion, *Off With Their Heads*, p. 54.

133. Robert Birchard, DeMille research notes, Pordenone (Italy) Silent Film Festival, 1991. The DeMille papers are now at Brigham Young University.

134. George C. Pratt, "Forty-Five Years of Picture Making: An Interview with Cecil B. DeMille," *Film History*, vol. 3, no. 2, 1989, p. 137.

135. Kevin Brownlow, *The War, the West and the Wilderness*, p. 132.

136. George C. Pratt, "Forty-Five Years of Picture Making: An Interview with Cecil B. DeMille," *Film History*, vol. 3, no. 2, 1989, p. 137.

137. Harvey O'Higgins, "To What Green Altar?" *The New Republic*, Feb. 15, 1919, pp. 80–81.

138. Bert D. Essex, review of *The Little American*, *Photoplay Journal*, July 1933, p. 33.

139. Wid Gunning, review of *Rebecca of Sunnybrook Farm*, *Wid's*, Sept. 13, 1917.

140. Robert Cushman, *Tribute to Mary Pickford*, unpaginated.

141. Mary Pickford, *Sunshine and Shadow*, p. 184.

142. Cari Beauchamp, *Without Lying Down*, p. 72. When the agreement for the two DeMilles was made, Zukor did not know that *The Poor Little Rich Girl* was going to be a smash hit. *The Pride of the Clan* and *Less Than the Dust* did not do nearly so well, according to Robert Cushman.

143. Robert Windeler, *Sweetheart: The Story of Mary Pickford*, pp. 102–3.

144. Frances Marion, *Off With Their Heads*, p. 50.

145. Review of *A Little Princess*, *Variety*, Nov. 16, 1917, p. 53.

146. Marcia Manon previously acted under the name of Camille Ankewich. Robert Cushman thinks her performance admirable: "one of the most compelling pieces of work I can recall on the silent screen."

147. Buckland usually worked with DeMille. In 1922, he designed Douglas Fairbanks's epic *Robin Hood*.

148. Chester A. Blythe, review of *Stella Maris*, *Photoplay World*, Mar. 1918, p. 35.

149. *Movie Weekly*, May 31, 1924, p. 18.

150. Sometimes known by its translated title, *The Star of the Sea*.

151. Cari Beauchamp, *Without Lying Down*, p. 81. Frances Marion's own book hardly mentions it and suggests the dual role was specially written for the film.

152. Booton Herndon, *Mary Pickford and Douglas Fairbanks*, p. 160.

153. Ibid., p. 242. (Unity actually dies near the end.)

154. Anthony Slide, in Richard Koszarski, ed., *The Rivals of D. W. Griffith*, p. 13.

155. In *Man, Woman and Sin* (1927), with John Gilbert and Jeanne Eagels, an M-G-M newspaper story directed by Monta Bell.

156. Scott Eyman, *Mary Pickford, America's Sweetheart*, p. 113.

157. Edward Wagenknecht, *The Movies in the Age of Innocence*, p. 11.

158. Arthur Lennig, "Mary Pickford's *Amarilly of Clothes-Line Alley*," *Classic Film Collector*, Spring 1978, p. 31.

159. Hazel Simpson Naylor, review of *Amarilly of Clothes-Line Alley*, *Motion Picture Magazine*, June 1918, p. 104.

160. Robert Birchard, Cinefest 17 program, Syracuse, N.Y., 1997.

161. Scott Eyman, *Mary Pickford, America's Sweetheart*, p. 101.

162. Ibid., p. 103.

163. Mary Pickford, *Sunshine and Shadow*, p. 250.

164. Julian Johnson, review of *Captain Kidd, Jr.*, *Photoplay*, July 1919, p. 102.

165. Jack Spears, "Mary Pickford's Directors," *Films in Review*, Feb. 1962, p. 84.

166. Review of *How Could You, Jean?*, *Variety*, July 5, 1918, p. 31.

167. Frances Marion, *Off With Their Heads*, p. 58.

168. Neil G. Caward, "Screen Gossip," *Picture Play*, Oct. 1918, p. 289. When shooting the last scenes of *Captain Kidd, Jr.*, there was a delay while sets went up; so they began shooting *Johanna*, then called *The Mobilization of Johanna*.

169. Booton Herndon, *Mary Pickford and Douglas Fairbanks*, p. 172.

170. Interview with Mary Pickford, conducted for Columbia University, Oral History Research Office, c. 1957, transcript pp. 80–81.

171. Kevin Brownlow, *The War, the West, and the Wilderness*, p. 108.

172. And later a fine cameraman in his own right.

173. Review of *Captain Kidd, Jr.*, *Variety*, Apr. 25, 1919, p. 83.

174. Scott Eyman, *Mary Pickford, America's Sweetheart*, p. 118.

175. "Pictures and People," *Motion Picture News*, Feb. 18, 1928, p. 497.

176. Review of *Nobody's Kid*, *Moving Picture World*, May 24, 1921, p. 383.

177. Scott Eyman, *Mary Pickford, America's Sweetheart*, p. 103.

178. Review of *Daddy-Long-Legs*, *Chicago Herald Examiner*, May 12, 1919.

179. Julian Johnson, review of *Daddy-Long-Legs*, *Photoplay*, Aug. 1919, p. 56.

180. Hazel Simpson Naylor, review of *The Hoodlum*, *Motion Picture Magazine*, Dec. 1919, p. 42.

181. Review of *The Hoodlum*, *Variety*, Sept. 5, 1919, p. 61.

182. Hazel Simpson Naylor, review of *The Hoodlum*, *Motion Picture Magazine*, Dec. 1919, p. 42.

183. Mary B. Mullett, "Mary Pickford Describes Her Most Thrilling Experience," *American Magazine*, May 1923, p. 108.

184. Unidentified clipping in Charles Rosher scrapbook, author's collection.

185. Review of *The Heart o' the Hills*, *Photoplay*, Feb. 1920, p. 113.

186. Sidney Franklin to author, American Film Institute Oral History, 1970, p. 135.

187. Frances Marion, *Off With Their Heads*, p. 67.

188. Burns Mantle, review of *Pollyanna*, *Photoplay*, Apr. 1920, p. 64.

189. "Pictures and People," *Motion Picture News*, Feb. 18, 1928, p. 497.

190. Frances Patterson, *Cinema Craftsmanship*, p. 105.

191. *The American Film Institute Catalog, 1911–1920*, p. 725.

192. Review of *Pollyanna*, *Variety*, Jan. 24, 1920, p. 60.

193. Marjorie Rosen, *Popcorn Venus*, p. 39.

194. Alma Whitaker, "Mrs. Douglas Fairbanks Analyzes Mary Pickford," *Photoplay*, Mar. 1928, p. 31.

195. No relation to D. W. Griffith, despite frequent assertions to the contrary.

196. Edward Wagenknecht, introduction to *Pollyanna*, Blackhawk Films release.

197. $1,160,962.45; figures from the Mary Pickford Estate.

198. Review of *Pollyanna*, *London Times*, Apr. 26, 1921, p. 8d.

199. Although many history books date *Caligari* as 1919, it was not released in Germany until February 1920.

200. From the Charles Frohman stage production '*Op O' Me Thumb*, by Frederick Fenn and Richard Pryce. Maude Adams was most celebrated for her portrayal of Peter Pan.

201. Jerome Weatherby, "He Grew a Foot in One Picture and Harold Goodwin Continues to Grow Fast in Public Favor. As for Acting, he says, 'Pretty Soft.'" *Picture Play*, July 1921, p. 50.

202. "Pictures and People," *Motion Picture News*, Feb. 18, 1928, p. 497.

203. And those of the George Eastman House and the Library of Congress.

204. Robert Windeler, *Sweetheart: The Story of Mary Pickford*, p. 118.

205. Alison Smith, review of *The Love Light*, *New York Globe and Commercial*, Jan.10, 1921.

206. Cari Beauchamp, fax to author, Jan. 18, 1997, p. 1.

207. Scott Eyman, *Mary Pickford, America's Sweetheart*, p. 136.

208. Frederick James Smith, review of *Through the Back Door*, *Motion Picture Classic*, Aug. 1921, p. 78.

209. Review of *Through the Back Door*, *Picture Play*, Aug. 1921, p. 66.

210. Frederick James Smith, review of *Through the Back Door*, *Motion Picture Classic*, Aug. 1921, p. 78.

211. Mary Pickford, *Sunshine and Shadow*, p. 138.

212. James Card, "The Films of Mary Pickford," *Image*, Dec. 1959, p. 124.

213. Gerald C. Duffy, "A Man of Few Words: Titles Are Bought in the Picture Business As Well As in Society," *Picture Play*, Aug. 1922, p. 23.

214. Adolphe Menjou and M. M. Musselmann, *It Took Nine Tailors*, p. 83.

215. *The American Film Institute Catalog, 1921–1930*, pp. 441–42.

216. David Robinson, review of *Little Lord Fauntleroy*, *Monthly Film Bulletin*, June 1974, p. 138.

217. Wid Gunning, review of *Little Lord Fauntleroy*, *Wid's Daily*, Sept. 18, 1921, p. 3.

218. Lewis William O'Connell to Robert Cushman, interview, 1971.

219. Kevin Brownlow, *The Parade's Gone By*, p. 229.

220. Alma Whitaker, "Mrs Douglas Fairbanks Analyzes Mary Pickford," *Photoplay*, Mar. 1928, p. 30.

221. Green went on to a prolific career, which included the smash hit *The Jolson Story* (1946). Jack Pickford, on the other hand, never directed for anyone but his sister.

222. Scott Eyman, *Mary Pickford, America's Sweetheart*, p. 141.

223. Ibid.

224. Review of *Little Lord Fauntleroy*, *Variety*, Sept. 23, 1921, p. 42.

225. Frederick James Smith, review of *Little Lord Fauntleroy*, *Motion Picture Classic*, Dec. 1921, p. 94.

226. Review of *Tess of the Storm Country*, *Photoplay*, Jan. 1923, p. 65.

227. Martin J. Quigley, review of *Tess of the Storm Country*, *Exhibitors Herald*, Dec. 2, 1922, p. 36.

228. *Tess of the Storm Country* was remade by Fox in 1932, with Janet Gaynor in the lead and the original plot reasonably intact. It was made again in 1960 for 20th Century-Fox with Diane Baker in the lead. This last version almost completely dispensed with the original plot.

229. And brother-in-law; Robertson's wife was Josephine Lovett.

230. Robert Florey, "Mary Pickford Tourne *Tess of the Storm Country* de Notre Envoyé," *Cinémagazine*, July 21, 1922, p. 83.

231. Ibid., p. 83.

232. *The American Film Institute Catalog, 1921–1930*, p. 667.

233. Edwin Schallert, "The New Mary Pickford: As Rosita She Is Doing Up Her Curls and Essaying a Real Grown-Up Heroine," *Picture Play*, July 1923, p. 47.

234. Ibid., p. 48.

235. Edwin and Elza Schallert, "Hollywood High Lights," *Picture Play*, Nov. 1923, p. 69.

236. Ibid., p. 69.

237. Scott Eyman, *Ernst Lubitsch: Laughter in Paradise*, p. 93.

238. Alma Whitaker, "Mrs Douglas Fairbanks Analyzes Mary Pickford," *Photoplay*, Mar. 1928, p. 30.

239. Scott Eyman, *Ernst Lubitsch: Laughter in Paradise*, p. 95.

240. Ibid., p. 95.

241. Gade had worked in Berlin and was a follower of Max Reinhardt. He had co-directed and co-designed the famous Asta Nielsen film version of *Hamlet* in 1920. He subsequently directed a number of films in Hollywood.

242. This sequence was included in Pickford compilations and was probably the only one she retained from the film.

243. Review of *Rosita*, *Photoplay*, Nov. 1923, p. 74; *Variety*'s reviewer (Sept. 6, 1923, pp. 22–24) considered Mary's acting better even than in *Stella Maris*, an opinion that Robert Cushman thinks is "baloney."

244. Frederick James Smith, review of *Rosita*, *Screenland*, Dec. 1923, p. 38.

245. "Pictures and People," *Motion Picture News*, Feb. 18, 1928, p. 497.

246. Gordon Gassaway, "What Makes a Good Screen Story?" *Picture Play*, May 1923, pp. 19–20.

247. Agnes Smith, review of *Dorothy Vernon of Haddon Hall*, *Picture Play*, Aug. 1924, p. 54.

248. Margaret Reid, "Looking on with an Extra Girl," *Picture Play*, Aug. 1924, p. 91.

249. Mary Pickford, *Sunshine and Shadow*, pp. 257–59.

250. Mary Pickford, letter to her cousin, Apr. 28, 1925.

251. Mary thought the subject far too similar to Colleen Moore's *The Desert Flower* (1925).

252. Tom McNamara was credited as collaborator; Hope Loring and Louis Lighton turned it into a script.

253. *The American Film Institute Catalog, 1921–1930*, p. 439.

254. Eileen Whitfield, *Pickford: The Woman Who Made Hollywood*, p. 241.

255. Harry Oliver was supervising art director, and the picture has his style.

256. Mary Pickford was furious when this enormous gasholder was constructed, as it ruined the sightlines on the east of the Pickford-Fairbanks studio. It was an eyesore and a bitter source of contention between Pickford and Fairbanks and the City of Los Angeles; it finally came in use for this production.

257. An odd thing about this sequence: in the weeping closeups Mary's wedding ring is distinctly visible.

258. Mary Pickford, *Sunshine and Shadow*, pp. 271–74.

259. It won the first Academy Award for cinematography.

260. Review of *Sparrows*, *Variety*, Sept. 22, 1926, p. 14.

261. Milton Howe and Elizabeth Greer, "News of the Camera Coasts," *Motion Picture Magazine*, Nov. 1926, p. 66.

262. William Beaudine to author, interview, 1969, transcript p. 26.

263. Hal Mohr to Robert Cushman, interview, Feb. 13, 1972.

264. Ibid.

265. William Beaudine to author, interview, 1969.

266. Surprisingly, considering Mary's antipathy to Lubitsch, he helped edit this film, according to evidence uncovered by Scott Eyman.

267. "Over the Teacups," *Picture Play*, June 1927, p. 48.

268. William Beaudine to author, interview, 1969.

269. Gloria Swanson had done the same for *Manhandled* (1924).

270. And sister of Frank Norris, who wrote *McTeague*, from which von Stroheim made *Greed* (1924).

271. The adaptation was by another Lloyd graduate, Tim Whelan, who later went to England as a director, and Allen McNeil, who had been a film editor for Mack Sennett.

272. John McGee, "Reel Reviewer," *Classic Images*, Dec. 1982, p. 33.

273. Norbert Lusk, review of *My Best Girl*, *Picture Play*, Feb. 1928, p. 67.

274. Kevin Brownlow, *The Parade's Gone By*, p. 234.

275. Adela Rogers St. Johns, "Why Mary Pickford Bobbed Her Hair: A Remarkable Insight into the Love That Existed Between Mary and Her Mother," *Photoplay*, Sept. 1928, p. 33.

276. Queenie Danciger, "What the Fans Think: Was Coquette a Success?" *Picture Play*, Dec.1929, p. 8.

277. The title "America's Sweetheart" was coined in 1914 by David J. "Pop" Grauman, father of Sid, who first put it in lights when he was presenting *Tess of the Storm Country* at his theater in San Francisco.

278. Robert Windeler, *Sweetheart: The Story of Mary Pickford*, p. 156.

279. C. A. Lejeune, *Cinema*, p. 58.

280. Ed Bernds, unpublished memoirs, chap. 7, p. 7.

281. Letter from Scotland in *Picture Play*, Feb.1930, p. 10.

282. Review of *Coquette*, *Photoplay*, June 1929, p. 54.

283. Review of *Coquette*, *Motion Picture Magazine*, July 1929, p. 62.

284. Mark Larkin, "Mary Returns to Herself," *Photoplay*, Mar. 1933, pp. 62–63.

285. "From the Mailbag" (letters), *Classic Images*, Nov. 1990, p. C12.

286. She played with Sir Herbert Beerbohm Tree in *Macbeth* (1915), supervised by D. W. Griffith.

287. Dorothy Manners, "What Is Doug Doing?" *Motion Picture Magazine*, Feb. 1931, p. 55.

288. Elisabeth Goldbeck, "The Woman That Was Mary," *Motion Picture Magazine*, Sept. 1929, p. 48.

289. Sime Silverman, review of *The Taming of the Shrew*, *Variety*, Dec. 4, 1929, p. 15.

290. Robert Windeler, *Sweetheart: The Story of Mary Pickford*, p. 162.

291. Robert Cushman saw it at the George Eastman House. He recently recalled that the film had incredibly long titles and was virtually unwatchable and earlier wrote, "Unfortunately, the silent version looks like what it is—a sound film with the track turned off and titles awkwardly inserted between the scenes. It was an early and all-too-painful confirmation that silent and sound pictures were two completely different fields." (Program notes, Mary Pickford Tribute, Los Angeles County Museum of Art, Mar. 14, 1971.)

292. Mary Pickford, *Sunshine and Shadow*, p. 186.

293. Faith Service, "Mary Pickford Starts *Secrets* All Over Again," *Motion Picture Magazine*, Feb. 1933, p. 88.

294. Mary Pickford, *Sunshine and Shadow*, p. 312.

295. They divorced in 1934.

296. Fifi D'Orsay actually came, like Mary Pickford, from Canada.

297. Scott Eyman, *Mary Pickford, America's Sweetheart*, p. 202.

298. He had appeared with Buster Keaton and in C. B. DeMille's romp *Madam Satan* (1930).

299. The vamp from *Sunrise* (1927).

300. Faith Service, "Mary Pickford Starts *Secrets* All Over Again," *Motion Picture Magazine*, Feb. 1933, p. 60.

301. Scott Eyman, *Mary Pickford, America's Sweetheart*, p. 203.

302. Ibid., p. 204.

303. Ibid. These are 1932 figures.

304. Scott Eyman, *Mary Pickford, America's Sweetheart*, p. 232.

305. Ibid., p. 233.

306. Hervé Dumont, *Frank Borzage*, p. 200.

307. The 1922 version had starred Norma Talmadge; the 1932 remake Norma Shearer. Both were directed by Sidney Franklin.

308. Hoffman, who worked rather in the Russian style, would go on to achieve the remarkable earthquake sequence for M-G-M's *San Francisco* (1936).

309. Scott Eyman, *Mary Pickford, America's Sweetheart*, p. 216.

310. Milo Anderson to David Chierichetti.

BIBLIOGRAPHY

BOOKS:

The American Film Institute Catalog: Feature Films, 1911–1920. Patricia King Hanson, ed. Berkeley: University of California Press, 1988.

The American Film Institute Catalog: Feature Films, 1921–1930. Kenneth W. Munden, ed. New York and London: R. R. Bowker Co., 1971.

Barry, Iris. *Let's Go to the Movies.* New York: Payson & Clark, 1926.

Beauchamp, Cari. *Without Lying Down: Frances Marion and the Powerful Women of Early Hollywood.* New York: Scribner, 1997.

Brownlow, Kevin. *The Parade's Gone By.* New York: Alfred A. Knopf, 1968.

———. *The War, the West, and the Wilderness.* New York: Alfred A. Knopf, 1979.

Card, James. *Image: On the Art and Evolution of the Film.* Edited by Marshall Deutelbaum. New York: Dover, 1979.

Chaplin, Charles. *My Autobiography.* New York: Simon & Schuster, 1964.

DeMille, Cecil B. *Autobiography.* Englewood Cliffs, N.J.: Prentice-Hall, 1959.

Dumont, Hervé. *Frank Borzage.* Paris: Cinémathèque Française, 1993.

Eyman, Scott. *Ernst Lubitsch: Laughter in Paradise.* New York: Simon & Schuster, 1993.

———. *Mary Pickford, America's Sweetheart.* New York: Donald I. Fine, 1990.

Frohman, Daniel. *Daniel Frohman Presents: An Autobiography.* New York: Claude Kendall & Willoughby Sharp, 1935.

Goldwyn, Samuel. *Behind the Screen.* New York: Doran, 1923.

Hampton, Benjamin. *A History of the Movies.* New York: Covici-Friede, 1931.

Herndon, Booton. *Mary Pickford and Douglas Fairbanks: The Most Popular Couple the World Has Ever Known.* New York: W. W. Norton & Co., 1977.

Higham, Charles. *Cecil B. DeMille.* New York: Scribner's, 1973.

Koszarski, Richard, ed. *The Rivals of D.W. Griffith: Alternate Auteurs 1913–1918.* Minneapolis: Walker Art Center, 1976.

Lejeune, C. A. *Cinema.* London: Maclehouse, 1931.

Lens, Sidney. *The Labor Wars.* Garden City, N.Y.: Doubleday, 1973.

Marion, Frances. *Off With Their Heads!: A Serio-comic Tale of Hollywood.* New York: Macmillan, 1972.

Menjou, Adolphe, and M. M. Musselmann. *It Took Nine Tailors.* New York: McGraw-Hill, 1948.

Patterson, Frances Taylor. *Cinema Craftsmanship: A Book for Photoplaywrights.* New York: Harcourt, Brace & Howe, 1920.

Pickford, Mary. *Sunshine and Shadow.* New York: Doubleday, 1955.

Rosen, Marjorie. *Popcorn Venus: Women, Movies and the American Dream.* New York: Coward, McCann & Geohegan, 1973.

Wagenknecht, Edward. *The Movies in the Age of Innocence.* Norman: University of Oklahoma Press, 1962.

Whitfield, Eileen. *Pickford: The Woman Who Made Hollywood.* Toronto: MacFarlane, Walter & Ross, 1997.

Windeler, Robert. *Sweetheart: The Story of Mary Pickford.* New York: Praeger, 1973.

Wood, Leslie. *The Romance of the Movies.* London: Heinemann, 1937.

Zukor, Adolph. *The Public Is Never Wrong.* New York: Putnam, 1953.

PERIODICALS:

American Classic Screen
American Magazine
Bioscope
Christian Science Monitor
Cinémagazine
Classic Film Collector
Classic Images
Collier's
Everybody's Magazine
Exhibitors Herald
Exhibitor's Trade Review
Film History
Film Quarterly
Filmplay Journal
Films in Review
Harper's Bazaar
Image
Ladies' Home Journal
Monthly Film Bulletin
Motion Picture Classic
Motion Picture Magazine
Motion Picture News
Movie Weekly
Moving Picture World
The New Republic
New York Dramatic Mirror
Photoplay
Photoplay Journal
Photoplay World
Pictorial Review
Picture Play
Screenland
Script
Vanity Fair
Variety
Wid's
Wid's Daily
Wid's Film and Film Folk

NEWSPAPERS:

Chicago Herald Examiner
Chicago News
Cincinnati Journal
Los Angeles Times
New York Globe and Commercial
Toledo News Bee

INTERVIEWS:

Lucien Andriot, interviewed by Kevin Brownlow, 1976.

William Beaudine, interviewed by Kevin Brownlow, 1969.

H. Lyman Broening, interviewed by Marc Wanamaker.

Olive Carey, interviewed by Kevin Brownlow and David Gill, 1976.

Sidney Franklin, interviewed by Kevin Brownlow, 1970.

Hal Mohr, interviewed by Robert Cushman, 1972.

Bessie Love, interviewed by Kevin Brownlow, 1972.

Roxanne Rogers Monroe, interviewed by Nicholas Eliopoulos, 1996.

Lewis William O'Connell, interviewed by Robert Cushman, 1971.

Mary Pickford, interviewed by Kevin Brownlow, 1965.

Mary Pickford, interviewed by George Pratt, 1958.

Mary Pickford, interviewed for the Columbia University Oral Research Office, c. 1957.

Karl Struss, interviewed by Robert Cushman, 1972.

Irvin Willat, interviewed by Kevin Brownlow, 1967.

Adolph Zukor, interviewed by Kevin Brownlow, 1964.

MISCELLANEOUS:

Ed Bernds, unpublished memoirs.

Robert Birchard, Cecil B. DeMille research notes, Pordenone (Italy) Silent Film Festival, 1991.

Ben Carré, unpublished memoirs.

Cinefest 14, program, Syracuse, N.Y., 1994.

Cinefest 17, program, Syracuse, N.Y., 1997.

Robert Cushman, *Tribute to Mary Pickford,* pamphlet, American Film Institute Theater, Washington, D.C., 1970.

Famous Players Film Co., pressbooks.

Theodore Huff Memorial Film Society, New York, notes.

Edward Wagenknecht, introduction to *Pollyanna,* Blackhawk Films release.

INDEX

Page numbers in *italics* refer to illustrations.

ACKNOWLEDGMENTS

This book came about thanks to a welcome change of policy by the Mary Pickford Foundation. During the past six decades, Pickford films had been rarely seen, and her place in film history had been seriously eroded. Even silent-film enthusiasts were hard put to raise much interest in a star who may have once been more popular than Chaplin but who was now a byword for quaintness. As a symbol of this loss of prestige, Pickfair, once regarded as the Buckingham Palace of Hollywood, was demolished by Pia Zadora. (*Her* place in infamy is secure!)

The Academy was approached by Keith Lawrence of the Pickford Foundation, and I was asked to write the text for the pictures in collaboration with Robert Cushman, Photograph Curator of the Academy's Margaret Herrick Library, who selected the photographs appearing on these pages. I accepted with enthusiasm, for Mary Pickford was a strong influence on my love affair with the silent film.

I am very grateful to the Pickford Foundation. Besides initiating this book, they introduced me to the remarkable Elaina Archer, now in charge of the Mary Pickford Library, who has been tremendously helpful, ensuring that I could see tapes of every extant Pickford film. It was encouraging to know how much she—a member of the current generation—admires Pickford's work. The Foundation also hired a celluloid sleuth, Christel Schmidt, who made some impressive discoveries in several archives.

I benefited enormously from the Pickford biographies written by Scott Eyman and Eileen Whitfield, as well as the study of Frances Marion by Cari Beauchamp. I read all three in uncut manuscript form. Each book I used is cited in the endnotes.

I had known Robert Cushman for nearly thirty years as the lone voice in the wilderness, trying to make people realize the outstanding quality of Pickford's work. He has proved an ideal partner, editing, checking, and rechecking facts and dates, correcting and entering the text into the computer, and ensuring that the pictures were all of the finest possible quality. And I thank Manoah Bowman for making such beautiful prints of those pictures.

I should also like to thank my editor, Elisa Urbanelli, and the book's designer, Carol Robson, both of Abrams; Bruce Davis, Ric Robertson, Mikel Kaufman, Linda Mehr, and Ellen Harrington of the Academy; Lynne Wake, Sherief Hassan, and Patrick Stanbury, my colleagues at Photoplay Productions; Bill Connelly, Jasmine Brunsuzyan, and Shahe Melelian of Producers and Quantity Photo; Dennis Doros of Milestone Films; Paolo Cherchi Usai of the staff of the George Eastman House of Photography; Maxine Ducey of the Wisconsin Center for Film and Theater Research; John Hillman; and Jeffrey Vance.

KEVIN BROWNLOW
LONDON, 1998